To good friend PAWNee
Senior sister of "KP" in the book.
Enjoy!
Best Wishes & Best Regards.
Bill Tompkins

Hood River, OR
Apr. 23, 2010

101 Road Patrol Tales

from a Chippie

of

the California Highway Patrol

by E. W. Tompkins Jr., CHP ID 6902, Retired

Copyright © 2008 by E. W. Tompkins Jr.

All rights reserved. No part of this book shall be reproduced or transmitted in any form or by any means, electronic, mechanical, magnetic, photographic including photocopying, recording or by any information storage and retrieval system, without prior written permission of the publisher. No patent liability is assumed with respect to the use of the information contained herein. Although every precaution has been taken in the preparation of this book, the publisher and author assume no responsibility for errors or omissions. Neither is any liability assumed for damages resulting from the use of the information contained herein.

ISBN 0-7414-4821-1

Published by:
INFI∞ITY
PUBLISHING.COM
1094 New DeHaven Street, Suite 100
West Conshohocken, PA 19428-2713
Info@buybooksontheweb.com
www.buybooksontheweb.com
Toll-free (877) BUY BOOK
Local Phone (610) 941-9999
Fax (610) 941-9959

Printed in the United States of America
Printed on Recycled Paper
Published August 2008

Dedication

To my family and extended family, who waited at home for me to return, and to those officers with whom I worked, especially those who backed me up so I could go home.

Table of Contents

Introduction	1
Getting Started	13
Tale 1 – Do You Want Fries With That?	15
Tale 2 – I've Got Mail?	16
Tale 3 – Missing In Action	17
Tale 4 – They Went Thata Waaay!	19
Tale 5 – Cutie Pie	23
Tale 6 – Mr. Big N. White & The Green Machine	24
Tale 7 – Mr. Glib	28
Tale 8 – The Great Haywire Patrol Tow Truck Caper	31
Tale 9 – Equal Opportunity Enforcer	41
Tale 10 – Mighty Friendly Of You, Friend	44
Tale 11 – Do You See That? No.	45
Tale 12 – Hell Hath No Fury	47
Tale 13 – Bouncing Chips	50
Tale 14 – Glug, Glug, Glug.	51
Tale 15 – A Friendly Wave Would Be Better	52

Tale 16 – Reds Rain	53
Tale 17 – Care For A Canapé, Old Man?	55
Tale 18 – It's Only Sticking Out A Little Bit	56
Tale 19 – "X" Marks The Spot	57
Tale 20 – You're Not Heavy, You're My Moped	58
Tale 21 – It's A Reach	59
Tale 22 – Helpless In The Act	60
Tale 23 – Bigger Is Not Necessarily Better	62
Tale 24 – Wadda Ya Mean, Woo-Woooooo?	64
Tale 25 – Construction Destruction	66
Tale 26 – Crying Wolf In The Rain	68
Tale 27 – Such A Deal He Has For Me	71
Tale 28 – A Bang Up New Year's Eve	73
Tale 29 – Such A Cute Puppy	75
Tale 30 – Stubborn Is as Stubborn Does # 1	77
Tale 31 – Stubborn Is As Stubborn Does # 2	80
Tale 32 – Ouch. Ouch. Ouch.	82
Tale 33 – Four Way, No Way	84

Tale 34 – Jacked Up	85
Tale 35 – I Love To Go A-Wandering	87
Tale 36 – Even The Meek Can Speak Mightily	88
Tale 37 – He Flies Through The Air….	91
Tale 38 – Like Shooting Grounded Birds, No Sport	94
Tale 39 – The Old Girl	95
Tale 40 – Definitely Not A Diamond Day	96
Tale 41 – Thar She Blows!	102
Tale 42 – Clothes Do Not Necessarily The Man Make	105
Tale 43 – Bike Ride	107
Tale 44 – Doctor Frustration	109
Tale 45 – Public Toilet	111
Tale 46 – What Goes Around Comes Around	112
Tale 47 – The Zs In The Night	116
Tale 48 – Man Of Peace	119
Tale 49 – If Only I Were On Commission	120
Tale 50 – Traveling Light	123
Tale 51 – Ugly American Deer	126

Tale 52 – Got Rope?   130

Tale 53 – Duck. Soup.   131

Tale 54 – Peddling As Fast As I Can   133

Tale 55 – Headless Chickenlike   137

Tale 56 – 'Cause You Did It   138

Tale 57 – Said To Contain   140

Tale 58 – Strangers In A Strange Land   145

Tale 59 – Recruits For The Three Stooges   148

Tale 60 – The Big Push   151

Tale 61 – The Big Rush   152

Tale 62 – The Big Oversight   153

Tale 63 – The Big Cry   154

Tale 64 – Fair Damned-sels   157

Tale 65 – It's Only A Disabled Vehicle   158

Tale 66 – Surprise! Surprise! Surprise!   160

Tale 67 – A Night To Remember   162

Tale 68 – Blondies Have More Fun, She Thinks   165

Tale 69 – A Slacker Gets His Due   167

Tale 70 – You Gotta Work With What You Know	168
Tale 71 – Auxiliary Days Off	170
Tale 72 – We Have Lift Off!	175
Tale 73 – Bull. Darn It.	177
Tale 74 – The Highway Hots Club	180
Tale 75 – Close, But No See-gar	186
Tale 76 – Group View	189
Tale 77 – I Wasn't Even In Heat	192
Tale 78 – Sad Hands	193
Tale 79 – Those Invisible CHP Cars	195
Tale 80 – Her Name Should Be Lucky	195
Tale 81 – Help From Heaven	197
Tale 82 – Flying Too High	199
Tale 83 – The Devil's In The Dirt	200
Tale 84 – Was I On Fire?	202
Tale 85 – Told You So, Too	204
Tale 86 – And Awaaaay, We Go	207
Tale 87 – Eye Think That's Funny	210

Tale 88 – Lunch, is served	211
Tale 89 – Bill's Thrill	212
Tale 90 – Care To Dance?	213
Tale 91 – Gentleman Jim Ain't Too Happy	214
Tale 92 – Public Acclamation	216
Tale 93 – They're E-v-e-r-y-w-h-e-r-e	218
Tale 94 – More Said To Be So's	220
Tale 95 – The Bunker	223
Tale 96 – The Only Thing Missing Is The White Flag	226
Tale 97 – Showtime	227
Tale 98 – Loose Lips Sink The Speaker	228
Tale 99 – Baby, Baby, Come To Me	230
Tale 100 – How Low Can You Go?	232
Tale 101 – Funny, You Mention It	233
You Pays Your Dime, You Takes Your Chance	235
Epilogue	240

Introduction

I can hear the woman's piercing high-low screams over the noise of the wind and the driven horizontal torrential rain that is interspersed with claps of thunder. And I am three hundred to five hundred feet away from her. I have just arrived at the scene of this dispatched accident call.

When the dispatcher gave me the call she advised the accident was an 11-83, radio code for an accident with unknown details. I knew an 11-83 could be anything from an aircraft crashing into a gas tanker on a freeway to the I-think-I-possibly-perhaps-kind-of-sort-of-heard-a-car-hit-another-car type report, but I could not understand why it was whomever called in this accident couldn't have provided just a bit of a clue so appropriate help, besides just me, could be rolled.

In front of me on this October Saturday afternoon on a usually busy two-lane rural highway in Fresno County, California, as best as I can determine in the fire-hose rain, are two occupied cars trapped between three downed utility poles. The poles are lying completely across the highway, blocking it. Apparently, the poles were blown down by the wind. The electric and telephone wires, their wire-support cables, and the poles' guy wires are broken loose and are tangled and snaked over the north-south highway. They are also wrapped around the front car. Each car is in its own section between the poles. The distance between the first downed pole in front of me and the third downed pole south of me is about one-third of a mile. The power lines had been arcing. Supposedly, according to training information, power lines arc three times before shutting themselves off. Emphasis on supposedly.

After quickly surveying the scene I radio my dispatcher. I describe the situation and request help: another unit to assist, and the utility company to do its thing. I tell her I will advise about the need for an ambulance after going to check on the welfare of the vehicles' occupants.

"All units are 10-6 (busy) on other crashes," the dispatcher replies, "There is no one available to assist you." Wonderful. (The old-timers would say with a condescending sniff: "What the hell. It's only one crash. Only need to send one highway patrolman.")

I request when a unit gets free that she send it to me to assist.

With that done, I button the top button of my raincoat collar, which partially protects a soaker towel I have around my neck, pull my hat with my rain cover on it down on my head, grab my trusty cigar box-sized first aid kit that contains only bandages, take a deep here-goes breath, and move into the downed lines toward the cars' occupants.

It certainly would be handier if I could have driven my patrol car up to the other cars if I needed other things, such as the radio, but the pole blockage killed that possibility. (In those days, we didn't have the handy portable radios today's troops enjoy. With a portable radio, I wouldn't be married to the patrol car as I was then.)

The woman's screams continue through the billowing sheets of rain as I advance toward her location.

I tippy-toe over the wet roadway through the tangled power lines and their cables, not knowing if I am going to get zapped or not. But I have to go. That woman's screams have my attention.

The first person I reach, because his door is mostly unencumbered by the wires and cables, is the driver of the screamer's car, an elderly male. He is cut in a multitude of places from the glass of his broken out driver's window. When the nearest pole fell, the power wire and support cable hit his window, firing the shards onto him as though from a shotgun. He is bleeding but not in a major way (that opinion could depend on who's doing the bleeding), and is otherwise in apparently good condition, especially given his seniority. Because the rain and wind are blasting through his window opening, I elect not to apply the bandages just then. They would have only gotten wet and not been effective. Unfortunately for me, I need to return to the patrol car through the downed wires. I have to get a plastic blanket to cover his window opening before I can bandage him.

The elderly driver's passenger, the screamer, is totally freaked out, but not otherwise injured. When the poles fell onto the roadway, the couple's car almost collided with the first pole, but didn't. But the then-charged electric lines fell onto and around the car. The lines began arcing. In doing so, the arc creates a loud snapping electrical buzzing pop, followed by a huge shower of sparks. In her case, this was happening on the car hood where she could see, and hear, very closely through the windshield. Because of the arcing, the screamer thought she was being electrocuted. She wasn't. The car tires insulated her inside the car. She didn't know that, or care. She just wanted out. But she couldn't exit due to the wires and cables blocking her door, and the elderly injured driver blocking the other door. (Luckwise, she should be glad she couldn't get out. If she stepped out when the lines were hot, and she had been touching the car, she would have grounded herself and been zapped big time. Perhaps cooked.)

I finally get her to understand the show is over and she is safe (I hope). I ask her to just sit there calmly. Help is coming from the utility company, I tell her.

"You know," I say, "I walked here through the wires and the rain, and I'm okay, so you're okay, too, right?"

"Yea… a… a ... h," she stutters, unconvinced.

"Okay," I say, "I'm going to go back to check the driver of the car behind you. Try to get calm. I'll be back."

"Ok... ay," she says.

As I walk away toward the other car, she resumes screaming.

Where is my help?

Arriving at the other car, I find a young girl behind the wheel. She is cool, calm, composed, and uninjured. She is just sitting there waiting for the cavalry to arrive.

"Is it safe to get out?" she asks.

"I think so, I walked down here okay."

"Are the other people injured? I saw you looking them over."

"The driver has multiple cuts and needs to be bandaged. But his door window is broken out, and the wind and rain are pouring in on him. I need to go back to my patrol car for a plastic blanket to use to put over the window to shield him from the rain. The passenger is frightened, because of the wires arcing and sparking."

"Oh, those wires sparked all right. They really sparked big three times," she says. "Would you like for me to go over there and sit with them to see if I can help calm her down. I can hear her screaming back here."

The girl leaves the sanctuary of her car and walks with me in the driving rain to the couple's car. She gets into the back seat through the driver's door, and immediately begins talking to the woman, trying to calm her down. I continue to the patrol car for the plastic blanket.

The woman resumes screaming.

Inside my patrol car, I take a blink of an eye respite from the rain and wind and call dispatch. I ask for an ambulance for the elderly driver and possibly his occupant, rerequest an assisting unit, and ask for the ETA (estimated time of arrival) of the utility company.

The dispatcher confirms the ambulance request, advises the utility company is en route, and again states all units are 10-6.

I get four yellow paper-lined plastic emergency blankets from my trunk. (We call them "44" blankets for the radio code of 11-44 used in connection with a fatality.) I return tippy-toe through the wires to the first car. The wind and rain are still turned on high.

I give each of the two women a blanket to wrap up in. (Surprisingly, the 44s do a reasonably good job of providing warmth.) I cover the elderly driver with another. Then I spread the fourth blanket over the outside of the open door, tuck the edges around the door frame, and close the door. He is now out of the cold rain and wind. Before I went around to the driver's door, I gave the first aid kit to the screamer, and asked the ladies to bandage the driver.

As I walk away to go south to the start of the accident scene, there are no screams. Progress.

By now, several cars are stopped where the poles first began falling over. With the torrents still sideways and pummeling hard, I walk through the wires—again—to contact the drivers of those cars. No one is hurt. They arrived after the poles were down. Since they can't get through, they just stop and remain there. All three drivers are trying to get to Fresno, and parked there waiting for the road to open! I tell them it is going to be a long while before that happens. They might want to consider finding an alternate route.

Now, I return through the wires to my unit, stopping along the way to check on the victims. The screamer has stopped screaming permanently. She and the young girl are talking. The male driver is bandaged quite nicely, and is patiently sitting behind the wheel waiting. All we need are my help requests to be filled.

As I pick up the patrol car mike to call dispatch again, the ambulance arrives. They, like us, like to have their rig by them with all their equipment available. When they see that they are going to have to walk with their gurney through the rain and wind, and through the wires to the number one car, they are less than enthusiastic about the situation. Both attendants look at me like I planned this obstacle course for them. But they take what equipment they can carry, and hike out across the wires to do their duty. With no rain gear on.

Just as the ambulance guys walk away, two of the utility company's two-man trucks arrive. The first thing the foreman tells me is to be careful walking through the downed wires. "They could be hot," he says.

Wonderful. Do I tell the screaming woman, now? I had assured her it was okay. Well, I thought it was okay, and I hoped it was okay, and I needed it to be okay, and I sure hope the wires are dead, because I have an ambulance crew presently going through them.

The utility men go about their business of finding the breaker switch for the downed lines. It is located somewhere south of the scene. The ambulance crew gets the car occupants out and back to the ambulance. Everyone is still working in unrelenting wind and rain.

Soon, the ambulance crew takes the victims away. The utility foreman returns to say that indeed, the power is off. (Yeah, boy!) They begin the work of clearing the roadway.

Abruptly, the wind and rain stop as if by magic, like a switch has been thrown to off. The sun breaks out from behind parting western clouds to make a beautiful pink, purple, gray, and white sunsetlike picture with the sun streaming through a hole in the clouds. It is a near idyllic scene, now.

Right then my requested help arrives.

The officer rolls up in his patrol car to where I am standing. Seated in his car, he rolls the driver's window down to speak to me. In the clearing air with the sunset picture, he looks at the empty cars at the scene and the utility crew working getting the wires and poles off the roadway, and says, "Why do you need help?"

Why me, Lord? Why me?

Because you volunteered, Tompkins. You voluntarily gave up your cushy bank assistant manager job and ten years with the bank, because you got the CHP bug from riding as an observer once a month with your good buddy, KP. Well... okay. But, it's his fault I am standing out here today in seemingly near-tornadic wind and pelting rain trying to help people trapped in cars over an accident scene that's a third of mile long. I only joined up to look good in uniform and for the coffee. (Joke.)

Long story a bit shorter: The bank I worked for near Fresno promoted and transferred me to the branch in Novato, California, north of the Golden Gate Bridge. My former wife and I moved into an apartment where we met KP and his wife. At the time, KP was a tire shop manager. But he'd always wanted to be a cop. He soon joined the CHP and was stationed locally where he patrolled the Golden Gate Bridge and environs.

At that time, civilians could ride in the CHP cars on regular patrol if they signed a waiver of liability and obtained the concurrence of the area office commander. I did that. About once a month, usually on a Friday or Saturday night, I would ride with KP. He frequently worked the graveyard shift (9:45 pm to 6:15 am), the action shift, I thought. I would ride with him and his partner. I'd be in the back seat with the drunk they arrested. ("Hey, buddy. They tow your car, too?" not noticing I wasn't handcuffed.)

Plain and simple: I got the "chasin' taillights" bug.

One Sunday in April, 1968, KP and I are riding in his car on the I-880 Freeway in the San Francisco Bay Area going to my house in San Leandro. My former wife and I had moved there a couple of years before when the bank again transferred me and promoted me to the local branch's assistant manager position. He and I were coming back from a day's fishing trip from under the Golden Gate Bridge, a favorite place of ours to fish.

The fishing conversation drops off. We ride along in silence when I decide to break the news to him that I plan to leave the bank to join the CHP.

"Guess what I did yesterday, KP?" I start off. (We began calling each other by initials, because he would call the bank and ask for "EW," a derivative of my name printed on my business card.)

"What?" he says, with no particular interest, keeping his driving attention to the busy freeway Sunday traffic.

"I filed my application," I say, purposely leaving out the important information.

"Uh, filed your application for what?" he asks, still focused on the traffic. (Years later, he said that he was thinking the application I filed had something to go with my bank job. That was the idea behind my withholding the info: suck him in.)

"For the department," I allow.

"For what depart... wha...what?

I thought he was going to suffer a convulsion. His driving attention drifted, I'm sure.

"Now, Bill. This job is dange... you've got ten years with... you have to work nigh... you're an assistant man...." He could not talk. He almost could not breathe. All the man could do was stammer and sputter.

From that time on, until just before I reported to the academy in Sacramento, he tried like the friend he was to talk me out of leaving what he thought was my exalted position with the bank. (Banker's hours? I thought farmer's had better hours than I did.)

His cajoling did no good.

All I could see was that if I passed all the tests and the background investigation, I could start at $100 more a month on the first day of the academy, and not even be able to spell highway patrolman, much less be one. The salary would go up. I would be eligible for an excellent retirement pension at fifty-five-years-old, instead of the bank's sixty-five-years-old qualification age to retire. That's ten more years of living—if I lived through the job. And on top of all that, eventually KP and I could work as graveyard partners somewhere in the state.

If I didn't make it through the academy, or the job didn't work out otherwise, or I got hurt, I could always go back to banking. But not to the one I resigned from: They were incensed I left. They were particularly incensed I left to go... go... go be a traffic cop? They would probably have been happier if I'd left to work for a competitor.

So, on January 27, 1969, with all my tests passed, my background exhaustively checked, my Marine Corps haircut back on top of my head, and a whole bunch of pounds lighter and in better condition from self-training, I reported to the CHP Academy in Sacramento at the tender age of thirty-one-years-old. I was starting sixteen weeks of intensive training for a job that was a major career change, and major lifestyle change for me, my wife, and our two daughters.

I was at the oldest eligibility age for a cadet. I had one shot at making it. If I flunked out, I was on the road back to banking.

My wife supported the career change. My sister and brother-in-law supported it. My dad, who was a former county corrections officer (read: jailer) and current reserve deputy sheriff, was against it. So was my mother. My folks could only see the fake mahogany desk, the suits, the accelerated climbing career I had enjoyed so far, and what they perceived as a safe environment. (Super stress is invisible; bank robberies are possible.) Eventually, all grew to accept it. Mostly.

When I graduated from the academy, I was sent to the East Los Angeles Area office in Montebello, California, to begin my career. From there, I transferred to the Los Angeles area's Santa Fe Springs office, near Whittier. Eventually, I transferred to Fresno, which is home. At Fresno, KP and I worked as graveyard partners sometimes but more often as adjoining beat partners on the afternoon shift, until we were each separately transferred from road patrol duties to other functions. I went to the San Joaquin Valley's supervising district office in Fresno to work in the investigative services unit investigating staged collisions and other related insurance frauds. KP was assigned as the CHP liaison officer to the California Bureau of Narcotics Enforcement.

Now that you know how I am able to tell these stories, carry on to read about things I saw, did, and heard in the twelve years of road patrol duties chasin' taillights.

"Good morning/afternoon/evening. I stopped you because you were speeding/were following too closely/were lane-straddling/failed to stop for the red light/stop sign/etc. May I have your driver's license and vehicle registration, please?"

I said those words, or a variety of them, to every driver I stopped in my twelve years working as a "roadie" for the California Highway Patrol enforcing the vehicle code, the penal code, and the other laws of the state of California.

As a "Chippie," I tried to make the contact as tolerable as possible for the driver and still get the job done. (I've received three tickets. I know what being on the receiving end of an enforcement stop is like.) It's a tough thing for a cop to do. We know when we turn the red light on we are going to affect the driver's freedom momentarily—it could be longer—and more than likely, his pocketbook, too, in a variety of ways: court fine, insurance rate increase, and possibly vehicle towing and storage charges. It is tough to have a pleasant businesslike contact under those circumstances. The best we can hope for is that we receive a neutral response; that is, drivers accepting their luck of the draw in a dispassionate way. Their fate, as it were.

Road patrol work is as interesting as it is sometimes frustrating, or dangerous. Working with people is an unknown quality at the best of times. In law enforcement, the officer never knows what kind of reception he or she will get at the initial contact, or what the outcome will become, during a stop. On a simple stop for speed where the actual speed that is paced is written down substantially to only ten miles an hour over the speed limit, thereby providing the driver with a big time break monetarily, but still correctly reflecting the basic violation, I have received nothing but bad mouth during the whole stop. Other times, I have arrested a drunken driver, stored the car as is usually required, transported the subject in handcuffs, as is also required, and then received a handshake at the jail thanking me for stopping the individual from driving while drunk. Some have even written letters to my commander thanking me for arresting them.

Go figure.

In selecting the stories included here, I tried to give a representational cross-section of the people, places, and events I encountered in my roadie work. Some incidents are funny or happy, some are ironic, some are sad, or even sadder, tragic. Some are unique things that happen outside the routine stereotypical events that people in general perceive highway patrolmen doing or encountering. You may find a surprise or two.

The job and the work isn't always like the TV show "CHIPS" or "COPS." Some days it is more like the old TV police comedy "Barney Miller" or the even earlier Keystone Kops movies.

But it is a heck of a job with a lot of individual responsibility and authority, sometimes with high drama, and other times in-the-trenches mud-slinging work with no thanks.

The dedicated officers working for the California Highway Patrol know that rain or shine, wind or calm, fog or clear, traffic or no traffic, blizzard or desert heat, riot or peaceful, holidays or workweek, canceled days off, getting off late to go home every shift for a week or longer, and court subpoenas in the middle of vacation days or on days off, that they will report for duty and do the job they volunteered for and are highly trained to do: protect and serve.

There are several caveats to consider as you read here:

Please know that I wrote these stories from memory without benefit of reports or notes. Time being the healer of all wounds and the grand hazer of memory, I must ask that you forgive me if you discover some discrepancy in the who, what, when, where and how. And please keep in mind that the stories are written to entertain you, not to detail the elements of a charge for prosecution.

Despite this being nonfiction, I have taken a bit of the so-called literary license given authors to make the dispatch talk and other conversation and events more understandable to you.

In several stories, such as the one that started this section about the woman in the car who thought she was being electrocuted, I have pointed out individuals who came forth to aid me, or others. All those individuals were recommended by me to my commander for a public commendation from the CHP. I commend them again here even today with heartfelt thanks.

A small FYI: A lot of incidents are told here about events that happened to people. The incidents beg the follow-up question of what happened to them after I left them. In some stories I have written what I knew, but in nearly all of the cases, like most police who are first responders, I handled the incipient incident, cleared the scene, and went on to handle something else or just resumed routine patrol. Seldom did I later learn of any event or consequence regarding those folks with whom I had the initial contact, so I have to leave you hanging, too. Sorry 'bout that, but it comes with the territory.

And, finally, an item of administration to help you enjoy the stories more: Police agencies and others use radio code numbers for the clarity of understanding, not for secrecy, which some people think is the real reason a code is used. The radio code the CHP uses is called the 10-code, because about one-half of the codes start with ten, such as the ubiquitous 10-4, which means I understand. (In the right context there is an implied element of "I will comply," as in the Navy's aye, aye, sir.) These radio codes conserve limited and therefore valuable air time, allowing more users to speak on the frequency. The codes starting with 11- generally mean there is a person involved.

Think how much air time it takes to tell dispatch the following situation in plain English: "Dispatch, I have encountered a minor injury two-car accident southbound Freeway 99, south of Blossom Avenue. I need an ambulance, two tow trucks, and a sergeant. I have a female prisoner in custody for drunken driving, and need another unit to transport the female to jail while I finish working the accident." (Fifty-three words).

Multiply that oration by the other patrol units working on the same frequency, and you can see that the beat officer would probably be standing in line to speak his or her needs and/or condition. Sometimes, when it is raining with the resultant increase in crashes, we are waiting in line, even with radio-speak.

The above filibuster of fifty-three words translated into radio lingo would be: "Fresno, I've encountered an 11-81, southbound 99, south of Blossom. I need an 11-41, two 11-85s and S-4. I'm 10-15X with a deuce and need an 11-48 unit to book." (Thirty words).

The last is easier, faster, much clearer, and less likely to be misunderstood.

Throughout the book, as the occasion calls for it, to give you the flavor of our lingo and to make the tale more realistic, I have included the radio code in the conversations, because, really, that is the way we speak. Following the code, I've included the translation at the initial mention of the word; thereafter, I figure you're informed and I drop the translation.

Now, go 10-8 (in service), and read on.

Getting Started

When a new officer graduates from the academy, the officer is book smart. He or she is steeped in the how-to of being a highway patrolman. But the newbie must learn to put the knowledge acquired to a practical use on the street. The application of this knowledge comes in the form of the routine encounter of incidents the new officer has during a thirty-day break-in period with another officer who is a seasoned road patrol officer, or in today's CHP, with a trained FTO (field training officer).

Due to the doubling-of-the-troops expansion program in progress when I enter CHP service, my seasoned break-in officer is from two classes before mine; he is about six months seasoned. But I take nothing from him because of his short tenure. I think he did a good job, and I'm alive today because of the things he taught me. (Thanks, Jim.)

What the new officer might hope for during break-in is to get practical experience in a progressively increasing degree of enforcement seriousness or involvement, thereby building an experience base. The ideal situation would be to start out thus: a verbal warning; a no-court involved fix-it ticket for mechanical or vehicle registration deficiencies (no longer available); an enforcement citation (read: ticket) for a moving violation; and lastly, a physical arrest and booking.

In regard to investigating accidents, the officer-in-training would hope for a single car property damage accident; a multicar property damage accident; a minor/moderate injury accident; a major injury accident involving hospitalization, and finally, a fatal accident with innocent party injury with the errant driver arrested for drunken driving.

Hit and runs fall in all those categories of accidents.

But because our duties vary according to the unintended and intended actions of others whose dealings are beyond our command or control, we pretty much get what we get when we get it, and not according to a hoped for schedule of what is desirable for training.

My firsts pretty much followed what is desirable as I recollect to write this, but there are a couple of exceptions. The verbal warning and the first ticket I issued were for speed stops on the freeway. I don't remember the detail of the stops, not even the speed.

But I do remember issuing the fix-it ticket.

Tale Number 1 – Do You Want Fries With That?

My break-in partner is driving. We are on surface streets in East Los Angeles about 1:30 AM. (The area is an unincorporated part of Los Angeles County, which the CHP handles, in addition to the freeways.)

A pickup truck enters from a side street in front of us onto the four-lane street in a business district where the stores front the sidewalk. Its taillights are out. My break-in officer gets closer and turns on the red spotlight. I flash the white spotlight across the rear window to add to the attention getting. The driver doesn't yield but continues driving on the lightly trafficked street. Just as my partner is going to touch the siren a bit, the pickup truck pulls into a Jack In The Box restaurant lot and enters the drive-up window lane. The red light is left on. We follow behind the truck in the drive-up lane. The truck drives to the order window (no speaker box then), and the driver places an order with the window guy. After placing the order, he pulls up to the pickup window. We then pull in behind him. My training officer instructs me to contact the driver to issue a fix-it ticket. I hesitate to go. I am embarrassed to make the contact in this situation. I think it would be more official on the street, though it is legal here because the violation was seen on the street. But I go.

I contact the driver at his window waiting as he is at the food pickup window. While he waits on his burger order, I write the fix-it ticket. Just as his order is being delivered to him, I have him sign up. I gave him his copy, and we clear after he gets his chow and pulls out.

The workers in the restaurant, and the few people sitting in their cars eating, are all loudly guffawing while we are on the stop. I suspect they are laughing at the situation and not the driver.

At the time, there was a frequently played TV commercial for Jack In The Box featuring various emergency vehicles from cops to fire department ladder trucks to ambulances. In super fast motion, the code 3 (red light and siren operating) emergency vehicles would blast into drive-in lane, order, pick up at the next window, and tear away as though their emergency run was barely interrupted by the no waiting in the drive-in lane.

The restaurant workers, and the others present, no doubt were thinking of that commercial during our stop in the drive-in lane, and laughed on reflection. Myself, I was still a little embarrassed.

Tale Number 2 – I've Got Mail?

I don't recall the events of my first drunken driver arrest. I should think that I would given I was, and still am today, very concerned about depriving anyone of their liberty and/or property. Since it was my first physical arrest, I should think it would have made a lasting impression, like the other firsts we all have. But alas, all I remember is the guy complained about me in an extended letter he sent to a state senator. The state senator sent it to the governor's office. The governor's office put a cover letter with it, and sent it to CHP headquarters, who sent it to my commander in East Los Angeles. The office opened a citizen's personnel complaint, and put the notice in my office mail box.

This is definitely not good mail. It is a complaint. I am still on break-in. Not a situation conducive to career enhancement, or for the immediate view, job retention during the probation period.

Answering the complaint requires me to respond in writing to each of the myriad allegations in his letter. (Nothing untoward took place; I handled the arrest in textbook fashion. My break-in officer was present.) The letter complained about the standard arrest procedures and processes (per training) that I followed. Mostly, the complaint was the driver was arrested. The department contacted the complainer, and performed a full investigation as is done with all personnel complaints. Ultimately, the complaint was found not sustained. Rightfully, so.

For some reason, people think if they complain about the officer, the department will withdraw the ticket or arrest. The department will not and does not interfere in the arrest or the court process. The courts govern the circumstances of the outcome of those situations. But the department fully and objectively investigates allegations made by a complainer on a personnel basis. If the facts determined by the investigation indicate a transgression by the officer, the officer is punished according to the seriousness of the misbehavior. All this is separate from the crime adjudication procedure, leaving the arrest or ticket to be still dealt with by the complainer.

Tale Number 3 – Missing In Action

I don't remember any of my first accident investigations, except I do remember handling my first fatality, or 11-44 as we call them using the radio code.

My break-in partner and I are working the graveyard shift. We are working the Pomona Freeway in the East Los Angeles area. It is summertime, about 2:30 AM on a Saturday morning. Dispatch calls to advise a taxi driver reports an overturned vehicle on the transitional ramp from the eastbound Pomona Freeway to the southbound I-605 Freeway. She gives the call to us as an 11-83 (you know about this type of call, already).

We roll to the location, and slowly drive through the two-lane transitional ramp looking for debris in the roadway and/or the overturned car. Even using the white spotlight, we see nothing to suggest an accident occurred. I call dispatch to advise "UTL T/C" (unable to locate traffic collision). I suggest she recontact the informant for more information. We resume routine patrol.

A bit later, dispatch calls again. The informant states that when he went through the ramp he saw the overturned car on the left shoulder of the ramp, but set way back from the curb. He says when he went through the lights from the car behind him illuminated the overturned car allowing him to see it. I acknowledge the call, "10-4," and we respond to check again.

This time at the ramp road, we drive over the curb onto the wide dirt shoulder and park. The headlights of the patrol car light up the overturned vehicle. It is a dark red convertible two-door sports car. It is lying on its left side, front end to our right, with the bottom facing us. Due to the gray color of the car bottom, the car is very hard to see at night, especially where it lies in the pool of shadow between nearby freeway lights. From our parked position, we see no one around. The car is reasonably together.

Exiting the patrol car and going forward, with an occasional vehicle whizzing by on the immediately adjacent ramp roadway despite our rear flashing amber caution light, we walk toward the far side of the car. Frankly, I walked with trepidation. I didn't know what I was going to find for my first fatal accident. Intact? Cut in half? Torn to pieces? Decapitated? What?

I assure you I was hoping for the first one: intact.

We do find the solo victim intact. (Whew.) He has been there so long, though, because of the car being hidden from the clear view of the passing cars due to the circumstances of the car's bottom non-color, and poor lighting location, that rigor mortis has set in. I am *greatly* relieved he is intact. A tidy fatal. But I tear up, anyway. I found it very sad someone could be involved in a traffic accident and die in a metropolitan area of more than 2.5 million people, without anyone witnessing the event to help the driver, or even report the incident.

Our investigation reveals the vehicle driver, the single occupant, probably drove into the curve too fast to safely negotiate it and slid into the left curb of the ramp with his vehicle's left wheels, which caused the car to flip up and over onto its top (convertible top was down), land, and then flip again, landing on its left side. At the time, seat belts were not required to be installed, or worn if installed.

The driver was ejected, and the car rolled over on top of him breaking his neck.

Tale Number 4 – They Went Thata Waaay!

Another first I remember is my first pursuit. Now, here is a first to remember!

In my thirty-day break-in period, which is running mid-month to mid-month, during which I am suppose to be exposed to all facets of road enforcement, I am the right front passenger officer in the patrol car for twenty-nine and a half days. While my break-in period is ending, and theoretically I am qualified to work by myself thereafter, that isn't going to happen. I am in a graveyard car. I have to work with my partner for at least the remainder of the month before I am eligible to sign up for another shift where I can sally forth on my own on the day or afternoon shift, if seniority allows. But I am not going to do that. I like graveyard. I intend to stay on it. (It also fits the schedule at home.) Maybe my trainer recognizes that situation and doesn't hurry along to allow me to drive, knowing we have time. While I had high-speed training, pursuit training, skid control training, and training for enforcement stop parking, etc., at the academy, newbies need driving experience in the black and white. It is a different type of driving than everyday driving. Maybe, the delay of my driving could be because my break-in trainer is… um… one of those people who are… uh… how do I say this?… hmm… prudently cautious? Yes. That's it. Prudently cautious.

When my trainer finally decides I can drive, he pulls to the curb of the main drag of East Los Angeles at four o'clock of a Sunday morning—for me, it is still technically Saturday night until daylight shows up—and announces I can drive.

"Really?" I inquire in surprise.

"Really," he says. "Now just be careful, Bill. Keep an eye out for the other cars. Watch it real careful when you're making a stop behind another car—don't rear end the violator's car!" (My mom's voice is ringing in my ears. She taught me to drive.)

Other cars? Another car? Sheesh. It is four o'clock in the morning. We haven't seen another moving car on the surface streets in East L. A. in an hour and a half, much less have the occasion to stop one. The area is so quiet it looks like the place has been evacuated. But I know why I am getting the cautious treatment. Of all the things an officer does *not* do on the CHP, damaging a patrol car, in or out of a pursuit, is at the top of the list along with not abusing anyone for any reason.

After the verbal admonition, we change places. That means we also have to swap the positions of our equipment: pinch book (ticket book), hats, flashlights, batons, and report boxes (form holders). All are jammed into the front bench seat crack (except the hats, of course) to keep them from becoming projectiles on fast turns and sudden stops. Some officers used to keep their machined, crosshatch-grip, heavy-duty aluminum flashlights between their legs with the handle jammed under "their equipment," and under their butt. But on those infrequent occasions when the front of the patrol car came up against an unmovable object, the officer would slide forward over that cross-hatching. Uh, uh, uhhhhh. Definitely not a place to secure a flashlight! No pun intended.

When the last item is securely in place, the seat adjusted, the inside and outside mirrors adjusted, and our seat belts cinched, I fire up the black and white four-door 1969 Dodge Polara with the 440-cubic inch engine, whose speedometer is marked to 140 miles per hour, though it goes faster than that. We sit there about fifteen seconds with the transmission in park mode as I think about where-oh-where do I want to drive this police Holstein.

At the very second I reach to grab the gear shift lever to change to the drive function, the front door of the bar we are parked in front of bursts open with a loud bang. A guy about twenty-five-years-old comes charging out the door on the short sidewalk to the patrol car's right front door where my almost-finished training officer is sitting. The guy's clothing is torn. His left eye is swollen and bruised. Blood is streaming from both nostrils, and his upper lip is cut and swollen.

He yells like we are across the street.

"Those guys (pointing to the side street next to the bar) beat me up and stole my keys. They're stealing my car behind the bar!"

My partner has parked us directly, and coincidentally, in front of *the* most infamous bar in East Los Angeles—the kind of bar every town seems to have that is a constant source of trouble to the police.

My partner yells back at the guy standing a foot away from him.

"Where are they now?"

"They're just leaving from behind the bar!"

"Jump in the back seat," my trainer yells to the guy, who is not searched. Bad cop work on our part, but procedure got lost in the alarm. And that's how cops get killed.

"Follow that car!" (True. Absolutely, true.) my partner yells at me.

And we are off.

I cut a power U-turn from the curb, smoking the tires. The U-turn terminates in the street alongside the bar. I put my foot into the 440-inch big block engine. The Dodge responds.

The victim yells, "There they go. Around the corner up there!"

The stolen car turns right and goes out of sight in a residential neighborhood. We turn right in time to see the stolen car turning left in the next block. We turn left in time to see it turning right in the following block.

The victim's car is a lowered, tan, two-door sedan. We are gaining on it a bit. The driver of the car keeps turning left, then right, left, then right, trying to lose us. I have the screamer (siren) on and the red spotlight up. My partner is flashing the white spotlight from side to side when he can get it on the car.

On a couple of turns, the evading vehicle hits the curb corner trying to make the cut. Sparks fly. The lowered vehicle bucks on the curb impacts.

"Those m-f'ers are destroying my car!" our victim yells.

Finally, the driver tries to make a run for it by going straight. Wrong move. The 440-cubic inch Dodge engine closes the gap. We are now right behind the car. But the driver doesn't yield. My partner gets on the PA (public address) microphone, and yells into the mike.

"Pull it over! Pull it over!"

Thinking that if we are a little off-set to their left, the PA system speaker mounted in our grille will be heard more readily, I use the Dodge's power, and simply swing out a little left and close up a bit. My partner thinks I am going to ram them.

Still with the activated PA mike in his hand, he yells into it, "Don't crash the unit! (patrol car) Don't crash the unit!"

I fall back behind the bad guys and continue on with them.

At this time, they must figure that we are along for the ride forever and aren't going to go away, and are pleading with them not to crash the victim's car. The driver brakes hard and swerves to the curb. We do, too. The doors of the car pop open and the two occupants hit the ground running. We do, too. And like every cop driver that bails out on foot pursuit, but knowing I shouldn't, I leave the unit with the engine running. Of course, in my case, I have no worries: A trusty guard is in the back seat.

I collar the driver, who should have gotten farther away than he did, but he is so drunk he can't run well. Only drive. Kind of. My partner captures the passenger, and is tussling with him on the right front fender of the patrol car when I return with my guy. In the end, we get them both handcuffed and seated in our thankfully still present patrol car.

We release the victim's car to him, but I request he take a taxi home. He is not in a condition to drive. He can return in the morning for his car.

Then I drive us to the jail to book the bad guys. After booking, we go to the coffee shop so my partner can regain his composure. Thereafter, I have no problem with my trainer for the rest of my time with him about my driving our patrol car.

Tale Number 5 – Cutie Pie

One beautiful spring Sunday about 2:30 PM, I am patrolling the section of Freeway 99 where it runs through downtown Fresno. As I approach the junction of a downgrade on-ramp to the freeway from the street above, I look to my right at the older blue sedan coming down the ramp to enter the freeway in the light traffic ahead of me.

The driver is tilting a can of beer to his lips. Open containers of an alcoholic beverage are illegal in a motor vehicle in California.

Looking to his left, I guess to check traffic to merge, he suddenly reacts with a surprised look, apparently noticing my black and white patrol car to his immediate left.

As his car enters the freeway directly in front of me in the shoulder lane, I put up the red spotlight. The driver yields to the shoulder without incident.

I approach the driver's window. Arriving there, I turn around to face the traffic for safety, and look inside the car at the driver. He is looking dead straight ahead with his hands on top of the steering wheel. He acknowledges my presence with neither words or motions. It is like I am not even there.

Looking past the driver, I see the cutest little four- or five-year-old girl. Her dark hair is in ringlets. She is wearing a beautiful white, frilly, lacy, Communionlike dress with white shoes and white socks. There is a gold chain with a locket around her neck. She has a smile that puts the sun to shame.

Before I can say, "Good afternoon, sir. The reason I stopped you…." to the driver, who is still looking straight ahead, "Cutie Pie," who is standing in the middle of the front seat (this is before mandatory seat belt days), bends down and tilts forward to look at me through the open window. Leaning in front of her eyes-ahead-driver, she says in her sweetest angelic teeny-tiny voice, "My daddy has a beer under the seat."

I let daddy go with no ticket after I have him pour out the beer and after I let him enjoy a counseling session with me outside the car away from Cutie Pie, his savior.

Tale Number 6 – Mr. Big N. White & The Green Machine

It is a summer day on the section of freeway that runs through downtown Fresno. I have been at work on the afternoon shift (1:45 PM to 10:15 PM) for about an hour when I get a radio call from dispatch of a reported 11-25 (traffic hazard) truck located at about the same section of freeway where I met Cutie Pie.

I respond and arrive promptly.

Indeed, I have a traffic hazard.

The hazard is a big rig eighteen-wheeler with a double set of aluminum cattle trailers hauling prized and expensive rodeo bulls. The bottom left rear corner of the rear trailer has fallen through, allegedly, because over time, the acidic bull urine ate away at the rivets securing the aluminum floor to the trailer sides.

The rig driver heard the loud bang of the corner giving way, and then the noise of it hitting and scraping the concrete roadway. He came to a stop in the shoulder lane of the four northbound lanes. The driver is super-reluctant to move the rig from the traffic lane onto the narrow asphalt shoulder for fear of injuring one of the high-dollar bulls that are on the broken bottom deck of the two-deck cattle trailer.

The driver tells me he has called his boss, and his boss is coming with another trailer so they can transfer the bulls from his trailer to the rescue rig.

"You're planning to transfer bulls from one rig to another on *my freeway*?" I ask skeptically.

"Yes, sir," he replies. "It's real easy. We just bring the other truck up real close in the next lane, and then make the bulls move over using an electric prod rod."

"We're going to be putting that other rig *real* close to yours, so there's no way a bull can get out on the freeway. Understand? Real close," I say.

I can see that we are going to be there awhile. I call dispatch to request CalTrans (California Department of Transportation) to bring out traffic cones to cone off the shoulder lane, the adjacent lane to it, and for safety, probably the lane next to that one. We'll leave one lane open on the freeway.

I am hoping to get this all accomplished before the after-work traffic comes through.

CalTrans arrives before the relief truck. They cone off three lanes. Meanwhile, about twenty to twenty-five people have either climbed over the freeway perimeter fence or jumped down the short distance from an nearby overcrossing and are gathered in the ice plant ground cover of the freeway embankment next to the shoulder. They aren't causing a problem, so I let them be, mostly because I am busy. It is illegal for them to be there.

Finally, about an hour after my arrival, the rescue rig and the boss arrives. The boss arrives in a white Cadillac El Dorado. He is wearing—and I am not making this up—white western boots, white pants, white western belt, white shirt with a white bolo tie, white western coat, and a white western hat with a white ribbon. He is a short, jowly, portly kind of man who is wearing dark aviator sunglasses under his white wide-brim hat. He has about a zillion cigars jammed into his shirt pocket, and one unlit monster in his mouth.

No question about it: this is Mr. Big N. White.

Mr. Big N. White ignores my presence when he arrives, and in fact never does contact me. He goes straight to his driver. In a few minutes, Mr. Big N. White stomps back to the rear trailer to check out the damage, all the while muttering "g-d" this, and "g-d" that. His driver trails him, studiously ignoring the full-time swearing. If the boss man's lips are moving, he is cussing at somebody or something.

While the first driver is occupied, I contact the rescue driver. I carefully and emphatically explain to him about *no loose bulls on the freeway*. He and I work together getting his rig up close to rig number one. Of course, I want the two trucks to be kissing, but both drivers tell me they can't do that. They have to have enough room to drop ramp gangway bridges into the doorway hatches of each deck of the receiving trailer. There is probably three to four feet of room between the trailers when they get into position. Both drivers assure me no bulls can, or will, get through the opening. Being a city boy, I am skeptical, because the opening looks pretty big, but I go with it.

With the rigs in place, the plan is this: The bulls on the broken bottom deck of the rear trailer will be prodded to go to the bottom deck of the receiving trailer. The rest of the bulls will be moved similarly to their respective compartments in the rescue trailer.

"Okay," I say, "Let's start. Carefully."

I move over to, and up on, the embankment in front of the amphitheater crowd so I can get a better overview. The rescue truck driver stands between the trailers to assist and supervise the transfer of the bulls as they move between trailers. Mr. Big N. White stands back behind the driver of the damaged rig, who is the person who is going to get the bulls moving.

The driver advances with his prod rod, sticks it through one of the many air hole openings in the rear trailer's side, and fires off a shot of electric shock. A lot of scuffling is heard, and a big "bawwww," but no bull moves to the rescue trailer. The driver gives another shot. More scuffling, another "bawwww," but still no bull moves to the other trailer. The driver steps up a little closer, fires off the prod again. Same results.

The whole time the driver is trying to get the bulls to move, Mr. Big N. White is still loudly continuing with the "gd-ing" and "sob-ing." Finally, he stomps over to his driver with the prod rod. He grabs the device out of the driver's hand with a "Gimme the g-d thing," sticks it through a different and lower air hole and fires it off.

Whomever, or *whatever* he hit, takes offense. And action. There is a very loud and long bellow, and a lot of scuffling of hooves, and then the fit hits the shan. The wet green stuff, lying on the aluminum floor of that prized-bull cattle trailer, formerly alfalfa hay before it was processed, comes exploding out through most of the air holes in the vicinity of the one the prod rod had been poked through. The stuff comes out like it has been shot from a jet engine. Of course, the only thing within range of the volume and velocity of that cattle caca was—tah dah!—Mr. Big N. White.

It splatters his sunglasses, his face, and the top side and underside of his white western hat. It spatters over all his other whiteness, including his boots, like spots on a Dalmatian, but green instead of black. And he isn't anywhere near as cute. A large green piece hangs like a flag from the end of his unlit monster cigar.

The crowd, save for the driver and myself, laugh and applaud and whistle. It is one of the hardest things I have ever had to do not to do the same. But I keep my professional composure. I don't know about the driver, because he had gone to pick up the prod from where Mr. Big N. White threw it down after stomping off to his Cad. Where the man went I do not know.

Eventually, the bulls are safely transferred, the traffic cones are picked up, and the roadway cleared and opened in time for the commuter traffic to pass through.

I went back to my patrol car and laughed and laughed and laughed.

Tale Number 7 – Mr. Glib

I am patrolling my beat this very nice fall Sunday afternoon in an unincorporated area of Los Angeles County that is principally a residential area.

People are out and about cutting their lawns, washing cars, tossing footballs around, and doing those and other various activities we do on the weekend.

I am motoring along slowly, really enjoying the fall day. If the top would have gone down like a convertible, I would have had it down. The weather is that nice.

I am on a very wide two-lane street that is bordered on the west side by middle-class homes and on the east side by a school building and its grounds.

Up ahead, about a half a block in front of the closed school's main entrance, a stocky man about fifty to fifty-five-years-old, is standing at the curb on the opposite side of the roadway. He gives me a single wave of the arm, which doesn't strike me as a come here wave, but more like a howdy wave. I return the wave and putt along. I am not hurrying.

He waves again in the same fashion. Hmm. Maybe it is a come hither.

At the time, we are using a fix-it ticket document. The violator's copy is a buff-colored card stock. Lots of people who had a card, on seeing a patrol car, would wave the card to indicate they wanted the officer to stop to sign off the document. But I see no document, no car. Still, I think this might be the case, since there is no sign of distress in the wave. Maybe the guy has the document, and he just didn't wave it. Probably for a driver's license violation, I think.

Unlike my usual style, I pull across the street going the wrong way (feeling Sunday lazy in the nonexistent traffic) instead of going past him and making a U-turn. I pull to the curb in front of the man and turn on the red light for the parking exemption. The man is wearing scruffy shorts, a sweaty T-shirt, and sports shoes. He is balding blond with thin wisps of disarranged hair. He has a puffy face with reddish cheeks, prominent front teeth that don't protrude, and a good start on a beer belly.

I roll the window down, leaving the air-conditioning on, because of the warm day, and say, "What can I do for you, sir?"

"Uh," he says, "Do you know anything about... uh... you know... about... um... you know... uh... you know, about...."

By the time he gets to the end of his sentence, my mind is trying to reach out to the guy, and determine exactly what it is he wants me to know about. About traffic laws? About getting a fix-it ticket cleared? About what?

"About what, sir?" I beg.

"Uh, about... you know... um... (snap the fingers, snap the fingers)... uh... about... you know... aaah, you know...."

I can't stand it. What does this guy want me to know about?

"About what, sir? What can I do for you?" I plead. Tell me. Tell me. Anything. Just tell me.

"Well, about... you know... ah... uh... (finger snap, finger snap)... hmm...." Now, he points his finger and pokes it in the air like he's keeping time to music.

The guy doesn't look like he is on drugs. I don't smell any booze. The engine heat blowing up from under the car in the day's warmth would be a telltale of his alcoholic beverage breath in a heartbeat if he had been drinking. He looks and sounds straight. He just can't get his question asked for some reason.

His stuttering and stammering goes on for a full four or five minutes! No lie.

Finally, my patience is almost zeroed out. My brain is fried from grunting for him to get the question asked.

"Sir, if you can't tell me what it is you need to know, I'm going to have to leave. I've got a lot of beat to cover."

"Oh... uh... uh, do you know... uh, do you know, uh, uh... do you know anything about CPR?" he yells in a gush. "There's a guy having a heart attack in the field over there behind the school!"

"*What?*" I yell, sitting up erect. What field? Where?"

"Over there. Through the school gates up there," pointing about three hundred-feet ahead.

I drop the trusty black and white's transmission into "D" for Do It, and race up the street and through the open wire-mesh gates, onto a grassy athletic field.

It is a large field. Very large. I stop to look around for the incident. I see a small group of people clumped together way on the other side from me. I guess that is where the heart attack victim is. I hope so, because I have wasted a lot of the heart attack victim's precious time with the guy out front, and don't want to waste anymore time by not locating the victim on the first try. Time counted—if the victim had any more left. I head for the group.

I get on the radio to Los Angeles dispatch. While I bump across the rough field, I request paramedics and an ambulance. I am trying to determine the location to direct oncoming help as I drive across the field. I don't know the name of the school. It's not something a traffic cop gets involved with and Mr. Glib didn't say.

Then I see a fire department engine company coming through the gate on the other side of the field, closer to the clump of people. The engine company beats me to the group by five fire truck lengths. Those guys rush off the truck with their emergency response bags and a tank of oxygen, which is much more equipment than I can deliver with my first aid kit and strong arms and lungs. Behind them I see the ambulance.

I call dispatch to cancel the equipment I ordered, explaining the on-scene response. I go over to the victim. He is very blue and hurting. Not a good sign. But the paramedics are working on him and getting him oxygen. In a few minutes, they load him into the ambulance, and leave code 3 for the hospital.

I never learned whether the victim lived or died, nor did I see Mr. Glib again.

Tale Number 8 – The Great Haywire Patrol Tow Truck Caper

I am compelled to write before I start The Caper that I, and others better situated to judge, think The California Highway Patrol is the finest traffic law enforcement agency in the world. Well-trained, well-equipped, well-commanded, well-run, and perhaps, arguably, well-respected by the public. But even The Pope experiences situations that start out bad and go down hill.

Such is the case here.

To protect the guilty in this tale—and the innocent—the names of involved parties are omitted or changed, and the city of location is not given. While I'm giving myself up here, I think I'm safe because the statue of limitations has probably run out.

Can it be that bad?

Yes.

A traffic officer, let's call him Kirk, formerly assigned to the area office involved, transfers back. Usually when an officer returns to an area he has worked before he is assigned to the graveyard shift, because those cars have paired officers in them for better safety at nighttime. Kirk, working in a paired car, would have a mentor who is familiar with the beats, their environments, their irregularities, and their dangers and thus is able to assist with the incoming officer's training and refamiliarization in an up-close mode. As in my assignment during break-in.

But at the time this incident occurred, the graveyard shift was fully-staffed. Since Kirk previously worked the area, it was thought by the powers that be that he could work afternoon shift alone, but as an additional car on the beat, something we call a beat partner. Sort of a medium distance mentorship.

At the end of the afternoon briefing, the shift sergeant says to me, "Tompkins, I'm putting Kirk on your beat. Let him get familiar with the area again. If something goes down, he can give you a call, and you help out. We want him to get reacquainted with that beat out there."

"10-4, sergeant," I acknowledge.

I get together with Kirk in the hallway before we leave the office. We agree to meet for coffee right from the git-go, so I can fill him in for openers. We meet for coffee, and we discuss the beat since his absence.

Leaving coffee, Kirk says, "Well, I'm gonna go wander around and see what's up. Give me a call for lunch, and we'll 11-98 (meet up)."

"Roge-O," I say, walking to my car.

"The beat out there" is not a freeway or highway beat, which we call line beats; it is an area beat. It is fronted on one side by a freeway, but the beat is a large—the largest of the area command—unincorporated area of surface streets with residences, apartments, businesses, schools, industrial parks, and warehouses. It even has (had) a large pasture where falconers fly their birds.

About an hour and a half after parting company, I get a car-to-car radio call from Kirk. His robust voice is at a whisper. It is so low I almost miss the call. I think he is hurt and needs help.

"888-12," he calls, "14, by." (He is 888-14, but on the radio officers responding frequently cut off the front area number in the interest of saving radio time. By the by: There is no 888 area.)

"Go ahead, 14," I answer in my usual voice.

Still whispering, Kirk says, "Uh, 888-12, can you, uh, 11-98 me east on the boulevard, and then where the railroad track crosses, follow that road that starts on the west side of track before crossing over. You'll see me."

"888-14, are you code 4 there?" I ask.

Still whispering, "888-12, 10-4. Just come on down."

"888-14, 10-4," I answer, very curious.

I follow his directions. Turning off the boulevard before the railroad tracks, I follow the unstriped, two-lane paved road parallel to the railroad track. The road, and the track, which is a siding, go into a developing business park, which is not visible from the boulevard because it is behind several large buildings. After about a two block distance, the road turns ninety degrees to the left, leaving the tracks to go straight on. The road goes for about another three blocks distance and ends in a cul-de-sac. About halfway down on the right, I see Kirk's patrol unit parked on the dirt shoulder.

As I get closer, I see a problem. Because of all the rain the previous week, the nude-of-grass red clay surface of the shoulder is slick. He stopped his car on the slick dirt shoulder, and then it slid on its own accord to the right like it was on ice. Because of the slight crown to the shoulder, the car slid about ten or twelve feet to the right. The right wheels are in a little dirt trough mini-ditch we call a bar ditch, which is located at the bottom of a split-post, four-strand barbed wire fence.

As I roll up to his location, Kirk calls on the radio without preamble, while still whispering: "Don't pull off onto the shoulder!"

I stop on the asphalt opposite his patrol car. He is sitting in the driver's seat. I get out, walk to the front of my patrol car, and stand by the edge of the asphalt bordering the red clay.

"¿Qué pasó, amigo?" (What happened, friend?), I say, smiling.

"Screw you, too," he replies, not smiling. "I pulled onto the shoulder to make a U-ee, 'cause I could see the road ended at the cul-de-sac, and there was nothing up there. I stopped to check over my shoulder before making the turn, and the car just slid into the bar ditch. I tried to drive it out, but all the wheels do is spin. This s--- is slick."

"Damn, man. From your whispered tone of voice, I thought you were hurt or something. Why were you whispering?"

"Well," he says in the tone of the old-timer he is to the boot (newbie) I am, "If you whisper car-to-car, the dispatcher can't hear you. I didn't want 'em to know."

"Is your unit damaged?" I inquire. If it is, he has to call a sergeant, and the sergeant will not be too pleased that Kirk's car is "high-centered," and out of commission for service to the motoring public, always our number one mission. At the least, Kirk will get a censurable incident report, and at the worst, some days off without pay that will cost some bucks.

"No. I looked out the passenger window. The right side is not touching the barbed wire, or the post."

Whew. There's a break, I think.

"What do you want to do?" I ask. I'm getting nervous here, because any minute either of us can get an accident call. While I can respond, he would have to either leave his car there locked up (a no-no, unless approved), and ride with me to help, or give himself up, and call the sergeant, while I depart on my own. Neither is an acceptable way to go for him.

"Is Big Truck Tow" (fictitious name) still working around here? I used to know all the drivers. Maybe they'd do me a favor," Kirk says.

"Yeah," I reply. "And I know most of them, too. Maybe they will," I say as I wonder what I am going to do on my free days off for participating in this incipient, semi-covert, borderline-illegal operation.

I call dispatch. I order one Big Truck Tow, "owner's request."

Big Truck Tow takes f-o-r-e-v-e-r to get there, it seems. And as luck will have it, I didn't know the driver. Neither did Kirk. The driver just recently started working for the company. But, uh, we "explain" the situation to the guy—Kirk from the seat of his patrol car, so his shoes don't get muddied. The tow driver volunteers to jump in as co-conspirator number three.

I pull my patrol car out of the way. The tow driver moves his tow truck ahead on the asphalt about three car

He gets the truck backed up okay, and then he tries and tries, but he can not get the bolt holding the pulley axle to the boom arm to loosen. Things look bad and time is evaporating.

Why neither of us has not received a radio call is amazing.

The tow driver finds a can of silicone spray in his truck, and gives the bolt several blasts of that. Once more he takes his wrench and cranks. The bolt gives and comes undone.

Hey, boy, we're rolling now!

The driver restrings the tow cable over the pulley. Then, he runs his tow cable from the top boom pulley (just restrung) to a swivel pulley (snatch block) attached to the upper bed of the tow truck. Continuing, he runs the tow line through an eye in the metal side panel of the tow truck's right side edge, down to a triangular-shaped cable guide loop attached to the bottom right hand edge of the tow truck. He sets that cable down, momentarily.

Now, taking another shorter separate length of cable, the driver slips and slides over to Kirk's patrol car. He gets down on his knees in the muddy clay, reaches under the car and loops one end of the extra cable around the rear axle behind the left rear wheel, and hooks that cable's hook to that cable. Then, still slipping and sliding, but now using the left side of the patrol car for support, he goes to the front and does the same thing to the left front wheel with the other end of the separate cable.

Walking backwards now, the tow driver, covered with clay mud on his feet, legs, and the backs of his elbows, brings the center of the cable attached to the patrol car to a "v." He then hooks his side-rigged tow truck cable's hook into the notch of the "v" of the patrol car cable, like drawing a bow string back.

He is now ready to pull directly sideways.

Clever, I think.

The driver revves up the truck engine from his rear operating station, hits the pull lever, and the lines tighten up.

Kirk and his patrol car begin to move directly sideways toward us.

Yeah, boy. We're almost outta here.

But an anomaly enters the action. (In situations such as this there always seems to be an anomaly!) Because of the combination of the slight shoulder crown, the muddy condition of the clay, and the low pulling point, the outside bottom side of the left tires (and the inside bottom of the right side tires) begin to plow the mud like scooping ice cream. The mud piles up in front of the tires to the top of the hubcaps. The low pulling point shifted the car's weight down to the left side, instead of down on the right side like it was when it was at rest in the bar ditch. Since the crown rises to the road from the bar ditch, pulling the car more is only going to gouge up more mud. Consequently, the tow truck is quickly unable to pull the car farther, because the car dug up too much mud in front of the tires.

After a loud cussing streak, Kirk says, "Let's cut the tow truck loose, and call the sergeant. Let's let this guy get outta here so he doesn't get into trouble." Kirk tells the tow driver it's okay to shove off.

The tow driver goes to his winch lever, and hits reverse to take the tension off the line so to make slack in the cable, which will allow him to disconnect his rigging from Kirk's patrol car.

The cable line doesn't move. Not an inch. The driver pulls on the cable. It's as taut as a high wire walker's wire.

The reason the cable doesn't move is because the cable has jumped the pulley, again. The cable is now strung so tight that even taking the pulley off, if it can be taken off, won't provide any slack. Now, the tow driver can not back up or go forward to create slack because he has married his pull cable to the patrol car's taut rigging.

This shows you what I know about clever.

"I'm gonna have to call the boss or the other driver to help. He can come over, put his tow cable on my cable, and just yank it out of the jam. Then, we can get some slack."

"Call the other driver," Kirk commands between clenched teeth.

The clock ticks.

The second Big Truck Tow rig takes longer to get there than the first did. We still haven't received any radio calls.

The Great Dispatcher In The Sky is looking out for us. We certainly need it.

Finally, tow rig number two arrives. We don't know this driver either. We are zero for two. But like the first driver, driver number two is game for the game, mostly because tow driver number one is asking tow driver number two to bail number one out of this flaming fiasco.

Big Truck Tow rig number two pulls along the left side of Big Truck Tow rig number one. The driver of the second rig winds out a little slack of his tow cable, jumps up on the first rig, and hooks his tow hook onto rig number one's tow line right at the point past the super-tight jam. The driver walks back to the winch handle, pulls it to "do it," and we all watch as his line tightens up and pulls on the jammed cable.

The jam does not come undone. The pull does not create any slack.

Thinking they need a different position on the jammed cable to get a better leverage bite on it, tow driver number two tries to remove his hook from the jammed tow cable. His hook will not remove.

Driver number two pulled so hard with his winch that the cable of rig number one became jammed tightly into the cleft bend of the tow hook of tow truck number two.

Both drivers cannot get the hook undone from the cable by hammering on it with a five pound hand sledge hammer.

I know we are going to get struck by lightning.

The situation is now this: Kirk is seated in his patrol car. The unit is parked at a slight left angle on the crown of the slick muddy red clay shoulder in such manner that the right front wheel is about three feet from the barbed wire fence on the right. The right rear door and rear fender are into the fence wire. There are mounds of red clay mud scooped up to over the top of the hubcaps in front of both left side tires. Big Truck Tow number one is on the asphalt road, left of and opposite of Kirk's patrol car with its tow cable jammed between the boom pulley and the boom, and with its cable hook securely and tightly hooked into a length of cable hooked to Kirk's patrol car's front and rear axles. Big Truck Tow number two is parked to the left of Big Truck Tow number one, and has its tow hook securely and tightly jammed onto Big Truck Tow number one's tow cable just past the pulley. No one can move or go anywhere.

Planning and execution by General Custer.

The tow drivers go to fiddle with the cable hooks and pulley to try to get something—anything—loose. Finally, Kirk calls from the open car window: "Go ahead, call the "f-ing" sergeant. I'll take the heat. What a "f-ing" deal!"

I call for the sergeant while the tow drivers continue to try to affect a change of status.

"Dispatch center, 888-12," I call.

"888-12, dispatch center, go ahead," the dispatcher replies.

"Dispatch center, 888-12 requests a shift sergeant at our '10-20' (location) at blah-blah."

"888-12, dispatch center, what is the reason for your request?"

"Dispatch center, 888-12, uh…exchange of information?" I try hopefully.

"888-12, dispatch center, 10-4."

Whew. Made it. I didn't have to blab over the air about a patrol car accident. No need to add to Kirk's embarrassment with the troops who customarily monitor calls to dispatch. They would be unmerciful in a situation like this. Especially, *this* situation.

While I am on the radio, Kirk finally waves the white flag and exits his patrol car. He slips and slides to the asphalt, cussing all the way about getting the mud on his

40

shoes. I remind him that it is the least of his immediate concerns.

While we wait for the sergeant, and the anticipated forthcoming butt-chewing (and possible summary executions), we entertain ourselves by diverting our attention to watching the tow drivers try to disengage something. (Equally surprising, they too have not received calls from their dispatcher.) They have nearly disassembled Big Truck Tow number one's boom and winch, and Big Truck Tow number two's winch. They are hammering, pulling, and banging without success. Things are apparently so bad, they are discussing calling someone from their shop to come out with cable cutters to severe the cable on each truck.

Right then, we hear a man's voice over our outside radio speakers.

"888-12, where are you?"

It is the sergeant. As we turn to look up the road to see if we can see him, we observe that he has already turned the corner and is coming our way.

"888-12, I see you," he says over the radio.

Before either of us can get inside my patrol car to the radio mike to warn him, the sergeant pulls onto the red clay shoulder to park. His car slides on the mud, down the crown, and into the bar ditch next to the fence behind Kirk's patrol car.

I immediately elect to get in my patrol car and get far, far away. And I did.

Tale Number 9 – Equal Opportunity Enforcer

In the formality of the jurisprudence system they are called intoxicated drivers. In the media, for the most part, they are called drunk drivers, though, I think correctly, it is drunken drivers. Chippies, such as myself, and most Californian cops call them deuces, because in the early California vehicle code, the section number was 50$\underline{2}$. When the code was revised, the department prevailed upon the legislature to ensure the new section ended with a two to preserve tradition, so the new number ended up being 23102 (a), thereby keeping the parlance going. Since then, the section has been revised. The new-new number is 23152, still ending with the traditional number.

In reality, outside the justice system, there are drunken drivers and there are intoxicated drivers.

The drunken driver is the one everyone is familiar with: slurred speech, staggering gait, and bloodshot, watery eyes, among other indicators.

The intoxicated driver is the one who has enough to drink to qualify on an objective chemical test basis (breath, blood, or urine) as being *legally impaired* and in violation of the drinking driver laws; drivers who blow, these days, .08 per cent on a breath test, or just above. (Back when I was first on the patrol, the legally impaired limit was .15 per cent, which was reduced later, to .10 per cent. The figures are read as point zero eight per cent, point one five per cent, point one zero per cent.)

These legally-impaired drivers are usually the so-called "social" drinking drivers who don't demonstrate, or greatly demonstrate, the exaggerated symptoms of intoxication usually associated with the stereotypical view of The Drunk Driver. It is these drivers who will stridently insist at the scene of an enforcement stop that they are *not drunk*, and sincerely question the officer's interest in them: "Why on earth are you bothering to stop me. I'm not drunk!" they say. It is these drivers, I think, who cause the most trouble for officers in their contacts with drinking drivers. They think they are wrongly stopped.

But it is these same drivers who greatly contribute to the injury and death rate just like the sloppy drunks do. Maybe more so, because, I think, there are more "socials" than "sloppies."

Please understand: I am not a temperance leader. I enjoy a cold beer with pizza, a glass of wine with dinner, drinks at the social occasions we all participate in and enjoy. But I drink in moderation. I don't drive until I'm sure the alcohol is out of my system, and I usually have a designated driver even when I think I'm clean. And I don't drink so much that I have to stay put for hours to achieve a zero blood alcohol level. (Nothing clears the alcohol out of your system except time.)

    I mention the above defense, because of the words below, which are not written as a boastful claim to some kind of body count to be painted in symbols under the window of my patrol car door like so many fighter planes shot down. The arrests mentioned below are to show the cross section of people who drink and drive and get arrested, who probably thought that they were not intoxicated/drunk, or impaired, but they were. Of course, there are always the ones who think they may be intoxicated and try to sneak home. They get caught, too.

    I don't recall any of the drivers described below being drunk within the common symptoms and understanding of the word.

    I arrested and booked Santa Claus in his red suit when he was coming from a mall Santa Claus stint; a Boy Scout leader in uniform with his merit badge banner, who was coming from a troop leader meeting; a new husband *and* wife who were coming home from being married in Las Vegas (I'd seen him drive into a gas station where they got fuel and switched drivers, after which she drove out in front of an oncoming car); a security guard in uniform, with gun, trying to drive his convertible (he was wearing a long, white silky scarf around his neck that was trailing in the wind a la The Red Baron); a semi-pompous university professor of English, who drew himself up to his full height and pshawed me when I asked him if he could say the alphabet. Announcing with the great vocal flair of a hammy Shakespearian actor, "Sir*rrr*. I am a university English professor," but he couldn't say his abc's in five attempts, thereby self-concluding, "I guess I *am* drunk."; a young fellow who can say his abc's backward, "Zyxwv, utsrq, ponml…" having memorized it in blocks of five letters, but couldn't get to "g" going forward; a guy in a wheelchair, driving a van equipped for the disabled, who, along with his very sober and capable female passenger, insisted that I deal with him as I would with any able person (talk about being regarded lower than whale poop, I had to wheel that guy into the jail. Did they give me a bad time? Big time for a long time); and finally, a petite female, about five feet tall and perhaps one hundred ten pounds—with the proverbial rocks in her pockets—who blew a point three two (.32), a personal career record for me for a live person, whose only fault was that she had stopped in the center divider of the eastbound Pomona Freeway when her car ran out of gas on New Year's Eve, and when asked, thought she was southbound on the San Diego Freeway. She did all the tests okay.

There are more: housewives in their bathrobes; politicians coming from fund raisers; kids from *junior* high and high school; teachers, and others from the whole gamut of society.

There are more that I wished I could have found and arrested. But they crashed first, injuring or killing themselves or other people.

My selfish theory is that it is easier to write a one-person arrest report than it is to have to investigate a fatality and write that report.

Tale Number 10 -- Mighty Friendly Of You, Friend

I make a "routine stop" for speed one nice afternoon on the freeway in downtown Fresno. It is a textbook stop. Up to a point.

A routine stop is this: The officer sees the violation of the vehicle code; moves into position to make the stop without the need to use the red light or siren; then, displays the red light and the driver yields the car to the right to an appropriate safe stopping place for both vehicles without incident; the driver contact is without incident or unpleasantness; the driver has a valid driver's license and current car registration for the vehicle driven (and, today, evidence of insurance); the driver follows the officer's instructions regarding safety on the stop; the errant vehicle is normal in all respects; the officer writes the citation for the sole original violation observed; without incident, the violator signs the citation in a businesslike manner, or a neutral or semi-friendly you're-just-doing-your-duty manner; and, the driver departs safely moving back into traffic without incident. A fast, fair, friendly routine contact.

The stop I mention here is exactly that with one exception. When the driver takes the copy of the citation from my hand after signing it, I say my usual, "Have a nice day," and stand there waiting for him to leave before I enter my car.

As his vehicle starts to roll away, the driver says, "I hope you die in traffic and your kids get cancer."

Tale Number 11 – Do You See That? No.

This is a graveyard shift weekend story. The time of the incident is about 12:30 AM Sunday, during the summer.

My partner, another former Marine, is driving. We are riding eastbound on a roadway with no street lights, and only an occasional car for traffic.

For some unknown reason, I look up through the top of the patrol car's windshield. About five hundred-feet above us, and a couple of blocks distant in advance of the unit, is a circular ring of revolving "hot white" bright lights. The lights, like us, are moving eastbound. They are directly over the highway.

"Uh, partner, do you see those lights up there?" I ask, wanting to believe, but not believing.

He uh-huhs without saying anything else but looks up, too.

We continue eastbound, periodically looking at the lights.

After a couple of miles, I say, "They're still there. Same position, same speed, same altitude. You do see them, right?"

Same answer as before to the same question: "Uh, huh."

I look at the speedometer. We are going forty-five miles per hour. We continue eastbound, and are now reaching the edge of the urban area. We are now on a four-lane section of the highway with street lights and a bit more traffic.

The revolving lights are still there. Same position, same speed, same altitude.

"Uh, partner," I say, "Do you think we ought to call this in?"

"No," was the immediate response. "Let's follow along some more."

"10-4," I say, continuing to watch the bright white revolving lights in the night sky.

By now, we have driven through the urban north area of town and are entering another stretch of two-lane road rural darkness. The lights above are as they have been all along.

All of a sudden, they disappear. Zip. Gone.

"No need to call it in," my partner says with a tone of relief of our not having to deal with them. "They're gone."

"10-4," I say, feeling like we have missed a great opportunity to report something different.

But unexpectedly, we see the lights again. Now, they are coming towards us! They are still over the highway and still revolving. My partner pulls the patrol car to the dirt shoulder alongside a vineyard we are by, and we crane our necks to look out through the top of the windshield. We hold this pain-in-the-neck position as the bright white revolving lights pass over the top of the patrol car.

I am fully expecting a cone of hot white light to come shining down from the object above and envelop the patrol car the same way as happened to Richard Dreyfuss' utility company truck in the movie *Close Encounters of the Third Kind*.

It doesn't happen.

What does happen is that we can read "Drink Budweiser Beer" written in the lights hung under the wing of an electric signboard airplane. The angle the plane was flying at in front of us prevented us from reading the sign properly. The angle only allowed us a distorted front or back view of the edge of the signboard's lights and not the message panel.

Man, am I glad we didn't call this event in!

Tale Number 12 – Hell Hath No Fury

The playwright William Congreve wrote, "Heaven has no rage like love to hatred turned / nor hell a fury like a women scorned." I believe that statement is as true today as it was in 1697 when it was written.

To illustrate:

The fog is already starting to come in one winter Sunday night in our part of the Los Angeles area when we are heading out from the office on patrol after graveyard shift briefing.

My academy classmate, Russ, who is driving, says, "Partner, it looks like it is going to be a long night in the fog."

"I hope not. You know I'd rather work in anything— rain, snow, wind, anything— but fog. But what I like and what I get are usually two different things."

He drives on to our freeway beat.

As required by the area office's SOP (standard operating procedure), we head out to check our beat of the Long Beach Freeway before going for our early coffee break. We take the transitional ramp from the Pomona Freeway to the southbound Long Beach Freeway. The Long Beach Freeway is already socked in. Heavily.

My partner elects to drive in the fast lane of the four-lane freeway. We collectively feel this gives us a chance against drunken drivers who pull into the shoulder *lane* and stop, thinking that they are on the actual shoulder. But our choice is no guarantee. The drunks can be coming the wrong way on the freeway, making our fast lane their slow lane.

You never know about drunks.

We are rocketing along about ten to fifteen miles per hour, checking I don't know what. We can hardly see the push bumper on the front of the unit much less the beat environment. We can see only fog.

All at once my partner exclaims, "We just passed a ped (pedestrian) in the center divider!"

"The hell you say," I say, looking back over my shoulder like I expect to see something. I do: thick fog.

"We didn't pass any cars in the divider," I continue. "Are you sure? What in the hell would a ped be doing in the center divider in this fog and at this time of night?"

"I don't know," he answers, "but there is one there. I'll turn around at the next ramp and go back. We'll check from the northbound side."

The center divider at this location is six feet wide on each side of a steel post braided-wire cable system from which green-painted metal cross-meshing four feet high is bolted to the cable. The six feet of width is just barely wide enough for a car to park in the divider if the driver snuggles the car up very close to the cross-meshing. If the driver doesn't snuggle the car in, passing vehicles, especially two-axle trucks that are allowed in the fast lane, will hit the door handles of cars parked in the divider. It is close quarters. Very close quarters, indeed.

We creep south to the first ramp we can exit at, and turn around to go back northbound in the fast lane. All this for a violation of the no-pedestrian-allowed-on-the-freeway law, basically, but maybe to save a life under circumstances that can go bad.

We don't know exactly where the ped is—if, in fact, my partner actually saw a ped. Maybe he just thought he saw a ped, because of the swirling, changing, thick fog patterns. I mean, why on earth would a ped be out here in this fog at this time of night? But we act like he saw what he saw. I put the white spotlight up, and train it on the center divider as we creep along in the fast lane with our rear deck amber light and four-way emergency lights flashing. With the white spot on, it is like driving in fog with the high beams on: We are mostly blinded.

The only saving grace is that it is Sunday night and there is almost no traffic.

Eventually, we see shadowy movement in the center divider, and then the outline of a man in dark clothes comes into our view. The man is on the other side of the center divider fence. My partner pulls into the six-foot-wide median and snuggles his side of the patrol car nearly up against the wire fence.

I exit to contact Mr. Mysterious. We want to make this as quick as we can, because we, the unit, and the ped are targets in this fog at this parked location.

"Hey!" I hail him. "What are you doing out here in the center divider in this fog? Are you trying to get killed? Climb over the fence quickly and get in the patrol car so we can get out of here. It's very dangerous."

"I can't, officer," the man replies civilly and earnestly. "I'm looking for a ring."

"Friend," I reply, "You're going to get us injured or killed out here tonight. Climb over the fence and get in the car, so we can take you off the freeway. Now."

"I can't, officer," he replies again, sticking to his plea. "I've got to find the ring. It's an engagement ring. My girlfriend got mad at something I said, and threw it out the car window when I was taking her home earlier tonight. I've got to find it. It cost six hundred and fifty dollars. I'm making payments on it."

"My friend," I say, "I don't want to add to your burden tonight. I really don't. But you have to leave the freeway now, and I mean *now*. I wouldn't want someone to have to work a patrol car crash with three injuries in this fog. That is, if we don't get killed. You either come over the fence, or I'm coming over to get you to arrest you for being a pedestrian on the freeway, and failure to obey a lawful order. We can work out your problem later. Now, come on!"

"Awww, officer," he says, and slowly starts to move to climb the fence to our side. At that moment, a car passes by him on his side of the fence. The car straddles the center divider pavement and the fast lane, leaving the hapless ped about three whole feet of room between him and the fence.

In nine and four-fifths of a second, if that long, the jilted ped is over the fence and in the right front seat of the patrol car. I jump in the back seat, and we haul out of there at a whopping fifteen miles per hour into the fast lane. That's real fun.

Partner: "Anyone coming?"
Me: "I dunno. Go for it."

My partner takes us off the freeway to the surface street below, where we take the ped to his car. Before leaving him, I suggest he contact the area office on Monday to see if they will escort him out here on the freeway to find his ring in daylight and better weather. I told him I would write a memo to alert them. I didn't think anyone would have the chance to get to the ring before he did.

He said good-bye to us without anger, but with great dejection concerning his and his girlfriend's action and the situation. He subsequently drove off. We went to coffee.

I don't know if he ever found the ring.

Tale Number 13 – Bouncing Chips

When highway patrolmen and other police go into restaurants to eat we are aware that all eyes are on us when we enter, when we sit down, while we eat, and while we pay and leave. It's like everyone has us under surveillance so they know where we are. Still, we don't like to call attention to ourselves the way I did on one occasion.

I'm sitting in a booth at a usual lunch break haunt. The place is busy on this afternoon. I order a turkey sandwich and coffee. The sandwich comes with potato chips in one of those little bags that are made out of some kind of plastic that should be used to armor tanks. The stuff is impenetrable.

I'm working on a report while I munch my sandwich. I stop writing momentarily, and pick up the chip bag. I pull at the seam to open it. And pull. And pull. All the pulling does is crinkle the wrapper with noise. I pull on the seam some more. And some more. Still, it will not open.

Finally, I *pull*!

The bag opens perfectly down its seam. It flattens out like a trampoline, and acts accordingly. It propels potato chips from my booth over into the booth behind me and into the booth in front of me, onto the floor, and certainly, onto my tabletop.

Usually, it seems like there are only two chips in those small bags. This one seems like it had a tractor-trailer load in it. Potato chips are everywhere I can see while I am slouched down almost under the booth table.

I apologize to all concerned, quickly finish my meal, and slither out to the patrol car to make a fast getaway.

Tale Number 14 – Glug, Glug, Glug.

This is another traveling beer-drinking story. It takes place on the same freeway ramp in Fresno where Cutie Pie's story occurred. It is a Saturday afternoon of another warm day.

Car "E," the errant vehicle to be, is coming down the same ramp from the street above. Car "HT," the good old Hi' 'Trol, is in the shoulder lane. The two cars parallel one another on the way to the ramp junction where Car "E" will merge in front of Car "HT." The two cars are some fifty to sixty feet apart side-to-side.

Driver "HT," the good guy in "the white hat," looks to the right to make sure driver "E," the errant driver-to-be is going to merge safely. At this time, the Hi' 'Trol observes driver "E" sucking on a can of suds. Driver "E" is now a confirmed errant driver.

Apparently, driver "E"-suds-sucker, catches something in his left peripheral radar that he suddenly thinks might be noteworthy. He slowly turns his head left toward me to look and verify and hope that what he sees is not what it is.

But it is.

Driver "E," is so suddenly taken with looking and seeing a cop while he is caught in the act that his open mouth gapes toward me in a look of total surprise. He also forgets to pull the can down from the drinking position; the beer continues to glug, glug, glug down his shirt front.

*Bus*ted!

Tale Number 15 – A Friendly Wave Would Be Better

Out in the very rural and desertlike west side of Fresno County, a rancher is working on his crop irrigation system when he stops for a moment to take a break in the late afternoon summer sun. He looks at the adjacent two-lane highway to see a three-axle, single-tank gasoline truck that carries, as I recall now, some 1250 gallons of gasoline. The tanker is approaching in one lane, and a pickup truck is approaching in the other.

As the two vehicles close on one another, the rancher sees the gas tanker swerve into the imminent path of the oncoming pickup truck. In doing so, the tanker truck lifts off the roadway, and nearly makes a full barrel roll to the left before crashing back to the roadway and bursting into a fireball. The pickup truck evades the tanker's swerve, and drives around the impact point to stop past the fire.

Because of the location of this accident, and the location from which I responded, it takes me almost an hour to arrive at the scene. The truck, and *the asphalt roadway*, are still on fire when I get there. The fire department is present, standing by monitoring the blaze as the hundreds of gallons of gasoline burn themselves out.

When the fire is out, the truck is a melted unidentifiable heap of metal lying in a burned hole in the roadway. The driver is very cremated.

The high-school-aged pickup driver was a friend of the tanker driver, who was also high-school-aged. The pickup truck driver states that the tanker driver may have been trying to say "Hi" with a let's-play-"chicken" movement. But if that is what the tanker driver had in mind, he forgot about the side-to-side sloshing effect of his load, something he wouldn't have in a car or pickup.

Even with baffles in the transport tank, it is hard to control that liquid-loaded truck when the load is severely sloshed side to side. As far as I know, the baffles are designed to prevent front-to-back sloshing, which would occur with the stopping and starting of the tanker. When the tanker wheel is cut sharply to the left, the inertia of the suddenly moved load accentuates the swerve with a catapultlike instant effort added and most likely, would cause the rig to roll over.

If all the tanker driver wanted to do is say "Hi," he should have just tapped the horn and given a country wave.

Tale Number 16 – Reds Rain

My partner and I are on patrol northbound on a surface street in East Los Angeles on graveyard shift when we observe a young male exit from the driver's door of a car parked with others at the northbound curb. The driver heads to cross the street to a pay phone booth. I write "heads to cross" instead of walks, because I'm not sure if what he did could be called walking. It's as though he is trying to walk on stormy ocean waves.

As we drive to his location and stop, he completes his journey to the phone booth.

We both exit the patrol car, and walk over to investigate him and his condition for a violation of the penal code section for being drunk in public.

The subject is now standing in the lighted no-door pay phone booth, facing inside. We can see that his right hand is in his right front jeans pocket. He is moving his hand around like he is fishing for something, pay phone change, maybe. We can't see his other hand.

I tap him on his right shoulder, and say, "Sir, turn around so I can talk with you."

He half-spins, half-turns, half-wobbles around (three halves and he still isn't whole!), and teeters backward against the phone shelf. Each hand is in its respective front pocket.

He appears to me to be totally wasted, but there is no smell of an alcoholic beverage. We think he is heavily drugged: He has that thousand-yard-stare-in-the-ten-foot-room syndrome. His lights are on, but there is nobody home.

"What's your name," I inquire.

"Blurnxyesuymmmmb," is similar to his mumbled reply.

"Sir," do you have any identification on you?" I try again.

"Mmlburbyymmblbmm," he replies. But now, his hands in his pockets begin to agitate briskly like he is really trying to find something. Then he stops, like he has found what he is searching for. He starts tugging his hands up out of his pockets, but he doesn't seem to be able to manage the coordination to get them out, due to his drugged state and the tight fit of his jeans. It is obvious he has no weapon in his pockets.

He stands there tugging and twisting his wrists trying to get his hands out. We stand there waiting for him to get them out for no other reason than to ease our handcuffing him.

At once, both hands come clear of his pockets. As they come out, something like five hundred barbiturate pills, known as "reds," explode in a shower up and out in front of him from his pockets. They are ejected like popcorn from an open popper. The red pills spray all over the phone booth floor, the sidewalk and us.

All he can say is, "Mbmmllbbbmmmm."

We book him for illegal possession of a controlled substance.

The worst thing: We think he drove the car that we saw him exiting.

Tale Number 17 – Care For A Canapé, Old Man?

Another summer night with another graveyard partner working the unincorporated surface streets of East Los Angeles.

We turn off one main street onto another, coming in behind a red convertible that has its white top down. Two males are in the front of the car.

The next main street has a red stoplight at the intersection. The convertible operator drives right through the red light like it is not there. He doesn't slow, he doesn't flash his brake lights, he just motors through like the red light is a green light and we aren't behind him.

No wonder, we soon find out.

When my partner and I walk up on the car after we stop it, we find both occupants zoned out to behind the moon.

On the chrome shift-lever console cover between the two bucket seats sits a clear plastic dish about five inches in diameter and maybe an inch deep. The dish is heaped almost to the brim with pills of many hues, shapes, and sizes.

Barring the different sizes, if you just glanced at the dish's contents, you might mistake them for mini-jelly beans. But they weren't.

There is an eclectic assortment of every controlled substance with which my partner and I are familiar on the street—and then some.

"Reds." Help yourself. "Cross-tops." Help yourself. "Whites." Help yourself. A veritable dry cocktail of prescription-only drugs.

The two occupants have been driving around enjoying the summer's evening, helping themselves from the dish like one would help oneself from an hors d' oeuvres platter at a party. "Why yes. I *do* believe I will have another. Thank you so very much. Do you care for one, Old Man?"

The two are so out of it they make no attempt to conceal their stash when we stop them or when we walk up on the car.

They both end up being guests of Los Angeles County for the night, and probably of the state for longer than that.

I am just happy to have them off the road.

The following four tales certainly make one ask the question, "*What* were they thinking?" I know they caused me to ask.

Tale Number 18 – It's Only Sticking Out A Little Bit

The vehicle code of the state of California allows a load on a passenger vehicle to extend only six inches from the right side of the car, and zero inches on the left. In short, one can't legally use one's passenger car to carry long things outside the car.

But some do.

I'm working about twilight on an afternoon shift out of the Santa Fe Springs Area office when I observe a Volkswagen bug proceeding on a narrow, tree-lined residential street. The vehicle periodically swerves severely to the left over the center line, and then rejoins the traffic lane of the two-lane roadway.

Man, I think, this driver is a good candidate to be a drinking driver.

When I stop the vehicle, I find that the young high school fellow, who is driving, is not drunk. Not even on drugs. He is closer to operating under the influence of a lack of judgment.

He is transporting an eighteen-foot pole vault pole in his VW bug. He has the pole stuck through the open right side passenger window. The bottom of the pole is anchored in the seat cushion crack between the upright back portion of the rear seat, and the bench seat's cushion in the area behind the driver's seat. There is about twelve feet of pole protruding from the window edge. About.

Each time he closes on a tree or parked car on the narrow residential street, he has to swerve to avoid unilaterally jousting with the other object.

I document his lack of judgment and require him to adjust the load in some manner to make it safe to transport and to be legal.

To adjust the load, so he can proceed home from pole vault practice, he prevails upon a resident bystander to be allowed to leave the pole there on the resident's lawn until he can return to get it in a more suitable vehicle: his Dad's station wagon. I also suggest he tie a red flag on the projecting end after he loads it.

Tale Number 19 – "X" Marks The Spot

I am working afternoon shift, again in the summer, but this time in Fresno. My beat is the highway that is the Fresno area's main thoroughfare to and from the nearby Pacific Coast.

I turn onto the two-lane state highway from a side road that runs through the myriad vineyards in the area. Up ahead of me is a motorcycle being driven at the sixty-five-mile-per-hour speed limit.

While the male operator isn't speeding, something doesn't seem right to me about the bike. I close up to check better. The bike is kind of wobbling a teeny bit, as though the wheels aren't exactly round. Also, the rear left bracket to hold the taillight, turn signal, and stop light assembly is broken. The lighting assembly is hanging down and is not working. The right side bracket is badly bent, but its lights are working.

At the bike with the rider, after stopping him for the defective lighting, I discover a new and different irregularity. The rider, who reports to me that he was injured in a motorcycle accident the month before, has his right leg in a cast up to just below his knee. He needs crutches to walk.

Where did he have the crutches, you may ask?

Mr. Ingenious placed the crutches in a "X" fashion across the gas tank. Each area between the cushioned armpit pad and the supporting "Y" bracket underneath that pad has been hooked over each of the rear view mirrors on the handlebar, one on each side. Of course, that will not keep the crutches from falling off. To secure the crutches better, the motorcyclist put a bungee cord around the "X" crossing of the crutches, and another bungee cord through that one, and then through his pants belt above his fly. In this manner, he tensions the crutches to keep them from falling, and also makes them flexible for steering when he turns the bike. The motorcycle doesn't steer too well, because the crutch ends hooked over the mirrors don't allow for a lot of slack going around corners, despite the scissoring effect of the "X."

He, too, is documented despite his persistent and civil protestations that he thought he had ingeniously solved his crutch transport problem.

To adjust his load in order to proceed, we take the crutches and put them together side-by-side. Then, we make a sling out of the bungee cords so he could sling the crutches at a diagonal across his back like a rifle might be carried.

"Why didn't I think of that?" he says.

I dunno.

Tale Number 20 – You're Not Heavy, You're My Moped

I am just preparing to exit the freeway onto a main street off-ramp at late afternoon of a midweek day. I am at the entrance of the down grade off ramp when I see a black Harley-Davidson motorcycle go through the signalized intersection of the ramp exit, and the main street of the surface street below.

The motorcycle is carrying a red moped motorbike (a low-horsepower motorized bicycle, but the name is actually an acronym for *mo*torized *ped*estrian) across the rear fender, resting against, and I hope tied to, the chrome sissy-bar (motorcycle lingo for the back rest for a rear passenger).

Because of traffic and my location, and the Harley's speed and location, I am out of position to stop the bike for the unsafe projecting load.

Even today, I would like to have a picture of that.

Tale Number 21 – It's A Reach

In the traffic law enforcement business one can never say one has seen it all, regardless of the years on the highway chasin' taillights. There is always someone somewhere who is figuring out a new and different way to make some Chippie's day.

For instance:

One Saturday, I see a car—a small two-door compact—motoring on a busy four-lane boulevard. The driver is splitting the lane line between the fast lane and the shoulder lane by putting about one-fourth of his vehicle into the fast lane, and riding in the shoulder lane with the rest.

Taking his quarter out of the middle, as it were.

There is no weaving. He is driving straight as a laser.

The cars in the fast lane overtaking this driver's car are the ones who are weaving. Those cars are swerving around the subject car and over the double yellow center line into the opposing fast lane, as each driver encounters the slower, but not slow, vehicle. It is the swerving traffic that actually catches my attention. I close up to check out the situation with a traffic stop.

The situation is this: The driver, returning home from the home improvement store, is carrying eight—count 'em!—eight two by fours, each ten feet long. Moreover, they are not tied to the roof, or slung under the car as I have seen others do. And they aren't all jammed together in the right front passenger window similar to the vaulting pole transport. No, siree.

Using what room he has to work with, the driver has slid the lumber through the two front windows, the driver's and the passenger's, across the front seat.

His car is about five feet wide, leaving five feet to project, or two and one-half feet of wood projecting on each side of the car. Almost a yard of lumber sticking out of each window.

But wouldn't that block the access to the steering wheel? you might ask. Yes.

The driver has the two by fours stacked in two stacks of four each and tied with string so they will not slide apart. By his sliding the front seat back a touch, he can sit back farther and still get his feet to the pedals, and he can put his hands under the lumber onto just the bottom part of the steering wheel to drive the car through the Saturday traffic.

The lumber, contrary to its description of being two inches thick, is only one and one-half inches thick, so he has six inches of lumber in height in front of him—from the top of the windowsills. He could have driven with his hands on the top curve of the steering wheel, I guess, but he would have had to hold his arms up over the lumber. That would have been tiring, I suppose.

I documented the violation.

To adjust his load, so he can leave, he prevails upon an employee of the gas station he yielded into to let him leave his lumber there while he goes to borrow a friend's pickup truck.

Sounds good to me. Wonder why he didn't do that first?

I dunno.

Tale Number 22 – Helpless In The Act

We are on a traffic stop in the city of Los Angeles one summer night on graveyard. My partner stopped an excessive surface street speed violator going westbound in our area beat in the unincorporated part of L. A. County, but the driver was slow to yield. He crossed the city limit line that ran through the center of the street of the signalized intersection three hundred feet east from where we are stopped.

I am standing back by our patrol car while my partner is forward with the vehicle occupant, writing him a ticket. We are code 4 (safe/okay), so I relax a bit. There isn't anything else going on this weekday early morning hour, and I am just looking around taking in what there is to see.

At that moment a green mini-bus camper comes into view northbound on the otherwise empty street near which we are stopped. I always wanted one of those campers, but I never seemed to get motivated to buy one. As I watch the camper van approach the intersection on the green light, I'm thinking how great it would be to have one to travel and camp in.

Then I notice a dark-colored pickup truck coming westbound toward the same intersection on a likewise empty street. It is coming toward our location. It is coming as fast westbound as the mini-camper van is going northbound.

But the pickup truck's traffic light is red.

Oh, no.

Oh, yes.

The pickup truck collides with the camper van at the rear right quadrant of the passenger side of the camper van. The camper van's doors pop open, including the hinged double cargo doors amidships of the van on the passenger side. The vehicle lifts, and spins on its rear wheels like a dancing circus elephant. The entire loose contents of the vehicle, including the two unseatbelted passengers (pre-mandatory seat belt days), are ejected in the two or three circular spins the camper makes before it falls onto its right side, where it spins some more while still sliding. It slides to a stop about two hundred feet from us.

The pickup stops in the intersection. Its front is crunched in, and steam is rising from under the buckled hood.

My partner cuts the violator loose immediately. He tells the man he will mail the ticket to him.

While my partner finishes with the violator, I call for an ambulance and the Los Angeles Police Department (LAPD). Then, we both run to the passengers of the crashed vehicles with our first aid kit and 44 blankets.

We come to the camper van passengers first. They are two thirtyish females. Both are alive with broken bones and severe cases of road rash, the skin abrasion one gets from sliding and rolling across a rough surface. I handle the two, who are one hundred feet apart, while my partner goes to the pickup truck driver.

The driver is still behind the wheel. He is alive with broken bones, too. My partner leaves him in the truck to avoid possibly creating more injury by moving him down to the asphalt to lay him out. He covers the man with a blanket to keep him warm, as I did with the females. None has any visible extensive bleeding.

As we start to set out flares, the ambulance and the paramedics arrive. Shortly behind them, an LAPD unit arrives to handle the investigation.

With all the help present, and after giving our statements to the officer, we return to patrol.

I decide I don't want a camper van any more.

Tale Number 23 – Bigger Is Not Necessarily Better

I am en route to meet another unit for lunch break one nice summer afternoon, and I'm motoring south on a four-lane city street approaching a signalized intersection with a two-lane side street.

At this time, I see a young man on a red moped (like the one that was on the back of the Harley) make a large circle and a half in the intersection. The cars on the four-lane street, which have the green light, have to stop to avoid colliding with this daring-do nonthinking young driver. I see him zip east on the two-lane street, and turn into the parking lot of a moderately-sized Saturday-busy shopping center.

I go after him by turning into the lot from the four-lane street. The chase is on. Well, kind of.

To start with, he doesn't know I am after him even though I have the red light up. Nor do the people walking, drivers in cars, and kids playing in the busy lot. The boy on the moped is zipping through the shoppers without real regard for their presence, going wherever he goes, and driving any way he wants. To the noninvolved, because of the quiet red light, I am just another car. I have to exercise great caution.

Reluctantly, I decide to kick on the siren. I mean, it is just a moped, but the kid is driving wild. But unlike the usual pursuit, I do not call dispatch (no requirement) to tell them I am in pursuit of…a moped! Usually, we put pursuit calls out so other units, monitoring the channel, will come to assist. But in this case, I ain't that dumb. I'd be the poster boy at every briefing. Those guys would still be laughing at me.

Now with the siren on, the drivers and the walkers cut me some slack. With the siren on, the moped driver knows I'm after him, and he uses the created slack to his advantage like most chasees do in a code 3 pursuit. He drives through the spaces between the parking lot's concrete bumper chocks at fifteen to twenty miles per hour, crossing the vehicular access isles. But I have to go up and down the isles at five to ten miles per hour. My car won't clear driving over the chocks. He's got me. I know he's got me, and he knows he's got me.

Finally, young Knievel Wannabe disappears into the sunset by cutting straight across the parking lot through the chocks. He gets out onto the four-lane street to zip away forever. I am still plowing my way through one of the busy access isles when I last see his dust.

It's the only pursuit in which I ever lost the suspect.

Tale Number 24 – Wadda Ya Mean, Woo-Woooooo?

It is a delightful, balmy, summer night in Fresno County. The kind of evening where it is nice to go for a drive and we are. My good friend KP and I are working the graveyard shift. We have not been busy and are enjoying the night of slow patrol as we mosey around.

About 4:00 AM on this Sunday, dispatch calls to snap us out of our reverie. She sends us to an 11-83 on the old state highway near a rural town in the south half of the county. We respond—to what, we don't know.

In this case, it is more of an incident than an accident, though technically, it is an accident. But, no matter, the driver doesn't see the need for a report. Right then.

The driver of the very sharp, mid-'60s, lowered, super yellow, two-door passenger car swung too wide when turning right to enter a short road that crosses a single railroad track paralleling the highway. He overshot the approach, probably going too fast, drove down a short moderate grade on the left side of the short roadway, and then went across the rounded-bottom dip of the railroad right of way, and up the right of way's embankment to the rails. The front axle of his sharp car is hung up on the left rail of the track. There is no damage to the car and no injury. All he needs is a tow truck, and then everyone can leave, including about twenty to twenty-five bystanders who have appeared from nowhere in the dark. (Where do*oooo* they come from?)

Given the hour of the night (or morning, depending on your viewpoint), there is no vehicular traffic to concern us, but we don't know about train traffic.

It is KP's "out" to handle the incident. (Partners rotate events to spread the workload evenly.) He calls dispatch, and advises that we have a car stuck on Such & Such railroad tracks. He requests a tow truck for the car, and asks our dispatcher to contact the railroad dispatcher to ascertain the status of possible nearby railroad traffic.

Shortly, dispatch calls. "65-73, Fresno."

Me: "Fresno, 65-73. Go ahead."

Dispatch: "65-73. Such & Such Railroad dispatcher advises the closest train is just leaving Bakersfield, and is not a hazard." (Bakersfield is about ninety miles south of where we are.) I acknowledge the train information, and request the dispatcher to get an ETA from the tow company so we'll know what we're looking at for a time factor between the tow truck arriving and the reported northbound train arriving.

In about five minutes, our dispatcher calls back. She advises the tow company reports that their truck should arrive in twenty minutes.

I "10-4" the dispatcher, hang up the mike, and turn in the seat to stand up outside the car to tell KP the info.

At that time, I hear—very close and very distinctly—"Woo-woooooo. Woo-woooooo."

I bolt from the patrol car, and run over to where KP is standing. We both look down the track, no doubt with our eyeballs springing from our eye sockets like in cartoons of old. There, about five miles south of us, but *very northbound*, is the bobbing headlight of an oncoming Such & Such Railroad freight train. (Locomotive headlights swivel up and down.)

Somebody or somebodies have made a big misstrake.

We yell at and motion to everyone to clear the area. My partner begins waving his flashlight in the emergency wave off side-to-side swing we are instructed to give trains to stop them. I run to the patrol car to get road flares, run back to the middle of the tracks, light two flares, and begin swinging them quickly back and forth making the wave off motion of a crossing "X."

The train keeps a-comin'!

The headlight on the front of a train that shows when its brakes are applied and in lockup is not lighted. The brakes are not applied. It takes a train about a mile to come to a stop under full emergency braking.

Here it comes, ready or not.

We both keep flagging with our flashlight and flares as long as we safely can, but ultimately, we have no success. Then we, like the rest, run for safety.

The freight train comes through about forty to fifty miles per hour. The front of the engine hits the right front of the car. At that very instant, my partner makes an exclamation of a scatological nature, throws his hat onto the ground, and stomps it.

The force and energy of the impact on the car is so quick and strong that it spins the front of the car to the left and out, and swings the right rear of the car in, hitting the train. That impact does the same thing, but in reverse, impacting the car again, and that impact creates another spin and impact into the now slowing train.

After the last impact, the train kicks the car loose. The car does a barrel roll down the embankment into the rounded-dip at the bottom of the embankment, and then rolls back up onto its wheels, settling on its suspension.

The driver runs over from his safe place of observation to look in total disbelief at his formerly show-sharp car.

In a matter of minutes—seconds, probably—the once pristine, undamaged, super-sharp passenger car is totally destroyed. It now looks like the Jolly Green Giant grabbed it and crunched it like a beer can.

Then, the tow truck arrived.

Tale Number 25 – Construction Destruction

The county of Los Angeles is doing construction work on a residential street in unincorporated East Los Angeles. They are doing something with sewer pipe. This particular street, which is under construction, has both ends of the street closed with multiple barricades and multiple signs that read "Road Closed."

But this early Sunday morning about three o'clock, the intoxicated young driver of a lowered two-door passenger car decides, according to his passenger, that he is going to take his regular route home despite the road closed signs. He drives between the barricades, knocking two of them down, and proceeds on the torn-up roadway, intending to drive several more blocks.

About mid-first-block in the road construction area, workers have cut a ramp down into the earth. The ramp goes down about five feet in depth to a trench that is about thirty feet long. The trench ends squarely at a wall of earth that the workers are probably going to dig out their next work day.

Sticking out from that wall of earth about two to three feet below the surface is an approximately twelve- to fifteen-foot length of two-inch galvanized pipe. The end has been cleanly trimmed off. I think the pipe is an old water line.

Our driver, moderately proceeding in his car on the closed street under construction, drives down the dirt ramp unintentionally, and crashes the front of his car into the wall of earth. Worse still, the two-inch pipe scrapes across the car hood, punches through the windshield, goes through the driver's right shoulder just under the collarbone, continues through him into the back of the front seat and on into the rear seat's back rest, pinning the driver in the car.

He is conscious, and anesthetized enough by the drink he has consumed earlier that he is relatively comfortable as he sits. Until the fire department starts cutting the pipe to get him out.

In order to get him out of the car, which is in close quarters, because of the dirt walls of the trench, they cut the pipe off fore and aft of him, leaving a section in his shoulder. It is determined by the fire department and medical personnel that it is better to leave the pipe section in the shoulder to keep more dirt out of the wound and to reduce bleeding, and to let the hospital people remove the pipe. Better for them, bad for him, especially when they work on the pipe, despite the pain easer the paramedics give him.

Every time the metal saw touches the metal pipe he sings louder than the cutting saw, and rightfully so. The fire guys keep working on the pipe little by little, and finally the pipe is cut on both ends. Then they have to separate the seat back and him from one another. Like the pipe pain, he let us know about the separation, too.

With the car still in the hole, he is removed with great effort and pain with the eighteen-inch-long piece of pipe projecting through and under the right side of his collarbone. They have to place him on the ambulance gurney just so to make the ride to the hospital.

I think all the fire department and ambulance people working on him that night were more relieved than he was when they got him out. I think they certainly felt they earned their money every time that saw touched the pipe.

I know I did, because I can still hear him.

Tale Number 26 – Crying Wolf In The Rain

I am working the afternoon shift on a beat that is the south half of the freeway that runs through Fresno County on another very rainy day of a rainy week.

I have been working this beat on and off over some four or five years by the time of this incident. I know the beat. At least, I thought I knew the beat.

About 8:30 PM of this dark and stormy night (had to do it), the dispatcher calls me.

"65-73, Fresno."

"Fresno, 65-73." I give my location. "Go ahead."

"65-73, we have a report of a dam breaking near Small Town." (Small town by the freeway, south of Fresno, and about ten miles north of my present location.)

"A dam breaking?" I ask questioningly, without benefit of a call sign while trying to rack my brain about where in the hell a dam is by the freeway near Small Town. The closest dam I know of is thirty to forty miles away in the foothills northeast of Fresno.

"Near Small Town?" I ask bewilderedly, again without call signs.

"65-73, Fresno. 10-4. The caller says the dam is breaking on the east side of the freeway."

Again, no call signs: "The east side of the freeway?" I repeat inanely with not a clue where any such dam is that she is referring to, or might be. "10-4, Fresno. I'll go see what I can see. 65-73."

Where do I check? Where is the flippin' so-called dam that's breaking? I've not a clue.

I drive north on the freeway in the moderate rain toward the general area described by the dispatcher. When I close half that distance, I see a large radiance ahead in this usually dark area. On this very dark night that radiance makes the area look like a space shuttle launch. Where is that coming from? I wonder.

On arrival, I find every TV station, and a radio station, with wheels to roll, has their communication equipment parked on the freeway shoulders. Both sides. Reporters, photographers, and their technical people are out of their vehicles standing on the shoulder in the rain. Their vehicles have their multitude of white outside lights on with their spotlight beams askew here and there.

The TV stations' news people monitored the call to me on their police frequency scanners, and rolled their equipment to the area, arriving before me.

I pull up behind the news trucks on the northbound shoulder and get out to look around. I thought maybe they knew something I didn't, and had located The Dam in the presently pouring rain.

They all come running to me, and in rapid order start firing questions.

"Where's the dam breaking?"

"Where's the dam that's breaking?"

"Can you tell us where the dam is that's breaking? We need to get shots of it. We have a broadcast at eleven."

"Where's it at, officer?"

"Hold on. Hold on," I say, putting my hands up in front of me with my palms out. "I haven't a clue where any dam is around here."

"But your dispatcher said a dam is breaking when she called you," someone said.

"That's true," I counter, "but I've been out here day and night for several years. I don't know of a dam, breaking or otherwise, out here. Let me jump back into my unit and take another swing through."

I left to drive up and down the immediate freeway area shining the white spotlight through the rainy darkness at topography that I knew didn't have a dam. I didn't see anything even remotely like a dam. I returned to the first group of reporters, who had been joined by those that stopped originally on the other side of the freeway.

As I get out and walk up on the group, someone says in my direction, "They found it. It's over there." The "it" is said like they found a body.

"They found it?" I query out loud to no one in particular. "Over there?" I query more. "Where over there?" I continue on. I go "over there."

"Over there" is a shallow ponding basin on the other side of the freeway perimeter fence. The basin is surrounded by about a two-foot high dirt berm. The basin is a catchwater hole, basically, about half the size of an Olympic sized-swimming pool, designed to take the run off water from some of the small town's surface streets. It is dry and invisible in the summer and usually can contain the normal runoff from normal rainfall. Tonight, it is well-filled with water, but not full. It is also invisible in the winter due to its location and darkness. It is not part of the freeway right of way but is located right next to it. If the berm around the basin should fracture, the water would run along the edge of the freeway perimeter fence, and not out onto the freeway, because the freeway roadbed is raised some feet.

The reporters all start returning to their vehicles. They are muttering in disgust that they had to roll out on this bad weather night and don't have a big dam-breaking story with film at eleven.

I wait until they all leave to be assured there is no accident with all the vehicles leaving the shoulder and merging into the moderate traffic coming by at freeway speeds. Then there would be film at eleven.

When all had left, I depart the dam-breaking scene ready to respond next year if I get called again. Now, I know where it is.

Tale Number 27 – Such A Deal He Has For Me

During the almost twenty-five years I served in the CHP, I received only one offer of a bribe.

That statement is not a complaint.

Sometimes, out-of-state drivers I stopped reported that in their state when an officer stopped them, the officer expects to see a fifty dollar bill behind the driver's license when it was proffered by the stopped driver. That embarrasses me, even now as I write this.

And that is a complaint.

But in my case, I'm not talking about a paltry fifty dollar bill. I'm talking real money: a thousand dollars. One Big One. A Big Bill, or as the bankers write it in their shorthand, $1.0.

All I have to do for the big moola is take the handcuffs off an intoxicated driver arrestee and send him back to the car he was driving so he can go to the appointment to which he was going to make a big bucks sales commission.

Do I have to write that I didn't do it?

On this early Monday morning at almost six thirty, the near-beginning of the day shift that I very infrequently worked, I encounter a leftover Sunday night drinking-driver trying to head home, although he is doing it very poorly. He is on the freeway through Fresno County at the very south end of the southern half of the freeway beat.

I stop him for driving really badly. He is weaving and lane-straddling, from almost the planted center divider, through the two traffic lanes, onto the shoulder, and then back the other way.

I give him the field sobriety tests, which he cannot do, and arrest him for deuce.

As soon as he is seated in the right front seat place of honor, he begins to offer the money.

His words are similar to, "Officer, I have to be at Such & Such company this morning to seal a big business deal to sell our product to a Japanese company. I have to be there. If I'm not there, my company loses millions of dollars of business, and I lose out on thousands of dollars of commission. It will affect my year-end bonus, too. If you let me go, I'll give you a thousand dollars."

All the way back to Fresno en route to the jail to book him, he repeatedly offers me the money, becoming more earnest in his offer the closer we get to Fresno. I have my tape recorder running to capture this lucrative proposal for use as evidence of a possible bribery charge.

A side benefit of his offer, he reports, is that if I let him go, his wife, whom he said was out of town, wouldn't know he had been out doing things with other people he should not have been doing as a married man. But that's his business. My business is removing drunken drivers off the road to insure their safety, and the safety of the others on the road. His driving is a perfect example of why he should be removed. He was a rolling crash looking for a place to land. But he is mostly concerned about not being present to make thousands.

At the jail, I tell him that the sheriff's deputies will probably release him on his own recognizance if his record is clean with no warrants, once they are assured the alcohol is out of his system. If they don't, he will have to call his friend to post bail for him.

I tell him also I don't think he is going to make his eight o'clock morning appointment time for his big deal. I suggest he use one of his two phone calls to obtain a short postponement of the deal time. He didn't think that would work because the representatives from Japan had planes to catch.

I ask him: If this deal is so important to his company and himself, why did he not keep himself ready for the deal this morning, instead of celebrating prematurely, and ending up being put into the pokey? I told him he was counting the pot, but the dealing wasn't done. He looked at the floor and didn't say anything.

I filed the bribery charge with the DWI (driving while intoxicated) charge. I don't know how he came out arrestwise, dealwise, or wifewise. I never got a subpoena to go to court, and I never heard from, or of him again.

Tale Number 28 – A Bang Up New Year's Eve

New Year's Eve. Official holiday for highway happenings.

Three Greyhound-bus-sized school buses, each said to be fully loaded with very young grammar school students on winter break, are headed for Disneyland in Anaheim for a special midnight celebration. The buses are traveling one, two, three, convoy-style.

As can be expected, the traffic on the freeway is heavy, and is stop and go at 10:30 PM. Lots of people are hurrying to get to their party location before the new year starts without them.

The buses stop in line in the southbound shoulder lane, because the traffic ahead of them stops. The traffic starts moving again. Bus number one starts rolling. Bus number two starts rolling. Bus number three starts rolling. Bus number one suddenly stops, because the traffic ahead did not proceed as the bus driver number one thought it would.

Buses two and three don't stop.

Bus two rear ends bus one; bus three rear ends bus two. Something on the order of 140 students are exposed to minor injury, and later, some do claim injury.

The multitude of parents following behind the bus convoy in a personal vehicle procession stop behind bus number three in the shoulder lane, too. The parents abandon their cars in the freeway lane, a very busy trafficked freeway any time of the day or night, and race forward to check on their Johnnys and Jennys, Billys and Sallys.

The scene is total chaos. Drivers, teachers, chaperones, counselors, and students—most all of them are out of the buses and are milling around on the freeway shoulder or the freeway with the parents from the cars.

Some people are walking out into the freeway lane to check the bus damage, some are jabbering to another person with both people standing between the cars, or between the buses. Some, including students, are walking along the outside edge of the buses and stopping to converse with uninvolved drivers passing by in other lanes who have to slow down due to the stop and go traffic.

Very dangerous acts and locations because when a crash is over, the accident potential isn't. There are plenty more drunks, inattentive drivers, and just careless drivers coming down the freeway to add to the injury and death stats.

Enter my partner and I in a graveyard unit assigned by L. A. dispatch to… you guessed it!… an 11-83. (*How* can there be *no* details?!) Besides being a traffic accident on a highway for which the CHP has responsibility, it is also a school bus crash. All school bus crashes in whatever way or place throughout the state are the CHP's responsibility to investigate. They are required to be c-a-r-e-f-u-l-l-y investigated and documented.

Right.

The buses have been moved from their points of impact prior to our arrival. Those locations are pertinent, but not terribly important. More importantly, each student is supposed to be diagrammed into the seat they were sitting in at the time of impact, including full name, age, address, and phone number.

But Little Johnny left his seat, and the bus, and has left with Mom and Dad in their car. Injured or uninjured? Don't know. Little Sally, with whom he was sitting, doesn't remember if it was Little Johnny sitting with her or Little Billy. The bus drivers don't know who was sitting where. The bus drivers are not even sure how many students they had on board. They *thought* they were full with forty-five kids in each bus, which makes 135 total. But a counselor said there were 140. Maybe. Some children claiming injury left before our arrival with unknown parties. ("I think he left with his aunty.") Some claiming injury were still there, but had changed seats; others had changed buses in order to sit with friends. Even if Little Sally knew it was Little Billy instead of Little Johnny sitting with her, she didn't know her seatmate's last name.

After a while, in spite of the chaos, we obtain what information we can, get the buses and the cars reloaded, and get everyone under way. None of the buses is inoperable as the collision damage is confined to the sheet metal only.

But small dent or large dent, if it's a school bus, any dent requires a full investigation.

We return to the office, so I can write and write trying to make sense of the partial information in order to leave some kind of intelligent report for the accident investigation desk officer to follow-up.

I wrote on the note that I attach to the report: "Good Luck and Happy New Year."

Tale Number 29 – Such A Cute Puppy

I exit the freeway one day on afternoon shift in daylight hours, and stop at the red light at the bottom of a ramp. Looking to the right, I see an older, worn, full-sized pickup truck with a worn camper shell on it. The truck is parked about two hundred feet to the right of the ramp. A man in work boots, blue jeans, plaid shirt, suspenders, and a very soiled wide-brimmed canvas work hat is standing by the edge of the left front fender.

When I look toward him and the truck, he waves at me with a buff-colored card. That card tells me that he wants me to sign off his fix-it ticket.

I turn right on the red light and pull in behind his truck.

Exiting the patrol car, I walk along the left side of his truck and camper heading for his location. When I am exactly opposite the left side window of his camper shell, with my attention directed at him, and my mind on his fix-it ticket, a very large, sharp-toothed German shepherd's head shoots out through the camper window and snaps at my face with a substantial growl and a loud bark.

I came very close for a need to change Skivvies.

As it was, my right cheek is wet with dog saliva that came from the dog's nose touching my cheek. I remember thinking if I had been just one silly little millimeter closer, I would thereafter be called, "Scar."

The dog's sudden snapping teeth and bark, causes me to jerk away violently to the left, knocking off my hat and ever-present sunglasses.

After regaining my equipment and composure (sort of) and wiping my cheek with my handkerchief, I continue toward the man, who is still standing by the left front headlight of his truck.

I can't get mad at the dog. He is doing his job guarding his master's truck. And I know from general experience that dogs do not like people in hats and/or sunglasses. But I would expect that the owner would warn me about the dog's presence. (Old joke. First guy sees a dog. He asks a second guy standing by, "Does your dog bite?" Second guy says, "No." First guy walks towards the dog, and the dog bites him. The first guy yells out, "I thought you said your dog didn't bite!" The second guy says, "I did. That's not my dog.")

Anyway, when I get to the man, he hands me the fix-it ticket, and simply says, "I forgot the dog was in the back."

Well, thank you very much. Your apology is accepted.

Tale Number 30 – Stubborn Is as Stubborn Does # 1

It is early in a summer graveyard shift in East Los Angeles. My partner and I are assigned to the Pomona Freeway between the east city limits of Los Angeles proper and the I-605 Freeway. I am driving.

We enter the eastbound freeway lanes into light traffic from the on-ramp of a major thoroughfare. We are on routine patrol. It is just another night with no place to go but back and forth on the freeway.

A big rig combination of refrigerated double trailers passes by on the freeway as we are coming up the ramp. The rig is in the otherwise empty shoulder lane of the four eastbound lanes. We are a hundred feet or so behind the tractor-trailers when we come onto the freeway at sixty-five miles per hour in the sixty-five miles per hour speed limit. The rig is substantially pulling away at our speed.

This is not good: The big rig eighteen-wheeler speed limit in California is fifty-five miles per hour.

Closing up a bit to about three car lengths (twenty-feet per length), I begin to pace the rig's speed. I determine the driver is at seventy-eight miles per hour.

I put up the red light. The driver yields to the freeway shoulder.

Walking up on the right side of the rig on the shoulder to the cab, I call the driver down to meet me. A relief driver is seated in the right side passenger seat.

When the driver arrives on the ground with me, I explain I stopped him for seventy-eight miles per hour.

"No way," he says, "I was at fifty-five."

"Sir," I say, "I came on at Atlantic Blvd. at sixty-five right behind you. You were pulling away from me then. I started a pace on you at about three car lengths from your rear trailer, and you held that seventy-eight until I put the red light on you."

"No way," he continues.

"Sir, give me your driver's license and registrations. I'm going to write you a citation for seventy-five for exceeding the truck speed limit of fifty-five." (The "discount" is to allow for speedometer error on the part of the driver and for fairness. Our speedometers are calibrated.)

"Write what you want. I'm not signing it."

Uh, oh. This does not sound like this will be the hoped for ubiquitous routine traffic stop. I go back to the right side area of the patrol car to write the ticket while my partner watches the men. The relief driver by then has gotten down from the truck, and is on the shoulder talking with the driver.

Ticket written, my partner and I go back to the former occupants of the vehicle. I explain the ticket to the driver just like I do with each driver I cite.

"I ain't signing it," he says firmly for openers, before I start to explain.

"Sir," I say, reading the print above the signature line on the ticket in the box where he is to sign: "It says, 'Without admitting guilt, I promise to appear at the time and place checked below.' All you're promising to do when you sign is to go to court to clear the matter."

"I don't care what it says, I'm not signing it."

Some months earlier, I cut an article from *The Los Angeles Times* regarding a reader's question about whether one had to sign a ticket. The printed answer was "yes," followed by an explanation such as I read above. I laminated the article, and stuck it in my ticket book just for these types of infrequent situations created by hard-headed people. I showed the article to him, indicating its source.

"I ain't signing your ticket."

The department's policy on these matters is this: Explain the signature line to the violator. If the violator still refuses, call the shift sergeant to explain it to the violator. If the violator still refuses to sign after that explanation, guarantee the violator's appearance in court by booking him/her into the county jail.

I call dispatch and request they roll our sergeant.

The sergeant comes out. "Did you explain the signature line to Mr. Stubborn # 1?" he asks on arrival.

"Yes, Sarge. I even showed him this article I cut out."

The sergeant looks at the article, hands it back to me, and walks up to Mr. Stubborn # 1, who is standing with his relief driver.

"Did the officer explain the circumstances to you of what is going to happen if you don't sign the ticket?"

"Yes," the truck driver says.

"Do you understand you will be booked into jail?"

"Yes," the driver says again.

"Will you sign the ticket?" the sergeant asks.

"No."

"Book 'im."

Then the relief driver speaks up. "For God's sake, Charlie, sign the f-ing ticket, and let's get out of here."

"I'm not signing the f-ing ticket now, or ever. They can go screw themselves."

"Well," said the relief driver, "give me the keys and I'll get the load delivered and come back to get you."

"You ain't takin' my f-ing truck, now, or ever, without me," Mr. Stubborn # 1 says.

"*What?*" the relief driver exclaims surprisingly and loudly. "If we don't deliver the reefer (truck talk for refrigerated) load of vegetables, they'll spoil and we won't get paid. They're gonna tow and store the truck if you won't let me have it."

"Don't care. I'm not signing the chicken s--- ticket, and you're not taking my truck!"

And so it came to pass, that Mr. Charlie Stubborn # 1, despite my best efforts, the efforts of my partner, the efforts of his partner, and the efforts of the sergeant, was transported in hooks (handcuffs) to the Los Angeles County hoosegow to guarantee his appearance, when his signature would have done the same thing.

His fully-loaded refrigerated trailers full of produce went to the vehicle storage yard driven by a tow driver. His relief driver went off into the dark of the night as a passenger in a taxi to some location (I know not where).

All this was for naught. Charlie still had to answer to the ticket charge in court, about which I never heard.

Why, then, did he do what he did?

Tale Number 31 – Stubborn Is As Stubborn Does # 2

It's a lovely fall Saturday afternoon as I enter southbound Interstate 5 (Santa Ana Freeway) in the City of Commerce area of Los Angeles County. Traffic, surprisingly for a Saturday afternoon, is light.

Up ahead, less than a quarter of a mile, is a big gray dog—a Greyhound bus. It is out in the fast lane (legally), zipping past what I judge is sixty-five mile per hour traffic in the adjacent lane.

I do some zipping myself, and shortly, I am directly behind the bus, inside the driver's view from the bus's mirrors, and doing what we call a "bumper check." I have him at eight-five miles per hour. I hold the pace for less than a mile.

I don't know if the bus is loaded or empty, but it doesn't matter. The rig is restricted to sixty-five miles per hour. It is just more unsafe if the bus is loaded.

Just as I start to move left a bit to provide a view of the patrol car to the driver and to put up the red spotlight to make the stop, the driver changes to the middle of the three lanes, and brakes with the brake lights coming on, which signals to me that my enforcement presence is now known. Slowing to sixty-five miles per hour, and then slower, the driver moves onto the shoulder and stops.

When I walk up to the bus's door, it is open. The driver is behind the wheel and not making discernable effort to step out to meet me. I have to ask him to come down.

He gets up and out of the chair, and moves toward the door and steps out. All done kind of slow. What the heck, I think, maybe he gets stiff while driving.

I tell him I stopped him for eighty-five miles per hour, checked by a bumper pace.

He makes no reply, just looks at me.

I ask for his driver's license and bus registration certificate. He moves with the deliberate speed of a sloth wakening from hibernation as he looks through all the papers for his driver's license in his loaded wallet. He looks at each and every side of each and every paper. Slowly. After a while, he produces the license, and eventually, the registration certificate from the bus.

"How many passengers do you have on board?" I ask.

"Forty-five," he says. He is fully-loaded. He tells me where he is going.

I tell him I am going to write him a citation for eighty in a sixty-five. I return to the patrol car.

When I return to the bus, he is sitting on the steps of the doorway. I ask him to stand up so I can explain the ticket to him.

He says, "I don't want to."

I move closer, and while he is seated, I explain the citation information.

"I'm not signing it," he says.

I do the refuse-to-sign drill, reminding him that if I have to guarantee his appearance, I will have to contact his company for a relief driver in order to provide for the forty-five passengers to continue the trip.

"I'm not signing it," he continues.

I call the sergeant. The sergeant comes out. He does the refuse-to-sign drill, and then he does the "Hawaii Five O" drill: (TV cop show at the time with the famous line the sergeant gives me.) "Book 'im, Dan-o," the sergeant says.

I call dispatch to request a Greyhound relief driver for a refusal to sign. The man who comes out is the driver's supervisor. He encourages Mr. Stubborn # 2 to sign the citation.

"I'm not signing," is the short reply.

The supervisor chews out the driver for delaying forty-five people due to his stubbornness. More importantly the supervisor continues, for holding the passengers on the freeway shoulder.

The supervisor takes command of the bus, and drives off. The employee who brought the supervisor out drives off. I drive off with Mr. Stubborn # 2. He is wearing hooks in his Greyhound uniform. I deposit him in the Los Angeles County jail to guarantee his court appearance to answer to the simple charge of speeding, when with his signature, he could have continued his trip.

Again, why?

Tale Number 32 – Ouch. Ouch. Ouch.

About twenty-five miles northeast of Fresno is a state park with a dam, lake, and recreation area. (It is one of several thereabouts.) The park lies in the foothills and draws a lot of boaters, picnickers, bikers, swimmers, and other visitors who are interested in relaxing and enjoying summer recreation there. And of course, some people drink alcoholic beverages when they are doing those activities.

Because the recreation area is in the foothills, most of the roads around the park are two-lane and curvy, rising and falling over hillocks as the road follows the topography of the land.

When the sun and the fun and the booze and a bike get together over those curvy roads, traffic collisions occur. Usually, for motorcycles, it is the run-off-the-road variety.

I was dispatched to one such motorcycle accident on a summer afternoon shift I was working.

The rider entered a forty-five degree dog-leg curve to the right where the roadway really narrowed between a large tall granite boulder by the pavement's edge on the right and the protrusion of a large clump of gnarly roots of a Valley Oak growing out of the hillside bank on the left. The biker entered the sharp curve too fast, and after fighting to keep control and trying to make it, he lost to the curve. He went down about one hundred feet out of the curve, and was dumped, with his motorcycle, on the right shoulder of dirt and weeds into the three-strand barbed wire fence strung along the highway right of way.

The fence controlled the livestock of a small adjacent ranch.

When the motorcyclist went into the barbed wire, the wire snarled around him and the bike, wrapping him and it in a tangle of wire and wooden posts.

I arrive at the scene before the ambulance. There isn't much I can do for the man because he is heavily protected by the barbed wire shield. His lower half is partially under the motorcycle. I reach through as I can and apply bandages in an attempt to stem the bleeding of some of the bigger lacerations. But it is a touchy—perhaps no-touch would better describe it—situation because of his entanglement with the wire.

He and his clothes are badly ripped. Luckily he is wearing a helmet, but he is dressed in a T-shirt, jeans, and sport shoes, not the leather jacket and leather pants and boots commonly recommended.

I decide it is best to wait for the ambulance. When I call the fire department, I ask them to bring heavy-duty wire cutters.

Shortly, the emergency help arrives. Everyone sets to work to free the rider from his torture chamber. But merely putting tension on the wire to cut it causes the former bike rider great anguish, as I learned earlier from trying to barely move the wire to put on bandages.

No matter how delicately the wire is handled, or how delicately he is touched or handled, he has a loud adverse and continuing reaction: "OwwwWWW!"

With great patience and skill, the fire people eventually get the wire cut, freeing the bike rider from his barbed wire torment. The ambulance folks probably used all the bandages in their rig on him. I know I used all of mine before they got there, which they removed to install new ones after the wire was off because they had better access to apply the bandages.

When they finally got him free, bandaged, and loaded on the ambulance, they headed for Fresno with Mr. Lucky.

I say with "Mr. Lucky," because if he had gone about another hundred feet, besides the barbed wire to deal with he would have landed in a very large pile of fresh manure, which had been collected and piled by the fence for pickup.

Out of all bad comes some good.

Tale Number 33 – Four Way, No Way

How many times have you pulled up at a four-way stop-signed intersection and automatically ascertained the informal rotation pattern prior drivers initiated among themselves without passing on the instructions? Too often to mention, I would suppose. Everyone usually takes his turn la-di-da. Automatically.

Enter a cop car in the sequence.

The cop pulls up to the intersection as the last car. Three cars are already there. But nobody moves. It's a standoff. Grass starts to grow. We've been there so long without moving it's almost time to hang the Christmas tree lights.

Behind our windshield, we can hear the brain wheels of the other drivers whirring: Let's see, the car on the right is supposed to go first. No, I'm on the right of him, he's supposed to go first. God, I wish he'd go, so we can go. What am I supposed to do here? Who goes first? Ad infinitum.

Finally, we go ahead out of rotation to ease the burden and spare the agony, besides, we only have an eight-hour shift, you know.

Legally (in California), any car can go after stopping, as long as the start off is safe and doesn't interfere with another car. But we do understand the rotation system. After all, we use it before and after work.

Tale Number 34 – Jacked Up

On another late summer afternoon, right around the area on the Santa Ana Freeway where the three-school-bus-bumper-car caper took place, another traffic-impeding event occurs. But this time it is only one vehicle.

I am trying to drive southbound on the three-lane freeway in the prerush hour afternoon traffic. But the traffic is slowing to stop and go, or just plain stop, and is backing up for some unknown reason.

The fast lane is mostly stopped, the middle lane is dead slow stop and go, and the shoulder lane is moving ever so slowly. Evidently, something is plugging up the fast lane.

The Santa Ana Freeway, also known as Interstate 5 at this location, doesn't have a median to speak of. What median exists is about one foot wide on each side of a double band of metal guard rails. That's it for median. The traffic lanes are narrower than usual, and there is a narrow paved shoulder, too.

I move to the shoulder using my rear warning lights and turn signals, and slowly drive the shoulder, trying to move ahead to see what the problem is.

The problem is a stopped car in the fast lane. It is up on a bumper jack at its left rear. The driver has the wheel off and is fiddling around with the spare tire in the trunk of the car.

Stop and go cars in the fast lane behind him are closing right up on the disabled car, and then are crowding over as they are able into the middle lane. Of course, the middle lane drivers don't want their way impeded; they aren't cutting the fast lane drivers any slack to get in. The shoulder lane people are holding their position, too.

The drivers are operating under Tompkins' First Physical Law of Driving: Any delay in driving is intolerable; intolerable driving will adjust for delay.

I park my unit on the shoulder, exit, stop all the southbound traffic, and leave the traffic stopped as I walk to the driver.

He can't get the spare out of the trunk. The nut holding the tire securing device seems to be welded to the bolt. It can not be loosened. I tell the driver to put the wheel with the flat tire back on his car, and to drive the car to the shoulder in front of my car. He can work on his car there better, safer, and Los Angeles can resume moving.

"But officer," if I do that I'll ruin the tire. It's only a puncture now. I can get it fixed. If I drive on the tire, it is going to cut the tire and ruin it."

I reiterate my instructions, and tell him to move on it. He glares at me in exasperation, but starts putting the wheel back on.

While he grumbles and remounts the tire, I direct traffic. I allow each lane to move out ten cars at a time—the law of trickle-through traffic direction.

Eventually, he gets the tire back on. I stop the freeway traffic again, and he drives the car on the bumping wobbly tire to the shoulder. I motion for everyone to move on, and walk over to the driver to see what I could do to assist him.

He is very angry with me.

I try to explain why it is better for him to be on the shoulder doing the job, instead of stopped in the fast lane of the freeway. He doesn't care. He is only thinking about saving the tire versus the cost to replace it. I can't make him understand that his life isn't worth the cost of the tire. Any one of those fast lane cars trying to squeeze into the middle lane that didn't clear his right rear vehicle corner could have knocked the car off the spindly bumper jack pinning him to the pavement, or worse, knocking him backward into the guard rail and crushing him.

Since neither event happened, he doesn't see the merit of my discourse. His only concern is about my making him trash the tire by moving the car. I give him the information to contact my office to get a form to make a claim against the state, because he acted under my lawful authority to direct traffic. The prospect of compensation for his cut tire brightens his demeanor. Shortly, he asks me to call a tow truck for him to come change the tire. I do so and then leave, hoping the traffic will pick up speed with my black and white gone.

For the cost of a tire, he risked his life and argued about it. Tells you how much he unthinkingly thought himself worth in dollars and cents.

Tale Number 35 – I Love To Go A-Wandering

I made a complete patrol check down the southern portion of State Route (SR) 99 Freeway that runs through the middle of Fresno County, and I head back northbound to go to dinner. Nothing is going on. All quiet on the freeway front.

It is dark, about two weeks after the time change from Daylight Saving Time back to Pacific Standard Time.

About a mile south of where I need to turn off to get to the restaurant at which I am to meet an afternoon shift beat partner, I see a small fire. It is back away from the freeway near the embankment for the overcrossing at that location in sort of an alcovelike area. I can't see the fire clearly because of the bushes that block the view.

We frequently see small grass fires along the freeway right of way. They are usually caused by lighted cigarettes thrown from vehicles. We call the fire department to do its duty for those.

This is not one of those cases. While this fire is set on purpose, it isn't arson, per se. Two intrepid European backpackers off to see the world on foot picked this location on the freeway right of way to pitch camp for the evening.

They have their nylon dome tents set up, their sleeping bags laid out within, and a pot of water boiling to hydrate their dehydrated meals. They have made the small campfire from twigs and leaves of the eucalyptus trees and other shrubbery growing thereabouts their camp. The only thing missing is a river view.

I contact the two explorers just before they ring their dinner bell. Only one spoke English.

I tell him they aren't permitted to be within the freeway right of way as pedestrians. It is a dangerous place to camp even if they are permitted to be there. All it would take is one sleepy driver, or an out of control vehicle, and they would be ex-wanderlusters. I prevail upon them to pack up and move out, and direct them to another location that is more suitable to their needs, but it is going to have to be without the fire.

I wait while they break camp, and use their hot water to hydrate, soak, and eat their meal, then direct them off the freeway to the acceptable location about a mile away. They are as happy with that move as I am.

Then, I went to my dinner, 'cause I was really starved after watching them eat.

Tale Number 36 – Even The Meek Can Speak Mightily

I am working the south end of SR 99 one weekday afternoon when I get a call from dispatch to meet the medical transport unit of a local children's hospital. The vehicle is a van with a raised roof cap and is reportedly stopped on the freeway shoulder northbound about in the middle of my beat. It is en route to Fresno.

I respond thinking the rig is mechanically disabled. It is not an ambulance. It doesn't have the medical or emergency vehicle equipment the vehicle code requires an ambulance to have. It just looks similar to an ambulance.

As soon as I pull in behind the rig, a nurse jumps out of the rear door and runs back to my driver's window. She is there before I have the patrol car's transmission in park.

In a rush of words, almost running them together, she says, "We're transporting a preemie (premature birth baby) on oxygen. The oxygen tank gauge is not working correctly. We think we are running out of O^2 (oxygen). Can you take us to the hospital code 3?"

"Absolutely," I say. "Let's load her up in the back seat with you."

The nurse and her driver quickly unload the oxygen tank equipment and the large, clear, storage box-sized lidded bassinet containing the preemie, and put it all in the back seat. The nurse gets in the seat behind me.

We are off code 3; red light on, head lights flashing, four-way emergency lights flashing, rear deck amber light flashing, and the siren on manual mode as needed.

With prudence, we zip up the freeway to Fresno, and then down onto the surface streets toward the north central part of town where the hospital is located.

The nurse is carefully watching the baby and the oxygen supply. When she is not, she is leaning forward resting on the top of the back of my upright seatback like an umpire behind the catcher. I don't know her or her name.

As usual, I catch a lot of red traffic lights, people pulling out of driveways oblivious to the world, and the usual run of drivers who do not pull over to another lane to get out of the way, much less yield to the right curb as required.

What code 3 cops normally experience when coming in behind a car is that the driver—usually driving over the posted speed limit and doesn't see or hear us come up—suddenly does see us and slows without brake lights in front of the patrol car to one-half the speed limit. While slowing down, the driver points in the rear view mirror and then to him or herself as if to say, "Me? You want me?" while trying to figure out what they did wrong while still rolling.

Sometimes after the driver slows, the driver just points at their right temple with their index finger, again inquiring, "Me? You want me?"

I have thought to myself out of frustration, hoping the finger was loaded, go ahead, pull the trigger. Maybe Dirty Harry of movie fame got his "Make my day" saying from working road patrol code 3 before he became a detective.

Today, all this empty-headed driving has been going on since we first began the run. As we get to within three or four blocks of the hospital, a driver ahead just slows to a complete stop in front of us on the four-lane divided street. We are in the fast lane. Another car in the slow lane is just creeping along as some do without yielding, and it is now blocking our way with the stopped car. The cars coming from the opposite direction are ignoring us.

Unexpectedly, the young ladylike nurse, no doubt in a pique of frustration, yells past my right ear in a total surprise to me, "Don't these f-ing people *ever* move out of the way?"

Regaining my physical and social equilibrium, I said, "No, and if they were inside here driving for help, or in an ambulance hoping to get to a hospital, I know they would wish everyone would move over. But they hardly ever do."

I proceed to grab the PA mike and demand the slow lane driver pick up his pace and move out of the way. He does, and we move on toward the hospital.

A bit earlier I had called dispatch to provide our ETA at the hospital. Now I ask the dispatcher to call the hospital to tell them to prepare for our arrival.

When we get to the hospital emergency entrance, personnel are standing by waiting to jump into action. They take the bassinet and equipment and hurriedly go inside with the baby.

I pull away to park the unit. I go inside to check on my baby passenger whom I had not seen. I wanted to make sure she arrived okay, in spite of the delays and stops caused by nonyielding traffic. She is an itsy-bitsy little thing, but in good shape with a fresh bottle of O^2 for her trip reward.

I leave to return to the beat to resume routine patrol, hoping the hearing in my right ear will soon return.

Tale Number 37 – He Flies Through The Air...

It's another balmy summer night in Fresno County. My buddy KP and I are working as graveyard partners on the highway SR 99 beat.

Shortly after the start of the shift, we receive an 11-79 accident call (injury accident, ambulance rolling). The location is the north end of the freeway where the highway runs through a cut between moderate cliff faces on each side. At the location the freeway is four lanes, two north and two south, with a planted dirt median of oleander bushes.

We respond and arrive quickly. Despite our quick response, we find on arrival the ambulance has already gone to the county hospital with the injured solo occupant of the lowered two-door passenger car involved in the crash.

The car is still at its point of rest, partially up the lower dirt embankment of the cliff face on the east side of the freeway. Each wheel is splayed almost to a position similar to "float pads." In the limited freeway light, when we look in the direction the car came from we can't fully determine the path it followed. We can see that it came through the oleander bushes from the southbound side, and came across the two northbound freeway lanes to its point of rest. There are no other cars around, so we think it didn't hit anything on this side of the freeway. Lucky thing, there.

A big rig tractor and trailer is on the other side of the freeway, near where the hole in the oleanders is newly made. We think it might be involved in the accident. We drive over to contact the truck driver.

The rig is not involved; the driver is a witness.

Still very nervous from the event, he says he was driving his combination of vehicles in the shoulder lane going southbound at fifty-five miles per hour when he decided to smoke a cigarette. He put the cigarette in his mouth, and brought his lighter up to light it. At that very second, the passenger car now at rest on the other side of the freeway flies, while on fire, across the front of the truck driver's windshield, pancakes in the center divider in front of the oleanders, then slides through the oleanders onto the concrete northbound lanes of the freeway in a shower of sparks and fire to its point of rest.

My partner asks the driver, "What did you do when you saw the car on fire pass in front of your truck windshield?"

The driver shakily replies, "I said holy s---! And the cigarette fell out of my mouth."

We took his information and cut him loose. He said he needed "a cup of coffee, or something, to steady his nerves."

We drove to the road above the freeway that runs along the top of the west side cliff face embankment. At that location, there is another road that joins the embankment road in a T-intersection. We discovered it was from here that the car started flying out over the freeway.

How do we know?

The steel guard rail, with the six-inch square wooden anchoring posts along the cliff side of the embankment road on the opposite side of the intersection entrance, is broken through. The wooden posts are also broken off. A small sapling tree about three inches in diameter on the freeway side of the guard rail is cleanly sheared off about three feet off the ground.

We now figure the car was going in excess of a hundred miles per hour when it came up the road approaching the T-intersection going toward the freeway below. The car blew through the stop sign, punched through the metal guard rail breaking the support posts, sheared off the sapling, flew off the cliff top, and while losing altitude, flew across the windshield of the eighteen-wheeler and across the southbound freeway lanes—without touching them—pancaked in the center divider, splaying the wheels, and then shot through the oleanders, across the northbound concrete freeway lanes in a shower of sparks and fire, and slid partially up the opposite cliff embankment to a stop.

Makes you want to yell, "Yeeee, hawwww!"

Thinking we have a solo fatal accident, we leave the impact scene to go to the hospital. Inquiring at the ER (emergency room) reception desk about the driver, we are told he is alive and not badly hurt. Amazing! We are granted permission to interview him.

While walking to the victim's room, my partner, whose out it is to handle an accident, tells me he knows what this guy is going to say.

"He'll say that he had nothing to drink; that he had not taken any drugs; that he was only going forty miles per hour when a dog ran out in front of him, or a car came around the corner making him lose control, and he didn't have any choice but to hit the guard rail. You know, the usual story we get."

I acknowledge with an "uh, huh."

At the victim's bedside, KP asks the driver what happened.

"Well, man, I was waiting on my girlfriend to come home from a party, you know, man. I waited and waited, man. She never came home. I got p---ed, you know, man. I really got p---ed. I left to go home, man. I was driving up the f-ing street, and I got more p---ed, you know man. I put my foot in it. I didn't give a s---, man. I hit the guardrail, and went over the cliff."

"How much have you been drinking tonight?" KP asks.

"Well, man, I had some beer while I was waiting on her, you know, man."

"How much have you had?" KP repeats.

"Well, man, I probably had a couple of quart bottles while I was waiting in the car. I hit on a joint, too, man. But I was in her driveway, man," the victim replies.

"How fast do you think you were going when you hit the guard rail?" my partner presses on, wrong so far with his investigative conjecture.

"Well, man, when I looked at the speedometer the last time, I was about one hundred and ten, you know, man."

Wrong again, man... uh... partner.

We left the hospital. KP made out what we call a courtesy report for the sheriff's office.

He turned the incident in as an attempted suicide.

Tale Number 38 – Like Shooting Grounded Birds, No Sport

It's November. I'm working the afternoon shift on the Santa Fe Springs' Interstate 605 beat. It is dark by five o'clock. I've had a very busy day with crashes, and I am behind in completing my reports.

To catch up, I back into the corner of a closed gas station by the exit/entrance to the freeway. This allows me to respond quickly if something else goes down, which I am hoping upon hope it won't.

I flip on the dashboard gooseneck light and commence writing. I want to get as much done as I can, because I'm still hoping to get off work by the end of the shift at 10:15 PM.

At 9:00 PM, I look at my watch. It's coffee time. I decide to skip coffee—What? A highway patrolman skipping coffee? Yes, it does happen—in the interest of getting the paperwork done so I can get off on time. I resume writing.

At 9:20 PM, a car exits the freeway at the ramp. I happen to be looking up at the time, pondering a thought to write. The car stops for the *green light*, and still on the green starts up and drives straight across the intersection at a diagonal into the gas station. It stops opposite my side of the unit about twenty feet away, driver's door to driver's door.

The driver leans into his open window and says, "Eshscuse me, offishshir. Caann you tell me howww to get to the Shandago Freeewayy?"

So much for report catch-up and getting off on time.

Tale Number 39 – The Old Girl

It's summertime, midweek, the graveyard shift in East Los Angeles, around one o'clock in the morning. Nothing is happening on the Long Beach Freeway, our beat.

It's one of those rare nights in L. A. when there are almost no cars on the freeway. I mean e-m-p-t-y. Nothing. That may be hard to believe for someone who has not experienced it, but it is true, nevertheless.

We have gone south from the Pomona Freeway to way past the end of our beat, turned around, and headed back northbound without seeing a single moving southbound car. Going northbound, so far, it is the same thing. Nothing.

But back on our beat, we have gone only a few miles when a yellow 1951 Mercury four-door sedan comes up the on-ramp from the surface street below. The car enters the freeway about two hundred feet ahead of us in the shoulder lane and stays in the shoulder lane of the four-lane northbound side. We are in the lane to the left of the shoulder lane. Both cars mosey along about fifty-five miles per hour in the sixty-five mile per hour freeway speed limit.

My partner and I comment to one another on the nice condition of the older car, and how happy we are to have a car—any car—in front of us.

We have no sooner made that statement when, with a puff of smoke and a hearty heigh-o, the driver stomps it and the car starts racing away: sixty-five, seventy-five, eighty-five miles per hour. What the…? What's going on? At one hundred five miles per hour, the car levels out after several miles. But before my partner, who is driving, can put up the red spotlight, the car slows without brake lights to fifty-five miles per hour, and resumes that speed.

We pull the driver over.

I approach the car on my out. When I get to the driver's window, I find a very sheepish-looking driver of about sixty-five years old, gray-haired and bespectacled.

I tell him, "I stopped you for your excessive speed, sir," and follow that with a question and a statement.

"What the heck got in to you? You were driving along there nice and prudent, then all of sudden you rocketed away. Did a bee sting you, or something?"

"Well, officer," he says, "I bought this car new in 1951. I was tuning it up in the garage tonight, when I got to wondering if the Old Girl still had it in her. After I finished the tune-up, I brought her out here to test drive her where I could go faster. When I saw no one was around, I opened her up. How fast did you clock me?"

"One hundred and five," says I.

"Good," says he, smiling, "she's still got it in her."

I gave the guy a verbal warning. For the conditions, he was not unsafe. I'm sure my decision had *nothing* to do with the fact that my first car, the one I first broke a hundred in as a teenager, was a yellow 1951 Mercury four-door sedan.

Tale Number 40 – Definitely Not A Diamond Day

Someone told me years ago when I was talking about having a bad day that "Sometimes you eat the bear, and sometimes the bear eats you." Those words also go hand in hand with John Denver's song lyrics of "Some days are diamond, some days are stone."

The events I am going to lay before you here were undoubtedly one of the worst days for myself and the others involved. Definitely a day when the bear ate us. A stone day. A bad day at Black Rock.

The 99 Freeway in northern Fresno County exits the county at the San Joaquin River and continues into the next county. At the time the north and southbound lanes crossed the river on separate concrete two-lane bridges.

Also here, the river area near the bridges is a de facto favorite swimming, picnicking, and party area for a significant segment of the local population.

All these factors, and others, come into play one hot summer Fresno day. Four men riding in a lowered four-door passenger car are northbound in the shoulder lane of the 99 Freeway, approaching the northbound bridge. They are overtaking a car that is in the adjacent fast lane and are closing the distance on a tractor-trailer rig ahead of the men's car in the shoulder lane.

The driver of the men's car, apparently not wanting to slow, judges that if he speeds up he can make it through the closing "window" between the fast-lane car and the shoulder lane eighteen-wheeler. The driver cuts the steering wheel sharply to the left to make a quick and severe lane change to quickly get in front of the fast lane car and shoot through the narrowing opening.

The sudden increase in speed and the quick cut of the wheel to the left are too much for the heavily-drinking driver to handle correctly. The car hits the left side wall of the bridge at about one-third the distance across the span and vaults over the top of the bridge railing, falling between the two bridges to the older dry flood plain of the river below.

The car hits the ground squarely nose first, and remains upright like some kind of metal pillar. The front doors pop open on impact, and the front two unseatbelted occupants (premandatory seat belt days) are ejected to the ground. The two back seat passengers, also not seat belted, remain inside the vehicle in the back seat. Their doors remained closed.

The four occupants of the car, all of whom are later found to have BA (blood alcohol) levels near point four zero (.40), some over, some under, are killed in the crash.

If I remember correctly, one of the passengers in the rear seat had a BA level of point five two (.52). That number means that over one-half of one percent of his blood is beverage alcohol. I've been told that at point five zero (.50) one can die from alcohol poisoning. I think the driver's BA level was point three eight (.38). Today's BA legal limit, stated in law and regarded by law enforcement and the courts as an indicator that you are legally intoxicated, is point zero eight (.08). The BA level in effect at the time of the incident was point one zero (.10).

The crash call goes out to the CHP office in the next county whose area of responsibility ends on the north side of the river. Nevertheless, they respond first, and then pass the call on to the Fresno area command, which assigns several units to the crash.

I am one of several officers sent to the scene and end up being assigned to investigate the quadruple fatal accident. It is my beat on which they were driving.

By the time I get to the scene, I am the last of four officers to arrive. Like the others responding, I have to go pioneering around a nearly four-wheel drive type rough dirt road behind a golf course and thread my way through the river area brush on unsigned dirt car tracks to find my way to the area under the bridges.

Before my arrival, the two fatalities in the rear seat of the car are removed to the ground. All four bodies are covered with the yellow blankets. Also, a Fresno unit at the scene calls dispatch, asks for the coroner's office to respond for four down, and also requests a tow truck for the crashed car that is still standing upright.

Our standing instructions regarding the handling of fatals is this: We are allowed to move them only so far as is reasonably necessary to affect a secure location for body integrity pending the arrival of the coroner. Since these four men are out of the car on the ground, out of traffic, covered, and in our immediate presence for protection, there isn't much more we should, or can do, pending the arrival of the coroner, who has been called. Therefore, we go about our business of investigating the crash, gathering measurements and vehicle information. The bodies are left to be searched by the coroner. We wait for him to obtain their identification documents, if any, that we need.

When the coroner did not arrive in what we at the scene regarded as a reasonable response time, dispatch is again radioed, and is asked to inquire for an ETA. The reply from the coroner's office through dispatch is that their van is en route.

When the crash originally occurred, some of the crowd at the river beach and picnic area, maybe one-half mile east of the scene, migrated to the scene to rubberneck. Before the fatals were covered with the 44s, someone in the migrated beach crowd recognized one of the fatals as being the significant other of a relative of someone at the beach. The person at the beach was notified that such and such individual was dead at the scene. That relative telephoned the living significant other, and the living one beat feet for the beach area and the accident scene. When she arrives at the scene, she is in a totally frenzied state, but she is restrained by friends in the crowd, and remains away from the scene center.

Though physically removed, her wails of anguish are very audible to everyone around.

By the time of her arrival, the word is out about the crash. More of the river beach fun seekers begin to drift down to the scene while we wait and wait for the coroner's van.

The day's summer heat is building. The hottest part of our day is around five o'clock. We are closing in on that time, and the probable one hundred-plus degree heat with low desertlike humidity.

The former rubbernecking attitude of the crowd begins to turn hostile, and that hostility starts to be directed specifically to the officers at the scene.

Some anonymous someone in the growing crowd of one hundred to 150 people says in a loud enough voice for all to hear over the rumble of the traffic on the bridge overhead, "Look at 'em. Lettin' 'em lie on the ground like some kind of dead animal meat."

Of course, the significant other of one of the fatals is still totally beside herself, and keeps crying and wailing that she wants to be with him. She is still prevented from doing so by her friends, but now and again an officer has to encourage them to restrain her as she tries to pull away. We can't let her go to the body despite any consideration to do so on our part; the coroner *must be* the person who handles the body. Plus, possible evidence has to be considered.

The restraint of the girl does not endear us to the crowd's heart, nor does their collective perception we have no care or regard for the dead on the ground.

The onlookers are in no mood for an explanation. Besides, it is collectively felt best by the officers not to try to explain what was *not* happening. No matter who might be at fault, we are the visible fall guys.

Sensing the ugliness building in the crowd, one of the officers calls dispatch and requests more officers for backup, just in case.

We again inquire of dispatch about the ETA of the coroner. Again, dispatch, and we, are told that the van is en route. All we can do is wait in the heat and the building tension, which is enhanced by individuals in the crowd verbally sniping at us with cuss words.

The still growing, and formerly mostly quiet crowd, pulling mass and energy from other river beach drinkers, begins to mill around and murmur while focusing their attention to the dead on the ground, the distraught wailer, and the officers whom they perceive are not doing anything regarding the dignity of the dead.

The officers present, and the two additional ones who responded to the backup call, are seriously considering circling the wagons to take a static defensive posture.

The crowd, most of whom have been drinking at the river beach, are hyping themselves up into a beginning hysteria regarding the treatment, or lack of treatment, of the fatals. The hysteria is fanned by the wailer.

Where in the hell is the damn coroner's van? This situation is getting very serious.

In a heartbeat, the crowd turns flat hostile, and it looks like they will charge and attempt to take the bodies. The collection of loose individuals (loose in more ways than one) seems to have coalesced into a single mass with one purpose. One can feel their energy of hostility and sense of determined action.

Hard as it is for me to believe, and later the other officers said they felt likewise, I am really considering unholstering my revolver to demonstrate a strong defensive posture. Pistol pointed down, of course! Nevertheless, we know that we cannot use lethal force against unharmed civilians. (Even barely against armed ones!)

Just then, the driver of a tractor-trailer rig in the shoulder lane of the southbound bridge above us fails to correctly judge the slowing and slow traffic ahead of him in the shoulder lane. Car driver rubberneckers in that lane are trying to look over the bridge railing to see what is going on below as they drive by. In all likelihood, the eighteen-wheeler driver is likewise occupied, because sitting higher, he can see better over the bridge railing.

The driver brakes his rig hard, leaving skid marks. To avoid rear-ending the last car in line he cuts his steering wheel to the right. The tractor hits the bridge wall, then caroms away to the left like a billiards bank shot. The loaded trailer jackknifes, levitates, and swings up past the tractor on the right side. The trailer flips over the bridge's concrete railing, falling to the ground below, pulling the tractor over the railing with it.

Because this new accident occurs at the south end of the bridge's tie to land, the combination of vehicles hits the bridge-tie embankment, rolls down the embankment at an angle, splitting the aluminum trailer apart and spilling its load of canned goods, while the tractor cab bursts into flames with the driver inside. Needless to state, all present, crowd and officers, are stunned.

The truck driver, evident in the cab, is screaming before being engulfed in flames. He is too far away from us, and it happens too fast, for any one of us on the ground to get over to try to get him out.

It is terrible to see and hear.

The formerly hostile crowd, which was nearly on a sensed verge of taking action against the officers, scatters afar when the truck comes over the side as if a live hand grenade has been thrown into their midst.

The truck accident instantly takes the tension out of the air. The accident is most unfortunate for the truck driver, but in reality, most fortuitous for the officers, and maybe even for the crowd. I have no doubt the accident's occurrence saved our bacon, and prevented a possible ugly, ugly outnumbered police versus drinking crowd incident.

The fire department is called for the truck fire. Dispatch is again asked to call the coroner's office.

About five minutes after the last call, the earlier called tow truck and the coroner's white van pull into the scene under the bridge. The coroner's van, which has *no* communication two-way radio, suffered a flat tire en route, and was delayed having the tire changed. The responding assistant coroner, a rather corpulent slow-moving individual, changed the tire himself without any sense of urgency, after all, he knew his clients had no rush.

After all is said and done, the scene is cleared of the five bodies; the two coroner vans (a second had been called); the fatals' car; the tow truck for the fatals' car; the fire department rig; the burned tractor; the tow truck for the tractor; the trailer; the tow truck for the trailer; the trailer's load of canned vegetables; the load-removal service truck; the formerly hostile crowd; and finally, the officers and their cars.

The scene by the river returned to the quiet, peaceful, environment it is.

Tale Number 41 – Thar She Blows!

It is mid-December in Fresno. It has been raining on and off for most of a week. The ground cannot—nay, will not—take any more water. Roadways are flooding. The runoff catch basins that help recharge the aquifer from which Fresno gets its water are flooding over their edges onto private properties and roadways. Slowly, the whole area seems like it is going under.

I am working 99 Freeway through the city on the afternoon shift. It's about 6:30 PM, and of course it is raining. The rain had begun that morning and continued moderately all day.

I start down a ramp to enter the freeway. This particular ramp passes under an overcrossing bridge right at the bottom of the ramp where the ramp joins the freeway proper.

At the bottom of the ramp, very adjacent to the right lane of the freeway, is a full-sized sedan with its lights on and the emergency four-way lights flashing.

The car is astride the concrete gutter between the slightly-raised asphalt shoulder next to the overcrossing's support wall and the merging area at the bottom of the ramp. There is a substantial pool of water straddling the shoulder lane from about the middle of the lane to about the middle of the ramp merging area. The car is not in that lake.

The light traffic passing by is using the lanes to the left of the partially-flooded lane.

I pull in behind the car, flip up the red spotlight to the let the occupants know it is a cop car, and then put the white spotlight on the car's rear view mirror.

I exit the unit, and make a right side approach to the passenger side, next to the overcrossing wall.

I have on my yellow slicker rain pants, slicker jacket with my gold badge pinned on my chest, a clear plastic rain cover on my hat, and a white soaker towel tucked around my neck partially inside the slicker jacket to catch drips. But I am out of the moderate rain, because of the overcrossing.

When I get alongside the passenger door, the window rolls down, and a well-dressed, well-coiffured, late middle-aged lady of the haute couture clan says, "Oh, officer, thank you so much for stopping. Something is the matter with the car."

Just as I start to lean into the window to speak with the passenger, another lady of the clan, equally appointed to the nines, with a gold neck chain attached to her eyeglasses, exits the car from behind the wheel and comes around the front to my location in a hurried shufflelike walk.

"Please get back in the car," I say. "It's not safe out here."

But she begins to talk as though I had said nothing.

"Ohhh, officer. We're late for a Christmas party at our church, and we *must* get there. The car quit running on the freeway. Can you please get us a tow truck, or something?"

"Ma'am, get back in your car. I can talk with you there."

"But, officer...."

Right then, an eighteen-wheel tractor-trailer combination comes through the shoulder lane about sixty miles per hour. All nine of the right wheels of the sixty-five-foot-long rig plow through the pooled water at the lane edge.

In the lights of the overcrossing, I can see the truck has created a tidal wave with a curl that would have put Hawaii's surfer's heaven of the Banzai Pipeline to shame. The wave curls up, out, and over the car, and down on top of Mrs. Dressed-To-The-Nines-With-The-Gold-Chain-On-The-Glasses-Going-To-The-Church-Christmas-Party-Who-Wouldn't-Get-Back-In-The-Car.

Seemingly, about five hundred gallons of pooled freeway rainwater, laden with oil runoff, cigarette butts, and other debris from the freeway land squarely and completely on top of the lady driver, drenching her thoroughly. Not a drop touches me in my rain gear, or her car.

With the water running off her head, her former Christmas party hairdo in matted debris-carrying-strings down her face with her chained glasses askew on her face, her clothes soaked and covered with cigarette butts and other debris, she balls up her fists, tightens her body with anger, and through tightly-clenched teeth says, somewhat to my surprise, "Shi*iiiit!*"

Merry Christmas to you, too.

Tale Number 42 – Clothes Do Not Necessarily The Man Make

My academy class partner and I are working the graveyard shift one Saturday night in East Los Angeles. We are driving along Whittier Boulevard, East L.A.'s main drag. At the time, it was four lanes with double yellow lines separating the eastbound and westbound sides.

We are in the fast lane westbound when Russ says, "Hey! That guy up ahead in the white Cadillac just about hit the car in the eastbound fast lane. The Cad swerved across the double yellows and the other guy had to swerve into the slow lane."

I hadn't seen the violation; I was looking someplace else.

My partner puts up the red spotlight to stop the Cad.

We are at the curb, and not yet stopped, but the Cad driver is stopped, out of his car, and back at our right front fender with his mouth in gear with the oft-heard, "Why aren't you out catching burglars and bank robbers? Why are you picking on innocent people? I pay your salary. I'll have your job...."

We both exit the unit, as is usual, and my partner contacts the driver on the sidewalk.

The driver is wearing exquisite, expensive, tailored clothes. He is wearing what seems to me like a $400 suit, $200 shoes, $20 tie, and a $100 shirt. His gold Rolex watch and two diamond rings are fit for a king. Even his hair and mustache are tailored.

My partner goes through our routine, during which time Mr. Indignant continues with variations of his previous offered themes. My partner explains the reason for the stop. The driver hotly denies swerving. My partner obtains the errant driver's operator's license, which the driver removes from an expensive wallet. My partner attempts to get a reason for the swerve, but receives only theme noise. He accompanies the driver to his car to get the registration and to take a quick look inside to see if there is some physical evidence to explain the swerve. None is visible. He then informs the driver that he is going to write him a citation for the violation.

The guy goes ballistic, yelling and screaming his aforementioned themes, jumping up and down, and waving his fists, but not threateningly to us, just demonstrative of anger.

My partner instructs the driver to go sit in his car, and he begins to write the ticket.

The driver does not go to his car. He stands there, continuing to rave and rant.

As my partner starts to write the ticket, rain begins. First, it is a quick drizzle, and in sixty seconds it is raining moderately.

When the drizzle begins, my partner again tells the violator to go sit in his car, and then my partner gets into ours, because one, ball point pen doesn't write on wet paper very well, but more importantly, two, neither of us had our rain gear with us.

But the violator just stands there in the rain.

From the right front seat of the patrol car, I watch him carefully, prepared to take action if need be while the ticket is being written.

It rains harder. My partner continues to write. The guy continues to stand in the rain.

The rain begins pouring. The guy stands there, getting soaked through.

My partner finishes the ticket, exits the car, and goes to the driver to get the ticket signed. As he exits the rain stops as if by command. Not a drop falls.

The soaking wet driver signs the ticket (surprising us both), all the while running off at the mouth. He is still denying the swerve. My partner gives him his copy, and we get back into the patrol car. It begins to rain again as we pull away from the curb to go to the office to get our rain suits.

The driver is still standing there in the rain looking at his ticket copy.

Tale Number 43 – Bike Ride

We are working graveyard shift, and are returning to our beat from a fringe-area call. It is four o'clock in the morning.

Driving on a near-empty residential street, we encounter a fellow on a bicycle pedaling in the same direction we are going. My immediate impression is he is going to work early. He may have been, but he is drunk within the common meaning of the word. Very drunk.

He is wobbling, weaving, and zigzagging severely with short jerks of the handlebars trying to keep the bike, and himself, upright. Based on what we see of his riding, we think the stunt driver is going to lay it down somewhere or hit a parked car and get dumped. Either way, he will get hurt. If that happens, we will have a drinking-driver-involved, solo vehicle (probably), injury traffic accident.

A bicycle, within the meaning of the California Vehicle Code definition of vehicle, is a vehicle. Surprise! So is a horse. (One can be arrested for drunken driving while on horseback.)

Since our job is to prevent injury and death to those using the highways, and since I've already mentioned it is a lot easier to write an arrest report than an accident report, or an arrest report *and* an accident report, we elect to make a drinking driver arrest whenever possible.

Let me say in defense of that statement that the arrest is for the safety of the arrestee and the general public who are exposed to the drunk's hazard while driving. Make that while the intoxicated driver is trying to drive. (The reduced paperwork doesn't hurt.) We try our damnedest to prevent drinking driver accidents by getting to the drinking driver before the drinking driver gets to someone else and causes a collision. (Notice: I didn't write accident.) We get to see the results of their irresponsibility up close and personal. We do everything we can to stop it. End of defensive diatribe.

My partner closes on the bike at the rear. I hail the rider on the unit's PA system. "Hey, rider. Pull over and stop," I say matter-of-factly, expecting an immediate response because of our eminent presence and proximity.

No response. He keeps pedaling trying to keep the bike upright. It is a chore. A couple of times he almost dumps it, but he manages to jerk the bike back to balance, how, I don't know.

"Hey, rider. Stop," I try again.

No response. Hmm.

We pull along his left side to "white door" him, so he can see the CHP emblem and patrol car. My partner makes sure we are way offset, so the rider won't zig into us.

I say loudly on the PA, "Hey! How about stopping?"

He turns his head to the left, and looks toward us. His eyes have no apparent focus. He is OTL (out to lunch).

My partner puts up the red spot, and turns it on the rider. Also, he hits the siren button quick to make the siren give one whoop. The guy keeps pedaling.

We both start laughing. Technically, we have a failure to yield, and are—ready for this?—in pursuit of a bicycle at five miles per hour. (Makes the moped sound swift.)

Should we put it out over the radio? You know how that goes.

Finally, my partner pulls ahead some distance from the rider, angles the patrol car to the curb and stops. I jump out to grab the rider when he arrives.

The bike rider gets the message. But before he gets to us, he brakes hard on the rattletrap standard bicycle, comes to a stop, and then he and the bike teeter over to the left. Ker*thunk*!

He doesn't get hurt; he is too lubricated to get hurt.

We arrest the rider for drunken driving and book him.

During the interview, the bike rider tells me that the reason he is riding a bicycle is because his driver's license is suspended for drunken driving.

And he wasn't going to work. He was going home from a bar.

Tale Number 44 – Doctor Frustration

I am working an area beat in the northeast quadrant of Fresno County one really nice warmish winter Sunday afternoon. The beat covers the lower foothills, the lower portion of the two-lane state highway leading to the higher elevations, and the ski areas.

Injecting business into this lovely day, dispatch calls to assign me to an 11-83 on the upper highway toward the ski area. The general location is described by the dispatcher as being about halfway between my foothill beat and the five thousand-foot elevation mountain area. That area is covered by a resident officer, who lives up there, but he is tied up on another crash.

I "10-4," and head up the highway looking for my accident. I haven't cleared my foothill beat area when I encounter a head-on crash that occurred just moments before my arrival. The vehicles are still rocking a bit on their suspensions, and steam is coming from the front end of each one. They are hooked together in front, and partially turned across the two traffic lanes, completely blocking the roadway. There is a line of *après*-skiing cars behind the downhill at fault passenger car, and two cars behind the uphill victim older pickup truck.

The errant young driver with the ski rack on top of his car is moderately injured. The victim driver and his wife, both elderly, are severely injured, with him possibly turning into a fatality. He bent the steering wheel with his chest from a concave shape to a convex shape. She bounced off the dashboard and the windshield. (premandatory seat belt days.) They are hurting and bleeding.

By the time I exit my car and get to midscene with my first aid box of bandages, the three injured are already being attended to by medical personnel. Luckily for me, and the injured, an emergency room nurse and a non-ER hospital doctor, unacquainted, traveling in separate vehicles, are coming back from a day of skiing. They are the first and second cars behind the wrongful driver's car. As soon as the crash occurred, they were out of their cars and over to the injured parties.

The nurse is comforting and watching over the driver at fault. The doctor is assisting both of the pickup truck victims.

The only hitch is the doctor has not brought his medical bag. The sole medical equipment on the scene is my bandages.

When I encountered the crash, I called for an ambulance without inspecting the injuries. I knew a head-on collision would require a trip to the hospital for someone, or several people. I also called for two tow trucks.

Some twenty to twenty-five minutes has passed since I went 10-97 (arrived) on the radio at the scene, yet the ambulance has not yet arrived. The fidgety doctor keeps looking at his watch, and then down the hill for the ambulance. He looks by using his stretched-out hand to shade his eyes from the sun, like a cavalry scout looking for a life-saving watering hole.

From time to time, the nurse looks questioningly at the doctor with The Look; the one medical folks give one another when things are not going the way they would like, or should.

Thirty minutes goes by. No ambulance. Forty-five minutes goes by. No ambulance.

The doctor can't take it any more. "For God's sake, where is the ambulance? These people need medical attention and quickly."

"Well, doctor," I say, "We go through this all the time, but that doesn't make it any easier. We don't have the equipment you have available to you in the hospital to help people. We have to try and save them out here with what we have until the paramedics or an ambulance crew gets here. You have to get used to it."

"My God!" he says. "How can you get used to it?"

"Because we have to. It's just one of those things we have to do," I say.

I go to the patrol car to call dispatch to ask her to obtain an ETA for the ambulance. Shortly, she calls back saying the ETA is ten minutes. I leave my outside speaker on so the doctor and the nurse and the others can hear the time update.

I have hardly hung up the mike when the ambulance pulls up. The crew rushes out and makes their way toward us. I direct them to the doctor and the nurse who can help them with the injured.

Eventually, the three injured are stabilized, loaded into the ambulance, and driven to Fresno. The tow trucks get the vehicles cleared, and that opens the road for the skiers to go home.

As the doctor and the nurse head for their cars to leave, the doctor comes back to me, shakes my hand, and says, "I don't know how you do it."

"It's tough, doctor. It's tough," I say. And it is. It truly is.

Postscript number one: The mountain unit cleared the crash he was working and responded to my original 11-83 call.

Postscript number two: Today, the CHP has many traffic officers on patrol who are certified paramedics and who carry their large emergency bag with them wherever they go—even off-duty.

Tale Number 45 – Public Toilet

All I am doing is going to coffee to meet an adjacent beat partner—not at a donut shop!

It is the beginning of the shift, early afternoon, nice weather, and midweek. The timing should have been safe enough, but of course when you drive a black and white, anything can happen at anytime. This is not a complaint, just a statement of fact.

I am driving east in a nice upscale neighborhood on a city street when I encounter… can it be?… a white porcelain toilet. It is complete with lidded water tank on the back, water in the tank and bowl, and a blue tab to make the water blue.

The toilet assembly is sitting upright, undamaged, dead-center in the middle of the intersection on top of—this is the truth, I am not lying—the access hole cover for the sewer system. I've heard of public toilets, but this is ridiculous.

To remove this possible impediment to motoring safety, and to…cough, cough…keep things moving, I cause all the light traffic to stop entering the intersection. Then, I commandeer two male driver "volunteers" from the stopped cars to help me move the lavatory fixture to an adjacent parkway, the area between the curb and sidewalk.

With that done they get back into their cars, I wave go, and the traffic moves on.

I get back into my unit, call dispatch to tell her to tell the city they have a toilet to pickup ("Pardon?" she says), and motor on down the road on my original mission.

Tale Number 46 – What Goes Around Comes Around

Just north of Whittier, California, is a run of foothills called The Puente Hills. In the little valley between two ridges of those hills at the time were avocado orchards and a golf course. The two-lane road through that east-west valley follows the twisty-curvy topography created by ridge lines, and their coexistent arroyos (dry gulches) that come down from the crest line above. The road is narrow with many sharp curves, most of which are blind, and has limited shoulder area with not many wide spots to pull over if need be.

The CHP office responsible for traffic enforcement of the area gets a lot of sideswipe, head-on, and run-off-the-road accidents on this two-lane highway. Whenever possible, the office assigns a beat unit out there, sometimes two. I liked working that beat, though it was a lot of work, especially on weekends with the road racers and drinking drivers. I liked the beat because it is outside the usual up and back of a freeway beat, is rural in the urban area, and always has something to do.

For example: One day I am on routine patrol out there going eastbound on that curvy roadway when an oncoming car comes into my view rounding the blind curve ahead. The car is completely to the left of the double yellow center line and is entirely on my side of the roadway, coming at me head-on. The incident would have been a head-on accident if I had been entering that curve, but in this instance, I was far enough back that there was no danger for me. But, if I had been just a little closer....

I stop in the roadway, turn up the red spot, and touch the siren a tad. The oncoming car corrects to its proper side of the westbound road and stops opposite my driver's door. The driver is a female high school student.

"Please pull ahead to the first place that you can pull over for two cars, and wait for me there. I'm going to write you a ticket for being left of the double yellow lines," I said. "We can't stop here."

The driver nods her head in the affirmative and drives away. I am not worried about her fleeing.

I go down the road about a half-mile to a wide spot, see-saw a turnaround, and head back the other way. I find her stopped on the roadway pavement in a wideish area directly in front of the entrance of a stop-signed T-intersection side road that descends sharply from the crest line. Because traffic is light to nonexistent and we can be seen in any direction for safety, I make the contact there.

I go to the girl's driver window to reinform her of the reason for the stop. I have just obtained her driver's license and registration when a small foreign car comes down the hill from the crest line and stops at the stop sign. My violator's car is blocking the other car's entrance to the valley road. Before I can advise the young lady to pull forward to let the foreign car pass, the car's driver opens his door, leans out, and shouts words to the effect of: "You G-D cops. You're always out here hassling everyone. Today, you're blocking the f-ing stop sign and hassling her. Get your G-D car outta my f-ing way so I can get outta here."

Two things you need to know here: one, I'm pretty even-tempered, and under circumstances such as the other driver's mouth, I usually consider the source together with the old saying about sticks and stones. That's what I do here. And two, cops are pretty much one-trick ponies—it is best to try to finish what you're working on before biting off more, especially if there is any chance that someone can get hurt.

The old saying of the military describes it best: "When you're surrounded by alligators nipping at you, it's hard to remember your original mission is to drain the swamp."

In this instance, I am concerned about the safety of an innocent party in the presence of someone of such uncontrolled anger.

I tell the girl to pull ahead. She does. Mr. Mouth takes off in a cloud of dust. After he left, I rejoin the contact with the girl, issue the ticket to her, and send her on her way.

Flash ahead three months.

I am parked under a large avocado tree, enjoying the shade immediately off the twisty-curvy valley road while trying to stay cool in the L. A. area heat. The engine is off and the windows are open. I am writing a run-off-the-road accident report that occurred earlier in my shift.

I suddenly hear the squeal of tires and look up. Coming westbound in my direction from around a curve made blind by an ridge line's dirt bank, completely on the left side of the roadway over the double yellow center lines, and so far to the left its left wheels are in the dirt of the shoulder of the opposing lane, is a small foreign car. The driver corrects the vehicle's handling by squaring it away in the left lane and then reenters his westbound right lane. As the car closes on my off-road location to go past me, I throw the reports over my shoulder into the back seat, fire up the engine, the red light, and the siren and go after the violator.

The driver, who looks at my parked unit when he goes past me, does not surrender immediately. He keeps his foot in it, such as it is, considering the car. But I don't try to catch up to him until the roadway stops being curvy and turns into a straight city street. It's right where I want to stop him. He yields to the curb.

Contacting the male driver, I tell him I've stopped him for driving over the double yellow lines on a blind curve. I ask for his driver's license and reg. He fumbles around looking in the glove box, and eventually comes up with the documents. Handing them to me he says, "The only reason you stopped me was because I yelled at you."

I didn't know what he was talking about. I had just contacted the guy. We had only normal conversation. What was with the yelling? I told him to stay in the car, and went back to the unit to write the cite. Finishing, I returned to the car, explained the cite, and requested his signature.

When signing it he says, "The only reason you stopped me was because I yelled at you. You had a girl stopped and you were blocking the road. I yelled at you."

When I handed him his copy of the ticket, my bell rang. All I said was, "I didn't see you until you came around the blind curve over the double yellow center line. I didn't remember you. I didn't remember your car. I didn't even remember when you told me you yelled at me when I first came up here. I remember you now. Have a nice day." I turned and walked back to the patrol car. What I said was true. Every word.

In the patrol car, though, as he was driving away, I smiled and smiled and smiled, and rubbed my palms together in great happiness. Today, I was a one-trick pony.

Tale Number 47 – The Zs In The Night

It is foggy in Fresno County.

How*wwww* foggy is it?

It is so foggy anyone of good sense is home enjoying a nice fire and a, uh ...cup of tea.

But I am not at home and neither is my partner. Neither is the driver of the reported accident near the county line at the south end of our Freeway 99 beat, nor are the several other drivers foolishly trying to make their way through this so-called valley tule (pronounced TWO-lee) fog this late night.

The dispatcher, sitting in her nice warm dry office, calls my partner and me to advise of—what else?—an 11-83. Someone called the CHP to say there was "an accident down there." That's all the dispatcher knew.

I "10-4" for us, and we start south turning on our radar eyes. Sonar would be better due to all the water in the air.

Did I mention it is foggy? I mean, it is ten to fifteen miles per hour fog if you drive it right. If you don't drive it right at those speeds it will be unforgiving fog as fog is.

We finally get close to the county line. By the grace of the fog gods, we find the reported accident. It is a solo vehicle, but it is not an accident. The car is not damaged. It is just stuck.

The front end of the dark-colored sedan is in the dirt center divider with its nose into the oleander bushes. The rear end of the car is sticking out two to three feet into the fast lane of the two southbound lanes. It appears the driver fell asleep and simply drifted off the roadway into the median.

The male driver is uninjured. He is standing in the center divider waiting for help.

I am greatly surprised there has not been a secondary collision, or more, with the rear end of the victim's car protruding into the fast lane and the dense fog.

My partner pulls our patrol car into the median divider parallel to the highway and past the 11-25. He pulls in as far as he can safely go to get our car away from the traffic lane and away from the victim's car, in case it is hit and bounced into ours.

I jump out, leaving my partner to deal with the driver (it's his out), and take a large bunch of thirty-minute road flares with me. Striking one off, I start walking from the incident site toward the oncoming traffic. I walk along the left roadway edge of the fast lane by the center divider. I slowly wave the lighted flare with an up and down motion with my extended left arm to the side hoping to warn those coming that (1) I'm here; (2) to slow down; and, (3) because I am here, to realize there must be a hazard for them to avoid.

A couple of cars that passed by the scene before I started laying the flare pattern did so in the shoulder lane while running twenty-five to forty miles per hour. That's way too fast for those drivers to react had they encountered me, or the hazard car, in their path.

When I am out about three hundred feet from the 11-25 car, I put a flare at the fast lane-median edge, and then, walking backward, "so I can watch the cars," I lay a flare every twenty paces, angling the line of flares toward the slow lane-fast lane stripping. This, in effect, cuts off the fast lane, keeping oncoming traffic away from the solo vehicle's rear end protruding into the lane. I hope.

Even though I am darting out into the fast lane to lay the flares, I am not able to see the oncoming cars. I can only hear them. Their tires make a roadway noise, albeit quieter than normal, because of the sound-reducing quality of fog. Of course, the drivers can't see me, either. Only when they are almost right on top of my location are they able to suddenly see the flare and me and then react.

At the start of the flare pattern when I'm laying the flares, the drivers overreact due to their speed and nearness to me. They encounter me in the fog without warning, or very limited warning. They brake suddenly and hard. The cars lose traction on the fog-wet roadway surface, and slide on the wet pavement. I can hear the zzzzzzzzz of the tires of the sliding car in the fog. But I can't see the car. When I hear a car coming in the very light traffic, I have to decide, in a game of dodge 'em, which way do I go? Fun.

The driver of a faster car behind a slow one suddenly sees the tail lights, or brake lights of the slower car, and brakes and overreacts, too, because the faster car is traveling way too fast for the reaction time needed to slow safely. They, too, slide. zzzzzzzzz. Here, I have two cars to dodge. Double fun.

It is very eerie and discomforting to hear a car you cannot see sliding in the fog. You don't know which way it is coming: at you, or near you, straight on, on making whoop-ti-do circles taking all available pavement. All my senses are straining through the fog, hoping to correctly determine where the cars are.

All I can do is hope that I will be missed and continue getting the flare pattern laid out, because as more of the flares are laid, the oncoming cars get more warning, and most slow down. But not enough.

There is no way to prevent the actions of these drivers at the scene, short of closing the freeway far ahead. But that would only move the problem "up there" for someone else. I have no way to communicate with the drivers who are not driving at a safe speed for the very limited visibility. I am therefore dependent on them to slow and stop in time when— or, is it if?—they see something, and yet I need a flare pattern two hundred or three hundred feet long to warn them of the crashed car projecting out into the traffic lane.

It's a foggy Catch-22.

Too bad there wasn't such a thing as an instant roll-out flare pattern: Lay it on the roadway, give it a kick, and in one roll the flares are lighted and safely laid out for the three hundred feet.

But in the end, I do get the flare pattern laid without anyone hitting the victim's car, or us, or me, or the tow truck that came out, or one another. But they nearly did. I thought I'd never get out of that place alive and uninjured due to the arriving, braking, and sliding of cars. But I did. With more gray hair and at least an additional year of age.

In the end, we got the scene cleared of everything and everybody, and resumed routine patrol, ready for something else.

But when I got home, I had a cup of... uh, tea.

Tale Number 48 – Man Of Peace

One day in Fresno County on a summer afternoon shift, I receive a call from dispatch about pedestrian on the freeway. All she can tell me is that the ped is reported to be somewhere around the middle of my beat, which is the south half of Freeway 99.

I didn't have a hard time locating, or recognizing the reported pedestrian.

I find him walking in the rough weedy right of way between the paved shoulder curb and the wire mesh fence marking the freeway boundary. He is dressed in open leather sandals and a gown of a very light white cloth. He has long brown hair flowing down to below the top of his shoulders. His hair is tied down around his forehead with a piece of cloth matching the gown. The head wrap's tails hang down behind his head.

I pull to the shoulder, stop, exit, and hail the man.

"Hello*oooo*. Will you come up here, please? Pedestrians are not allowed on the freeway."

The man turns toward me the instant I call. He walks up the embankment, and onto the paved shoulder. Arriving, he says nothing. He just stands there looking in my direction.

"Sir, pedestrians are not allowed on the freeway. Do you have any identification?" I ask.

"No," he replies without elaboration. He then sits down on the curb.

I stand back to evaluate the subject: He is about twenty-eight to thirty years old, white, 5' 8," or so tall, and maybe 160 pounds. While he is oddly dressed that is no violation of law. He has good bearing, good eye contact, is clean and clean shaven.

The singular quality I notice most is that he radiates a great feeling of peace and tranquility. The radiated feeling is strong; strong enough I think I can feel it against the skin of my arms in a short-sleeve shirt, and on my face and throat. Truly. Similar in strength to someone barely pressing on one's arms.

Standing by him, I do not see or feel that guarded defensive posture common to most people when they encounter law enforcement.

I see no reason to change the situation. It is not illegal per se to wander, to dress differently, or to be different. He has not been a hazard to freeway traffic walking where he was by the right of way fence.

We are close to an exit. I direct him to leave the freeway there, and volunteer to transport him off. He declines the ride, and asks if he can walk off. I agree. He stands up without ado, walks back down the embankment to the weedy right of way again, and heads toward the exit.

I never saw him again, nor have I ever met another person who seemed to have so much peace about them, or emanating from them.

Tale Number 49 – If Only I Were On Commission

I am back on the road at the very south end of my Freeway 99 beat after my dinner break. I am traveling northbound toward Fresno on the old 99 about a quarter of mile to the east of, and parallel to, the new Freeway 99. It is fall and it is dark.

I'm driving the speed limit heading to rejoin the freeway, whose access is some miles ahead. I happen to look west to the freeway, and observe the lights of five big rigs traveling close in a convoy. They are overtaking and passing my parallel position. Since big rigs are required to travel fifty-five miles per hour, and I am driving fifty-five miles per hour on this highway, they obviously aren't driving the truck speed if they are overtaking and passing my position.

Now, I did not make a habit of running speed paces on parallel highways. It is not a safe practice. The officer has to look at the target violator(s) while the officer's patrol car is moving straight ahead on his or her roadway. Such a situation is a formula for mishap. I very, very seldom did it. But tonight, this group needs immediate consideration.

I begin a parallel pace.

The five rig group is running seventy-eight miles per hour, twenty-three miles per hour over the limit for combination of vehicles. I have to pace them four or five miles because the highway I am on doesn't have a connection to access the freeway until that distance ends.

Reaching the access, I enter the ramp to the freeway, and come in right behind the last truck.

I decide to stop all five trucks together. This is tricky, and also not a wise thing for one officer to do. It's how highway patrolmen get hurt. But these rigs, and this convoy, are flagrant violators, and are bordering on reckless driving given their speed, size and weight, stopping distances at the paced speed, and the moderate traffic. They are passing everything on the freeway, and they are doing it from the shoulder lane and the lane to the left, which they use to leapfrog ahead.

I proceed to make the multiple vehicle stop. There is nothing illegal about it.

Immediately on my entering the freeway, the convoy's speed drops to fifty-five miles per hour, and they hold their positions. This action tells me they know the speed limit, their speedometers work, and so does their CB (citizen band two-way) radios.

I close up in my lane to the driver's side of the cab of the last truck, which is in the shoulder lane. I hail the driver on my PA system. He rolls his window down. I tell him I am stopping the whole group, and to pull in behind the leader when I stop him.

I work my way up the line hailing drivers and instructing each to pull over behind the leader when I stop him. There is no side road to escape.

At the cab of the front rig, I hail the driver, and put up the red spotlight. By now, I am pretty sure the driver knows of my presence, and my expressed instructions to the other drivers, through the convoy's CB radio communications.

The leader yields to the shoulder, and the other drivers follow in behind: two, three, four, and five. All the rigs are from different companies.

I pull in front of the first rig and stop, and exit the patrol car with my ticket book. I go to the right front fender of the patrol car, and watch and wait. The drivers start forward.

The driver of the first rig is not a he, but a she. A rough and ready she. I suspect she is the self-appointed wagon mistress of the group, and she is hot about the stop. And that is an understatement.

In a reverse of the western movie theme, I sense she could consider forming a posse then and there to lynch the officer. She clearly states she thinks I'm lower than Dead Water in Death Valley (282 feet below sea level). She calls me every name she can think of, some more than once. And she has no embarrassment about being explicit: She thinks I am chicken s---, unfair, illegal, incompetent, cowardly, and a class A a------ for running a pace on them from a parallel road out of their vision (and awareness).

I feel I understand her mood and words sufficiently to the point I call a backup to come hold my hand. I fear she is going to work herself up to incite her men to riot and possibly ruin my day.

The backup arrives quickly (a novelty: Someone close by and not tied up!) and stands guard. I start writing the five truck-trailer combination of vehicles' tickets that require the registration information for each vehicle (tractor and semi-trailer, or tractor, semi-trailer, pull trailer with maybe a one-axle removable dolly under it), plus the driver's license information. It is a tedious, laborious, and time-consuming endeavor, especially done under the continuing machine gun word stream of Madam Mouth.

While I am writing, driver number one also accuses me of stalling to cause them to lose more time.

Finally, I finish and return everything to everyone. I do not check their log books or inspect their vehicle's equipment (lights, air brakes, tires, etc.) though I could have. Contrary to her earlier allegation, I did not want to tie them up longer, despite the continuing flak and denigration from The Fearless Wagon Mistress. If I could have wriggled my nose and thus completed all five tickets at one time, I would have done so to be shed of The Leader Lady.

All the drivers return to their rigs and pull away. My backup and I clear and return to patrol.

Even though each of the drivers was very upset about my stopping them collectively, I never got a subpoena to go to court from any of them.

Tale Number 50 – Traveling Light

It is a very hot summer Saturday afternoon of over one hundred degrees in Fresno County. I am working the north half of Freeway 99.

I receive a call from dispatch: Meet the man at the freeway exit to such and such surface street. No other information is provided. I respond and exit the freeway at the prescribed ramp.

Across the street by the on-ramp, standing in the shade provided by a decent grove of eucalyptus trees, is a man about twenty-years-old. His is wearing only a yellow brief-type bathing suit and a pair of Zoris/Go-Aheads/shower shoes—whatever you want to call them. He waves the I'm-the-guy wave.

I pull up and invite the subject into the cool of the patrol car's air-conditioner. (I didn't search him. Where would he have a weapon hidden?) I ask what assistance he requires.

"I need you to find my wife," he says.

"Pardon?" I query.

"My wife has been driving up and down the freeway looking for me. I have been on the freeway overcrossing waving at her each time when she came through, but she didn't see me. I need you to find her, and get her stopped, so I can get back in the car."

"How is it you are here in your bathing suit, and she is out there in the car?" I ask ever so curiously.

He tells me the story.

He and his wife are moving from Sacramento to the Los Angeles area. Shortly after leaving Sacramento, an argument started between them. The argument continued to fester all through the trip to Fresno, roughly some 180 miles.

At the overcrossing where I met him, he told his wife, who was driving, to exit the freeway, because he had to urinate. As his urinal he selected the grove of eucalyptus trees where I met him.

She exited the freeway and stopped the car at the requested location. He got out and walked into the grove to take care of his business. She, apparently with her boiler still under temperature and pressure, drove off. He was left there as is where is. He didn't even have a dime for a phone call (pay phone cost at the time). To call the CHP, he had to beg money at a near-by gas station. He is definitely on hard times.

When she drove away, he walked out to the middle of the overcrossing and waited, hoping her temper would cool down and she would return for him.

She did return. But he guesses she couldn't remember which ramp she had dropped him off at, because he could see her driving up and down the freeway going out of sight northbound, and then passing through southbound, again going out of sight. (She could not see the grove of trees from the freeway because the roadway was sunken.)

Each time she passed under the overcrossing, he jumped up and down and waved and shouted like a lost hiker reaching out to the rescue helicopter. But she didn't notice him and motored on.

I obtain the color, make, and model of their car from him and call dispatch. (He didn't know the license number. The dispatcher obtained it from the system.) I ask her to put the information out as a BOLO (Be On The Lookout) for our area officers, and to the beat officers in the counties north and south of Fresno County. Then, he and I zip out on the freeway ourselves to see if we can find her.

After two hours of patrolling north and south, including going into the next county north to look and sitting on the ramp where I found him waiting for his wife to go by, I give up. There have been no reports from any of the other counties' freeway units. It seems fruitless.

But what am I to do with Mr. Light Baggage?

I call dispatch to ask if they have a resource for the fellow whose story they know too well by now. I am told to stand-by. They will check and advise.

We do our standby while parked on the ramp, just in case. She is still a no-show.

After an extended wait, dispatch calls back.

"Traveler's Aid Society advises that if you will bring 'your client' by their office," the address of which she provided, "they will assist your victim as they are able."

I dropped my client off at the location given. Before he walked away wearing his swim suit and Zoris, I gave him a ten dollar bill to help him in his predicament.

I never heard from him again, nor did I hear if he and his wife made contact.

Tale Number 51 – Ugly American Deer

Ninety miles north of Fresno at the terminus of State Highway 41 is Yosemite National Park, a world-renowned geographical splendor that draws visitors from all over the globe.

Yosemite visitors frequently arrive in Fresno, rent a car, and drive north on Highway 41 through the foothills, mountains, and the two mountain towns along the way, to visit the park. Such is the case here.

On this nice summer day, five Japanese tourists in a rental car are motoring through the last town before going on to the park's southern entrance. Their car hits a large white-tailed deer jaywalking across the very busy four-lane highway running through the town. All five tourists are moderately to seriously injured, because seat belts were not yet required to be worn.

The lone CHP resident officer stationed in that mountain area of Madera County (larger staff now) responds to the crash. The local ambulance also responds, calling another ambulance to assist. It is determined the local emergency facility is not equipped to handle five people with injuries these severe. The victims are transported to a large regional hospital located on the north side of Fresno, nearest to where the ambulances are coming from, some thirty-five miles away. That hospital is adjacent to my beat.

I am just arriving near the edge of my beat after leaving afternoon shift briefing when dispatch calls me: "65-14, Fresno," the dispatcher says, calling my beat number and giving her dispatch center location.

"Fresno, 65-14 Such and Such streets. Go ahead," I say giving my location.

"65-14, Madera County resident post requests you go to the north side hospital for an assist to him. He requests you get page one information for a crash he is working involving Japanese tourists who hit a deer downtown."

"Fresno, 65-14. 10-4."

Page one information. That's the first page of the accident report. Such a request means to get the name, address, phone number, and driver's license information of the driver, and of each passenger in the crash, and their placement. But by implication, because I am there at the hospital, the request also means obtaining the hospital information, including the nature and extent of injuries. And it also means I have to take each person's statement as to who was driving, and what events they saw. Page one information, therefore, while it sounds like easy-in, easy-out, is really about one-half of the accident investigation. The remainder is the scene information and diagram, locating and interviewing witnesses, storing the car, and arranging for the disposal of the 44 deer. (No yellow blanket.)

A few moments later, right after I made my U-turn to head to the hospital, the same dispatcher calls back.

"65-14, Fresno."

"Fresno, 65-14. En route to the hospital." I am thinking she is calling to cancel me, and to advise the resident post officer is coming down.

"65-14. 10-4. By the way, there are five injured and they don't speak English."

"By the way," she says, "there are five people and they don't speak English!" I'm en route to get personal information and statements from five people who don't speak English? No problem if they speak Spanish. We can cover that. There are lots of Spanish speakers in the hospital and at our office. But Japanese?

I arrive at the hospital's ER entrance and go in. The ambulances have preceded my arrival, unloaded their patients, and left. I am supposed to include the ambulance information in my end of the report: which companies, their arrival times, their departure times, etc. I later call dispatch to tell them to advise the resident officer that the ball is in his court on the ambulance info.

The atmosphere of the emergency trauma room is controlled chaos. The ER doctor and nurses are trying to find out from the patients where they hurt when it is not obvious by a visible wound. The only immediate way to determine where they hurt is the touchy-feely way: The doctors touch it, the patient feels it, and then advises in Japanese pain that it hurts there. This is not a satisfactory method for anyone, especially the patient.

What to do? What to do?

I go to a pay phone and call dispatch. We have a dispatcher of Japanese ancestry working that day, though she is not handling the frequency I am working on. I ask to speak with her. I don't know if she speaks Japanese, or if she does, if there is a dialectal problem that would prevent communication. Of course, she is working 2:00 PM to 10:00 PM like I am. She can't leave if she wants to; she has the radio.

The dispatcher tells me she belongs to a church attended by many Japanese-speaking members. She agrees to try to locate and obtain a volunteer to come to the hospital to translate. I tell her such a person, or persons, will be greatly appreciated, because right now they are all John and Jane Does, numbers one through five, who are conversing with the doctors only in Japanese pain. She advises she will call back.

"10-4."

After about an hour, during which time the doctors and nurses progress in treating what they can how they can, the dispatcher calls back. A gentleman from her church is coming to help. He will meet me at the ER entrance.

"Rog-O!" I inform the medical trauma staff. They are elated to say the least.

About 3:30 PM, the church member arrives. He goes right to work in the ER. Going from one injured person to another with the doctor, he obtains each victim's limited medical history, a list of the drugs they are taking, a list of drugs they are allergic to, and their specific complaints of pain and discomfort. This cannot be done without him. He goes from ER to the X-ray department, back to ER, and back to X-ray. The man works tirelessly. He goes to wherever he is needed in the hospital to translate.

I can't do much but wait; wait until a victim is in a position in the flow to talk with me when the translator is also available. It is a slow process because their medical treatment needs override my investigative needs. As it should be.

At nine o'clock of the evening, things are starting to stabilize. But despite their injuries, the chief complaint of the victims is that all their money, clothes, and passports are still in the mountains. To alleviate their anxiety, and at the same time facilitate my job, I make arrangements to get their stuff.

I call my dispatch center in Fresno, who calls the dispatch center handling the resident post in Madera County, who calls their officer. He agrees to contact the tow driver to ask him to open his tow yard. The resident officer travels to the tow yard, gets the gear (all listed on the vehicle storage inventory form), and ferries it downhill to a mutually-agreed-upon rendezvous point with a regular flatlander Madera County patrol unit. That unit delivers all the bags to me at the hospital ER entrance door.

In short order, it's a done deal.

They have their gear, and I have documented proof in the English language section of their passports of their names and addresses and other identifying information. Moreover, I and the hospital personnel, now have their in-case-of-emergency reference.

I leave after midnight to go to my office to end my shift and go home. I have no report written, only notes. The volunteer translator is still working when I leave.

The next day about 8:30 AM, I return on my time to check on the patients and see if anything else is needed. Nothing is worse than being sick when away from your home, much less being severely injured in a place that doesn't speak your language, and where you have no friends or family.

At the time, I don't remember if I was on days-off that day, or scheduled to return for the afternoon shift again. Since the report was not written, I suspect I was scheduled to return. No matter. What matters is that the translator is still there, and had been all night. But now, he is accompanied by his Japanese-speaking wife.

They have everything under control. The kind helpful couple have arranged with several gracious members of their church to take the victims into their homes as each tourist is able to be released from the hospital. The tourists now will have a home away from home with friendly, caring people who speak their language. The only thing better would be if those folks could heal the victim's wounds.

With nothing more I can do, I thank the Japanese couple heartily, as have the hospital staff several times, I'm told, and return to my home.

As is usual with most of the things we handle, I don't learn about the ultimate outcome of the tourists. I hope they recovered quickly and got home.

I did ask my office to provide the assisting couple with a public commendation for the desperately needed help they graciously volunteered to provide that afternoon, evening, early morning, and morning. Maybe even into the afternoon, too. I don't know.

I do know that whatever was done for them was not enough.

Tale Number 52 – Got Rope?

I am patrolling the south half of Freeway 99 in Fresno County one Saturday afternoon when I spot a pickup truck parked on the shoulder. Since part of our job is checking disabled and/or abandoned vehicles on the freeway, I stop to check it out.

As I roll up on the shoulder behind the pickup, I can see someone sitting near the front of the truck on the shoulder curb. I get out, and walk up on the right side of the pickup truck.

The person sitting there is a man of about forty-years of age. He is crying hard. To his left side, nearer the front of the truck, is a pile of avocado-colored metal that looks vaguely familiar. I ask if the metal pile belongs to him.

"Yes," he says, through sobs, "I... just... bought... it... at Sears. It is... it was... a microwave oven... over a conventional oven... slide-in unit. I bought it for our house."

Long story shorter: He bought the oven slide-in unit, and put it in the cargo area of the truck to take home. He stood its back against the rear of the cab by the pickup truck's rear window. He didn't tie it down. He thought it was heavy enough to stand unsecured. He was riding in the shoulder lane when he encountered a slower vehicle. He swerved into the left lane, instead of merging smoothly, and the combination oven unit, which he said cost $800, hopped out of the truck bed and committed suicide. Luckily, no other car hit it, and no one was injured.

Around four hundred years ago, George Herbert wrote, "For the want of a nail the shoe is lost; for the want of the shoe the horse is lost; for the want of the horse the rider is lost...."

I'm thinking this driver never read George Herbert.

Tale Number 53 – Duck. Soup.

You would think the one occasion that would be safe from the rigors of a roadie's life would be an officer's lunch break. Not so.

I am on my chow break one day in a restaurant I had never been in before. The place is located in a small town south of Fresno. I went to the restaurant after interviewing traffic accident victims who were taken to the town's hospital from an accident on the freeway. I was *waaay* past my usual lunch hour and I was hungry. Instead of holding out to hit a regular haunt, I followed the old sailor's motto: Any port in a storm, and the closer it is the better.

I go in and seat myself in a booth. I can spread out and work on the accident paperwork while I wait and I while

I eat. Shortly, the waitress comes by. She takes my order, and then leaves. I begin to work on the report.

While writing, I look up to think about some aspect of the accident I am trying to sort out in my mind. I see the waitress come alongside me from behind and go past me carrying someone else's order. It's a single bowl of soup. She is carrying it in the center of a large metal serving tray that she has balanced on her right palm and forearm.

She gets as far as the second booth past mine when the tray slips, thus allowing the bowl of soup to also slip. I can't see what is transpiring because her back is to me. But I see her quickly reach down to pull the bottom of her apron up, hunch her shoulders, stretch up on her toes and bow her legs.

The soup bowl, and plate underliner, hit the linoleum floor at about a forty-five degree angle tipped toward her. And me. The angle, the curvature of the bowl bottom, and the momentum from the drop, aims and accelerates the soup, and launches it as a coherent mass through the arch of her legs. The trajectory could not have been more refined if a computer was used.

Arcing up from the floor, the mass of beef-barley soup passes over the right shoulder of the man sitting with his back to me in the booth in front. Not so much as a drop gets on him. Thereafter, in slow motion, the large globule of soup continues on to me.

I can see it coming. But there is nothing I can do. In the manner of following too closely behind the car in front of you, speed and distance are not in my favor. The blob of soup hits me squarely and forthrightly in the middle of my chest, and then slides down to my lap. It splatters everything on and around me that is available to be splattered, including the traffic accident report I have partially completed.

The waitress runs back to me saying, "Oh, my God. Oh, my God," and begins to vigorously wipe my chest and… uh, lap, with a towel she carried.

Most of the diners present stood and gawked and laughed a little, and then went back to eating.

I had to take the towel from her hand. She was… uh, too exuberant in the wiping. When I took the towel from her, she realized what she had been doing and turned stop sign red and hurried off to points unknown.

In the end, I got reasonably cleaned up so I could leave the restaurant. For privacy from other chippie's ears, I telephoned the sergeant from the restaurant's pay phone to request to go home to change uniforms due to a "toxic" spill. Permission granted.

I never had the occasion to return to that restaurant, even though I wanted to know how the waitress came out. Especially since we were almost good friends at the time.

And I'll tell you one thing: Given the choice, I'll take the potato chips over the soup.

Tale Number 54 – Peddling As Fast As I Can

Back around 1979 or 1980, the department bought several vehicles of one model of a smaller car of lower horsepower to use as test cars for the purpose of evaluating their cost of operation and use in the field.

Headquarters wanted to try the cars out under road patrol conditions to determine whether the car would be adequate as an enforcement tool, and also, whether a lower horsepower car was cost effective.

Patrol cars by definition are work horses. They are driven hard and braked hard frequently, and sometimes are operated twenty-four hours a day for multiple days in a row. Anything that contributes significantly to reducing fleet expenses without greatly affecting vehicle performance or officer's safety, would be beneficial to lowering operational costs, a big part of the departmental budget.

I don't remember the make and model of the test car, but I remember the engine size: It was 318-cubic inches, substantially smaller than the 440-cubic inch engine size of our then-used patrol car.

The Fresno area office was assigned one of the cars to test, and one day when cars were assigned at briefing by the sergeant, my luck runs out: I am assigned the infamous test car, which by then is not liked by anybody in the office who has driven it.

I would have been happier in a VW bug. From reports, I knew the test car didn't have enough acceleration power to pull a kite up to fly, but I drove it for eight long hours.

Near the front of the afternoon shift, I am going north on one of the main north-south rural roads. The road has a posted speed limit of sixty-five miles per hour.

I am momentarily looking away from the roadway when a car passes by me going southbound at a high rate of speed. When it whizzes by, I redirect my attention to look in the rear view mirror. I estimate the speed at over one hundred miles per hour, and it isn't slowing.

Maybe the driver has high speed tunnel vision drivers get around one hundred miles per hour. Or, maybe the driver recognizes the car I am driving has a squirrel turning a spin-cage for a motor, and he isn't worried about me catching him.

I make a power U-turn to go after the violator. Strike that. I *try* to make a power U-turn to go after the violator. The unit turns as quickly and as deftly as an aircraft carrier in a high sea. Finally getting turned around and heading southbound, I rock in the seat using the steering wheel to pull myself back and forth trying to transfer momentum to the car. It starts to roll. Slowly.

Among other words, I yell, "Yea, mule," but it doesn't do any good.

Looking south on the two-lane highway that has no other traffic, I can see the car still rocketing away, greatly increasing the distance between it and me. While mine is moving, it is only thinking about going that fast.

Finally, it gets moving.

About three-quarters of a mile ahead of me at a major rural crossroad, I see the dot of a car stop for the stop sign I know is there. The car waits briefly for the cross traffic I see pass though the intersection in the opening between the vineyards at the location. The driver signals a left turn, and turns left.

I'll never see it again, I think. But I press on, foot to the floor though not achieving too much hurry. Soon, I arrive at the same stop sign and turn left, too.

The car is not in sight. No surprise there.

I decide the chase is over. (How can it be a chase when the chasee doesn't know the chaser is back there?) The phantom is gone. I drop the speed down and resume routine patrol mentality.

I have gone only about half a mile when I see the car in the circular driveway of the second house from the corner from where the stop sign is. There are two houses along this stretch of immediate roadway, both upscale ranch-style houses on large farming acreage. The person I presume to be the driver of the car—I never did actually see the driver—is standing outside the car talking to someone on the front steps of the house.

What the hey, I thought at the last minute driving by the house, I'm going to give it a shot. But I had driven past the driveway entrance from the direction I was coming, so I wheel in from the other direction into the circular drive. Mr. Inconspicuous.

I pull up nose to nose with the other car and exit to contact the presumed driver.

Now, probably at least five minutes have passed from the time I last saw the car, not the driver, just the car. Maybe more than five minutes.

Since I can't identify the driver, not having seen him or her, and since I lost contact with the car, I could not write a citation for the high speed. But I could give a verbal warning, saving face to myself.

When I get out of the car and walk toward the two young men of about twenty-five years of age, they stop talking and look at me quizzically. I'm sure the fellow on the step thought I was coming to his house for something related to him, and so did the car driver. Why shouldn't they think that? To me, it seemed like a year had passed between my arrival after the chased driver's arrival.

"Are you the driver of this car?" I ask, pointing to the one in front of the unit.

"Uh, yes. Can I help you, officer?" he solicits, maybe thinking I am inquiring about buying the car because of the small for sale sign legally taped to the corner of the rear window. In his mind, why else would I be there? Enough time had gone by since we passed, and I showed up here, he could have grown a beard. This contact definitely is not contemporaneous to the time of the observed violation, which is why when we see the violation, we stop the driver as quickly as possible.

The fellow on the step sighs with relief realizing I am not there for him.

"Yes, you can," I reply. "You blew past me coming down here in excess of one hundred. That's way too fast, way over the speed limit, and way too fast for the area. May I see your driver's license and registration, please?"

He gets them out. Everything is fine with the documents.

"Why were you driving so fast?" I ask.

"My sister dropped me off at the garage to pick up the car. I had it tuned up and had the carburetor rebuilt. I was just checking it out, sir."

"I'll tell you what I'm going to do," I say, starting my sales pitch. "I'm going to give you a verbal warning on this. You stopped at the stop sign properly, and you signaled your turn. There was no other traffic. And, your documents are okay, too. Check it out on the dynamometer next time, not on public streets. Okay?"

"Uh, yes, sir."

With that, I return to my unit, and go on down the road protecting the traveling public of Fresno County in my highway patrol Nopoopmobile.

That kid would not have been near as dumbstruck as he was about not getting a ticket for one hundred if he had known about the squirrel motor.

Tale Number 55 – Headless Chickenlike

We are returning to our graveyard beat from booking a drunken driver this summer's night. My partner and I are working a large unincorporated area surface street beat near Whittier, California.

We are only a mile or two from our beat when we stop for a red light at an intersection that leads to a regional shopping mall's parking lot. Naturally, the place is closed since it is one thirty in the morning.

Waiting for the light to change, and with no other traffic around, I start watching one of those compact parking lot sweepers that is mounted on a mini-pickup truck frame. It is actively sweeping the mall's parking lot.

Having worked graveyard a lot when the sweepers are sweeping, my partner and I have seen other sweepers sweeping before. They usually drive up and down sweeping the lots in a methodical manner, like a harvester harvesting wheat. Up and down. Back and forth.

This sweeper is not sweeping methodically.

He is sweeping like a doodle bug on turbo: circles, figure-eights, slaloms, destroyer-laying depth charge zigzag patterns, sailboat sailing tacking patterns. Everything, but straight.

Hmm, could he be?

Our intoxicated-driver investigative curiosity is piqued. (It is contrary to California vehicle code law to drive intoxicated on private property, including your own property.)

We turn into the mall drive and head to intercept the sweeper.

It is an effort.

The guy is not trying to evade us, he is just driving *cwazy*. Finally, we come at him head-on—at a distance!—sweeping our red and white spotlights back and forth and flashing the headlights from low to high and back.

He gets our message and stops.

He is not intoxicated. He is drunk, blitzed, smashed, stoned, feeling no pain, pickled, swacked, crocked, stewed, soused, and polluted. He is plastered, snockered, tanked, potted, bombed, ripped, shellacked, zonked, stinko, three-sheets-to-the-wind, blasted, blotto, and stiff. Did I mention crock-o?

And he was booked accordingly.

Tale Number 56 – 'Cause You Did It

Of the approximately twenty-four years and six months that I spent in the CHP, about twelve years were spent chasing taillights. In those twelve years, while stopping cars for violations of the state vehicle code, I heard a lot of drivers tell me: "The only reason you stopped me was—

"'Cause I'm a truck driver, you know I have the money to pay the ticket."

"'Cause I'm a Cadillac driver, you know I have the money to pay the ticket."

"'Cause I'm a Mercedes driver, you know I have the money to pay the ticket."

"'Cause I'm a BMW driver, you know I have the money to pay the ticket."

"'Cause I'm Mexican, you know I don't have the money to pay the ticket."

"'Cause I'm black, you know I don't have the money to pay the ticket."

"Because I'm a school teacher, you know I have the money to pay the ticket."

"'Cause I'm a student, you know I don't have the money to pay the ticket."

"Because I'm well off, you know I have the money to pay the ticket."

"'Cause I'm poor, you know I don't have the money to pay the ticket."

"'Cause I'm driving a junker, you know I don't have the money to pay the ticket."

"'Cause I'm driving a new car, you know I have the money to pay the ticket."

"'Cause I work for (insert the name of any national company whose name is painted on the vehicle), you know I have the money to pay the ticket."

"'Cause I'm a guy, and you know I have the money to pay the ticket." Also: "Cause I'm a guy, I know I can't get out of a ticket like the girls can."

"'Cause I'm a women, you know I can get the money from my husband to pay the ticket." Also: "I bet blondes get out of tickets with you."

"'Cause I got beer in the car, you know I have the money to pay the ticket."

"'Cause I've been drinking, you know I have the money to pay the ticket."

"'Cause I'm smoking, you know I have the money to pay the ticket."

And so on. Each with an ax to grind in defense of a driving error they committed in my presence.

I can't speak for other police agencies. But I can speak informally on behalf of the CHP as I think I knew it when I was working, and as I think I know it now, and I can certainly speak for myself in the past regarding the reason we stop vehicles: The usually unseen driver of a very visible vehicle commits a driving violation of a section of the California Vehicle Code in our presence that we can articulate specifically to the driver, and is stopped accordingly. Period.

The only reason you "was" stopped is 'cause you did it.

In regard to the money thing, the CHP is not financed by any money from tickets. None. The fines and other fees assessed by the courts go to the county in which the violation occurred, and other entities, under a formula of which I am not informed. The CHP is not part of that formula.

The department is financed entirely through vehicle registration fees collected by the department of motor vehicles.

The defense rests, honorable reader.

Tale Number 57 – Said To Contain

In my former life before joining the Chippies, as you know, I was a bank assistant manager.

In that capacity I used to sign for bags of coin shipped by the Federal Reserve Bank (FRB) to my branch. The coin bags had tags attached to their necks, and among other information on the tag, was the amount of coin in the bag with this government disclaimer: "Said to contain."

In other words, the FRB wasn't guaranteeing the amount of the coin in the bag; only that it was stating such a sum could be there, but it was to be counted as though it was correct.

A nebulous situation for a bank, isn't it? We had to believe the total stated ($50, $200, $500, etc.). After all, the FRB was the government. You know, as in, trust us, we're the Feds.

Well, I worked for the government, too, and I want you to trust me. I have some hearsay stories here I heard from other government agents, so you can trust me about the stories.

Yeah, right.

In truth, I don't know if they are factual in any aspect. However, they are of interest to repeat, true or not.

For example, it is said there is a report of a motorist who rented a motorhome for a tour of the West. He was driving on US 101 Highway in the middle of California by the Pacific Ocean when nature called him. He is said to have put the vehicle on "automatic pilot"—cruise control—and gone back to the motorhome's bathroom to take care of business.

He was rescued by the paramedics when they responded to the crash.

Another motorist is driving on the same US 101, but in Northern California. He is enjoying music from a tape cassette. The tape plays out, and he wants to change tapes. The others are locked in the glove box.

Not to be one to waste time by pulling over, unlocking the glove compartment, getting the other tapes, and locking it back—you guessed it!—he removes the key from the steering wheel ignition while rolling along. This action locks the steering wheel in place. And the wheels. He hurriedly tries to unlock the compartment, get the tape, and get the key back into the ignition to unlock the steering wheel before things deteriorate.

Good plan (?), poor execution.

At the location the driver elected to try this magician's quick switch, the highway separates at a big hole. The southbound lanes go around the hole one way, northbound lanes go another.

He went between the lanes, thereby joining the injury accident statistics of California.

Another?

A two-man graveyard unit pursued a national pizza chain delivery driver who was allegedly driving recklessly in order to deliver a pizza in the chain's formerly advertised delivery time of thirty minutes or less. The officers effected the stop about a block from where the pizza was going.

They hook up the driver for reckless driving, leave his car at the curb with his permission, and drive the block to the pizza's intended destination. Then, the passenger officer takes the pizza they had brought along, goes up to the pizza buyer's apartment and rings the bell. The renter comes to the door. Standing there is a fully-uniformed CHP officer with the hot pizza.

The officer says, "Compliments of the highway patrol, sir," turns, and walks to the patrol car without another word.

As they drive away, they see the guy is still standing there in his doorway with the pizza, staring in amazement.

More?

An officer on patrol on surface streets encounters a pickup truck stopped in the middle of three lanes of a surface street expressway. The pickup is the first vehicle at a signalized intersection. It has a tall camper shell on the back and the hood is up, but the hood can't be seen from the rear because of the camper shell.

Apparently, the truck is broken down.

The officer pulls in behind the pickup, and goes forward to check what's up.

The driver of the pickup is standing on the front bumper leaning into the engine compartment fiddling with the carburetor. He tells the officer he's "almost got it."

The officer tells the driver he will use the push bumper of the patrol car to push the truck from the intersection to the shoulder so the man can work on the truck there and be safer.

The driver says, "Okay."

The officer goes back to the patrol car. He snuggles the push bumper up against the rear bumper of the pickup truck, and gooses the gas to give the pickup a quick start, and just enough momentum to roll to the curb.

The pickup rolls across the wide intersection toward the curb.

At the curb, the driver was still standing on the bumper with the hood up. He had been hurrying to get the carburetor fixed before the officer pushed his truck and was still working on it when it was pushed. Now he jumps from the truck like a stuntman leaving a runaway stagecoach.

The truck jumps the curb, rolls over the sidewalk, and crashes into a concrete block wall of someone's backyard fence.

Lots of paperwork on that one for a sergeant somewhere.

How about this one?

A graveyard unit in a mountainous area is responding to a property damage hit and run call. En route, they encounter a pickup truck with a camper on it stopped in the northbound single lane of the two-lane curvy mountain road. The truck is parked on the no-shoulder roadway with no lights on, and no reflectors on the curve before or after the truck.

This situation is something we encounter with drunks, who think they are on the shoulder but are in fact in the traffic lane. We see this mostly on the freeway where they have parked in the shoulder lane.

The officers bang on the camper door and shout "Police," hoping to wake anyone inside who might have been asleep.

There is no response.

The officers train the white spotlight through the camper door window to light up the inside of the rig, though they could not see through the curtain.

No response.

Obviously, they can't leave the vehicle where it is, so they call a tow truck.

When the tow driver arrives, he opens the locked cab with his door lock pick tool. The officers bang on the cab's nonsliding rear window hoping again to raise someone, if someone is inside.

Still, no response.

The rig is towed to the tow company's fenced storage yard, and locked in the yard for the night pending claim by the owner.

Late the next morning, a Sunday morning when the tow operator didn't customarily come to work, the pickup driver, apparently very drunk the previous night, opens the camper door and steps out to start a new day. Big mistake.

As the guy steps out, the tow company's junk yard dog nearly eats him alive.

The tow company owner figures the dog smelled the guy in the truck when the rig was brought in, and lay under the truck all night long just waiting for Mr. Partyman to show himself outside.

Ouuuuuu-wee, I bet that hurt.

Okay. The last one for now.

Three friends arrange an overnight fishing trip to the mountains. As fisherman do, they left bright and early in the morning, and drove to their favorite lake, which was located in an adjacent county.

They are engaged in fishing that afternoon when one of the three dies of a heart attack.

The two survivors consider the situation, and figure they can't do anything for their friend. They decide not to ruin their long-planned trip.

They seat the deceased in the middle of the front seat of the pickup truck they all traveled in and lock the doors. They know the chilly day and cold night temperatures will assist them in their endeavor. They then go about their fishing business.

The next afternoon, it is time to head home. They load up the gear, get in the truck with their buddy, one on each side, and drive back to the city located in county where they live.

The first police agency they go to is a CHP office.

They pull into the parking lot to contact the information officer at the front desk. They tell him the whole story. The desk officer doesn't believe them. He goes outside to find a very dead guy sitting in the middle of the truck's front seat.

The desk officer calls the county sheriff's office and the coroner. Both agencies are incensed because the guy died in a different county, no one was notified of the death, the date and time of death were undocumented, the dead guy was moved to another county without notice or permission, and then he was taken to the wrong place when he was brought in.

I was told it all got straightened out.

Tale Number 58 – Strangers In A Strange Land

The first really tense moment of the tense moments I've had while working highway traffic enforcement occurred about a week after the Newhall, California, gunfight massacre on April 13, 1970, in which four highway patrolman, one of whom was a classmate, were allegedly killed by two well-armed felons.

That incident is *very* present in my and my partner's minds during this episode.

My graveyard partner and I are assigned by the shift sergeant to take a package from our East Los Angeles Area office to the near-by Santa Fe Springs Area office. We don't know exactly where that office is because we are both new to the area, and just haven't had a need to know, but we "10-4" anyway, and start off to deliver the package with some casual and incomplete instructions.

Consequently, at 11:30 PM, we are southbound on the I-605 Freeway from the Pomona Freeway in territory unfamiliar to us.

As we are discussing the merits of calling Los Angeles radio dispatch to ascertain clearer directions, we are passing a truck-tractor with two gasoline tank trailers. The driver hails us by shining a flashlight beam through our windshield. We come alongside his cab. He rolls his window down and yells what we thought was going to be a question about how-to-get-from-here-to-there.

Instead, he yells, "Two guys in a white over red car waved a gun at me! They're about a quarter of a mile ahead of us. It scared the crap out of me."

Whoa, baby! This is how the Newhall incident started; a vehicle occupant brandishing a weapon at a car on the freeway. We go to alert-alert mode.

We race ahead, and at a distance get behind the car. While doing this, I call dispatch advising them of our situation and location. Because we didn't know where we were on the 605, we are thankful to pass an exit ramp from which we obtain our location information from freeway signage.

I request backup, a check for wants on the license plate, and a registration check to insure the make of the car on the registration is the make of the car we are stopping.

If something goes down at least investigators will have the correct make of car to look for, and a possible registered owner. But we know there is no guarantee the ownership registration is current, or true.

Just as we are getting ready to turn on the red light and make the stop, the car exits the freeway. It goes down a two-lane off-ramp on the ramp's left side exit lane. The car stops as the lone vehicle at the bottom of the ramp at a signalized intersection. The car's left turn signal is blinking.

As we "creep" up behind the car to put the red spotlight on, the traffic light changes. The car turns left. My partner turns on the red light, and we get prepared physically and mentally to make a felony stop, a stopping procedure for high risk cars we have been trained to do.

I hail the car on the PA system, and order the driver to yield.

The car yields under the unlit overcrossing of the I-605 Freeway. (Where are those freeway lights when you need them?) We move to felony stop mode: doors wide open, us behind the doors down under the red and white spotlights, headlights on high beam, partner with his handgun drawn, me with the shotgun.

My partner gets on the PA: "Occupants! Toss out the gun. Put your hands out the windows."

No response. We can see silhouettes rustling around in the car.

Again, "Occupants! Toss out the gun. Put your hands out the windows."

This time, the passenger door opens, but the passenger does not exit. He is the subject the tanker driver identified as the brandisher of the pistol.

He is on my side.

My partner on the PA: "Passenger! Put your arms out the door with your hands in the air before you exit."

At this time, the passenger stands up and faces us. He has the gun in his right hand with his arms to the sides of his body. He begins moving his hands and arms around for some stupid reason. He finally raises his arms over his head.

The gun is now pointed up.

My partner on the PA: "Passenger, drop the gun! Drop the gun!"

The passenger then lowers his gun hand similar to the military position of port arms; the right arm at a diagonal, the gun at the hand's position for the salute-to-the-flag posture. He points with his left hand at the gun, as in you-mean-this-gun?

My partner gets down to basics on the PA: "Drop the f-ing gun! Now."

The passenger bends down way forward and slowly drops the gun to the sidewalk in front of him. He then stands upright, puts his hands back up, and starts slowly advancing toward my position at the car.

I still have the shotgun leveled in the notch of the doorway, but my finger is off the trigger. As he advances, I can see his mouth is moving like he is talking. But I can't hear him because of the rumble of the traffic passing on the overcrossing on the freeway above.

We also couldn't hear the radio dispatcher inquiring about our well-being.

"Are you code 4 yet?" she inquires unheard.

She is holding the frequency open for us, barring all other patrol car radio calls, which can be a problem if someone else is in a dicey situation, too, and needs to call for help. But with her holding the frequency open, this allows us radio access in case things go south.

In a few more tense but uneventful moments, we take both of the vehicle occupants into custody for brandishing a gun and other charges related to the situation. Then we acknowledge to dispatch we are code 4 with two in custody.

At that time, our backup arrives.

The alleged gun-waver is a sixteen-year old wise guy with a toy gun. He and the driver were having "fun with the trucker," he says. They were intentionally delaying yielding to us while rustling around inside the car because they were trying to hide the open containers of beer they had. We considered they were getting more guns than the one brandished.

That kid will never know how close he came to getting shot and killed in the name of fun by a twelve gauge double-ought buckshot load of pellets when he got out of that car with that gun in his hand, and moving it around while he raised his hands over his head.

It is stops like this one that make it right that we may retire at age fifty.

I was ready that night, but we were just recently off of break-in.

Tale Number 59 – Recruits For The Three Stooges

Blue sky, white clouds, warm sunshine—a lovely, lovely winter afternoon in the Los Angeles area. This is the kind of near-balmy winter day that brought the thousands of people from other places who now live here.

I receive a call about 3:30 PM of an 11-83 westbound on the Pomona Freeway. Another 11-83; another accident to report to with no details.

I respond.

On arrival, I find two lowered, two-door passenger vehicles parked on the westbound shoulder. The occupants are standing by their respective damaged cars.

I pull in behind the last car, exit, and head for the accident victims. Walking forward alongside the damaged cars to contact the people, I notice the unusual crash damage to the cars.

The windshield *and* the rear window of *each* car is shattered. The fenders of both cars have welt dents along their tops only. The hoods have welt dents. The headlights *and* taillights of each car are broken out. I could not see any normal collision damage. All the damage is high on both vehicles.

I ask the front car driver what happened.

"He started it," he says, pointing to the other driver.

The other driver responds, "We were just having fun. It was only a snowball. We were coming back from the snow."

After the stories come out it is like this: Driver number one is traveling in the lane left of the shoulder lane, slowly overtaking driver number two's car in the shoulder lane.

The occupants of the two cars do not know one another.

At driver number one's instructions, his significant other, sitting in the passenger seat, throws a snowball at the left side of driver number two's car in the shoulder lane. Driver number two takes offense. He takes his significant other's large paper cup of soft drink and ice she was drinking, and tosses it out his driver's window at and onto the snowball thrower's car.

Score at the end of the first quarter: six to six.

The driver of the snowball-throwing car now fires the International One-Finger Sign of Peace in the air. The other driver responds in kind.

Each now has made his conversion, the score is seven to seven.

Driver number one pulls to the shoulder. Driver number two does also, indicating he understands the rules of the game these two are making up while driving.

This act signals the start of the second quarter.

Both drivers exit their vehicles for the new kickoff, and meet in midfield with their team: the always-ready roadside adjuster tool—a tire iron.

Since the kickoff really belongs to the Snowballer, he walks up to the front of Soft Drink Thrower's car and bashes out a head light. Soft Drink Thrower walks over to Snowballer's car and responds in kind. Snowballer then massages Soft Drink Thrower's windshield. Soft Drink Thrower responds in kind.

New score update: 21-21.

As in a comedy routine where the comedians cutoff one another's neckties in turn, these upstanding rational (?) citizens of the road, licensed to drive in California, thereafter take turns massaging the other's car with a tire iron in a tit for tat exercise in stupidity and destruction.

The score remained a tie, but with much higher numbers.

Finally, when they stopped, and reality returned to the oatmeal they had for brains, they realized what they had done. They then decided a CHP accident report was in order, forgetting for just a silly moment the word "accident" means what is says: *American Heritage College Dictionary*, 1a. "An unexpected, undesirable event. b. An unforeseen incident. 2. Lack of intention; chance...."

I heard their stories, surveyed the damage, and graciously declined taking an accident report. I tell them it is doubtful their insurance companies will pay to fix the damages since insurance companies are in the accident indemnification business, and not in the mutual combat damage redemption business.

I do tell them I will be happy to call the Los Angles County Sheriff's Office (LASO) for them so each can file felony vandalism and malicious mischief charges against the other, but I felt in all likelihood each would go to the calaboose when the reports were taken by the handling deputy sheriff.

They thanked me for responding, declined my offer to call the LASO, wished me a nice day, and departed in their battered vehicles, more knowledgeable perhaps, but doubtful if any smarter.

I don't believe there are freak accidents. I believe there are only accidents. (In most cases, they should be called "carelessnesses.") It doesn't matter what the nomenclature of the accident is if one is injured or killed. Freak or not, you are injured or killed. The manner of how the event occurs may be less frequently known than more commonly known ways that injure or kill. That doesn't make it a freak, just infrequent. So, I say there are no freak accidents. Just accidents, which in most cases can be avoided.

Here are incidents I investigated in which people were killed. Some might say they are freak accidents, and pose questions that are "whys" to ask.

Tale Number 60 – The Big Push

Judging from the evidence, because there is no complete witness, an elderly man, alone in his vehicle, is driving a minibus uphill on a narrow, steepish, two-lane mountain road when the vehicle stops running for reasons unknown. Again, judging from the evidence, the minibus stops in the single lane and the driver puts the parking brake on. He then gets out, releases the parking brake, and runs back to the rear of his vehicle to push it uphill a short distance into a dirt turn-out area. At that moment, a witness to the last event rounds the corner in his car some distance downhill from the minibus's location. The witness sees the minibus roll backwards, knocking down its former driver and running over him, and continuing to roll backward into a small ditch and cut bank on the left edge of the roadway.

The man is dead when the witness reaches the scene.

The ironic thing to note, and it is patently obvious at the scene, is all the driver had to do is sit in the driver's seat, and using the regular hydraulic unpowered foot brake, slowly roll backwards to a very adequate stopping place *downhill* and behind him on the dirt shoulder.

Why then did the man attempt to push it uphill to get it off the roadway?

Tale Number 61 – The Big Rush

An elderly couple, with the wife driving, is in a rush to get to a strip mall post office to beat the mail truck's pickup time at the curbside collection box. As they approach the strip mall corner, they see the mail truck is already at the mail box.

The female driver hurriedly drives the post office access driveway that leads to the inside corner of the L-shaped strip mall where the post office is located. She pulls up a short distance behind the mail truck, driving the left wheels of her car up on the strip mall sidewalk. The area between the sidewalk and the flat parking lot surface is shaped like the coving edge of a linoleum floor, but in this case the area is filled in with asphalt to make the concave slope.

In a rush, she throws the older heavy-framed station wagon's automatic transmission into park, and exits the driver's door, leaving to give the letter to the mail truck driver. The car is parked at a slight angle.

But immediately on exiting, she notices the car is rolling backwards. She has not put the automatic transmission into park, but into reverse. The creep of the transmission, the slight parking angle, and the slight difference in height between the raised edge of the sidewalk and the lower parking lot surface are enough collectively to allow the car to roll backwards easily.

Instead of jumping into the car to apply the brake, this frail, possibly one hundred pound infirm lady runs to the back of the station wagon, and puts her back to the tailgate against the car with her arms outstretched to the sides in an attempt to stop the car from rolling.

While she does so, according to a witness, she yells to her husband, "Step on the brake! Step on the brake!"

Her paraplegic husband is sitting in the right front passenger seat, his legs paralyzed. Knowing he can't just step on the brake as his panicky wife requests, he raises his left leg with his hands, and throws his leg to extend it over the transmission tunnel hump in an effort to hit the brake with his foot.

His foot hits the gas pedal.

The vehicle shoots backwards knocking his wife down, rolling almost all the way over her, killing her and pinning her under the car.

Why didn't she just get in the car and step on the brake pedal?

Tale Number 62 – The Big Oversight

A mother about thirty-five years old and her seven-or eight-year old daughter are riding in their car on the freeway in the lane to the right of the fast lane.

It is a nice clear day, and they are riding with the traffic flow.

Ahead of them a couple of hundred feet, but in the adjacent lane to the right of theirs, a truck-tractor is traveling pulling a set of almost empty flat bed trailers.

Behind the big rig, and a short distance behind the mother and girl's car, is a witness traveling in the same lane as the truck.

As the group is riding along, the witness notices a large piece of metal bouncing up and down on the back of the rear flat bed trailer. The metal piece is later found to be about one-quarter of an inch thick, and about twelve inches square. All the sides of the metal plate are jagged from having been roughly cut out of something by a cutting torch.

The witness continues to watch the metal plate bounce and after a while moves to the shoulder lane, and drops back a little farther for consideration of safety. The witness didn't like the bouncing plate situation.

The mother apparently did not notice the hazard, or did not recognize the situation as being a hazardous one.

After a bit more traveling and bouncing, the witness said the slipstream from the tractor caught the metal plate on a good bounce up, and sent it sailing. According to the witness, the metal plate sailed like a Frisbee back and to the left toward the mother and the daughter's car. Upon reaching the front of their car, the plate turned vertical and went through the windshield directly into the mother's face, killing her instantly.

The car drifted out of control and ran off the freeway shoulder into the perimeter fence. The girl was uninjured physically. Mentally, I don't know about.

Why didn't the mother see the metal plate bouncing and move away?

Tale Number 63 – The Big Cry

Back when motorhomes were just becoming popular but still not numerous, a very average married couple, probably of less than average means, decided to become entrepreneurs in the motorhome rental business. They bought an almost-new motorhome to rent out. They figured the rental income would enhance their financial status. They also reasoned they would have the motorhome for their free use because ultimately, it would be paid for by the rental income.

Accordingly, they place an advertisement in the local newspaper to set their financial plan into motion. They are very happy when their first prospective renter calls to make an appointment to inspect the vehicle prior to agreeing to rent it.

The couple is sitting in their front room when they see the renter-to-be arrive, park his car at the curb in front of their yard, and come to house to make inquiry.

After discussing the terms of the rental, the prospect asks to test drive the motorhome. The couple agrees and gives him the keys. Neither one of them is going to ride along for security; the husband is infirm with a disability, and the wife doesn't feel comfortable riding alone with someone she doesn't know.

But they aren't worried about the security of the motorhome. They have the man's station wagon as collateral. He has even given them the key to make them feel better about his taking the motorhome out alone.

The prospect backs the RV out and departs. They return to their front room to watch TV while they wait for his return.

When about five or ten minutes passes, the husband notices movement in the back of the station wagon. He directs his attention more closely to see a person climb from the rear cargo area over the rear and front seat backs, and into the front seat. He sees the subject get behind the steering wheel, and drive the car off.

They both get a terrible sinking feeling when they see the car leave. But hoping against hope, they wait an hour for the rental prospect to return with the motorhome. When he does not, they call the sheriff's office, which forwards the stolen vehicle report request to the CHP, which handles all car theft calls in the unincorporated areas of L. A. County.

The CHP sends me to the couple's home to take the report.

When I arrive at the very plain, ordinary concrete block home, two sheriff deputies' patrol cars are parked out front. One of the deputies is walking out the front door going to his car. He is shaking his head.

As he passes me on my way into the house, all he says is, "They're destroyed."

As I enter the house, a second deputy, standing with a sergeant, points to the kitchen. He didn't have to do that. I can hear the sobbing, wailing, and groaning from the doorway.

The middle-aged couple is sitting at their round kitchen table that is covered with a worn plastic table cloth of red and white squares. They both have their heads cradled on their respective crossed arms on the table. Indeed, they're destroyed.

It takes a full hour with all the solace three law enforcement officers and a female neighbor who looks after them can muster to get them to return to some level of stability.

When we get them to that point, I address the matter of the stolen vehicle report. I am trying to fill in the form in between their joint independent bursts of deep crying, accompanied by that stuttering in-breathing deep criers do to catch their breath.

I hate to bother them. But I am trying to get their information to complete the stolen vehicle report for their signature. Once signed, I can then have it broadcast in a hope of catching the thief.

When I ask about the name of the insurance company covering the motorhome, they both break into deep sobbing like they were when I walked in.

Somewhere in the middle of this renewed deep heartache the man blubbers out, "We-e-e- don-n-n't haaave annnyyyy! We-e-e didn-n-n't haaave a-n-y-y-y monneyyy le-e-eft after-r-r-r get-t-t-ting it."

I look at the other occupants. If ever in my life I thought I had seen utter dejection, it was only the kindergarten variety compared to the looks on the faces of those present, including the look of the so-called hardened police officers.

A consensus concludes a visit by the paramedics is in order to evaluate the couple's vitals because all present are concerned about the couple's welfare.

The paramedics respond. They are instrumental in getting the couple to achieve a limited state of emotional stability, which assists me in finishing my business. With the signed report in hand, I return to my unit to call dispatch to broadcast the stolen vehicle report.

I left the couple with the sheriff deputies, paramedics, and neighbor and went back to patrol, hoping to coast for the day because I wasn't in much shape mentally to be really functional.

I don't know if the thief was ever located or the motorhome recovered.

Tale Number 64 – Fair Damned-sels

A town on the west side of Fresno County is holding its annual harvest fair. Besides the agricultural exhibits there are the usual carnival rides, midway with its games of skill, and food and drink booths.

My buddy KP and I, are among the several paired units assigned to patrol the area while the fairground is open this late summer Saturday night.

We are about two hours into our graveyard shift when we receive one of those accident-with-no-detail calls. We respond to the rural main road location of the accident to find what is commonly called by some, a grinder—a two-car head-on collision.

A mid-thirties solo male driver in a pickup truck was southbound on the two-lane rural road in the darkness. The driver drifted into the opposing lane and hit the oncoming passenger vehicle nose to nose. The estimated combined speed of the two vehicles at impact was around 120 miles per hour.

As I have mentioned previously, the wearing of seat belts was not mandatory at the time, so the installed lap belts were not worn. Consequently grandmother, age about fifty; daughter, age about thirty; and daughter/granddaughter, age about twelve, all coming from the fair, which I "guesstimated" from the carnival trophies in the car, were killed outright.

The errant driver was not killed, in fact, he was barely injured.

But, he was drunk.

The victims' car was on its roof in an unplanted field off the highway in the rural darkness. The headlights were on. The radio was playing happy peppy music. The three generations of bodies were all jammed together on the driver's side roof, probably as a result of the vehicle coming to rest after a roll over. The fair trophies were in and around the car.

While the happy lively music played, because we didn't have enough awareness to turn it off, and the inside of the car was lighted by our flashlights like some kind of room in a Halloween house, we helped the coroner untangle the bodies, unload them from the car, and load them into his van.

That was not fun like the fair was.

Tale Number 65 – It's Only A Disabled Vehicle

While on routine patrol one afternoon on northbound 99 Freeway south of Fresno, I spot a mini-pickup with a camper shell stopped in the oleander-planted center divider.

I stop to check it out, because the vehicle was not there on my southbound pass.

Pulling in behind the truck in the median (even *I* don't to stop there unless forced to), I see a male of about thirty-years-old squatted by the left front wheel. He has an elbow-type tire iron in his hand, and is working at the wheel hub cap.

Must have had a flat, I think, as I get out.

When I exit the patrol car, he stands up, and moves to the area in front of the truck.

That's unusual, I think.

As I continue to walk toward the truck, he moves a little farther away from it.

He turns to face me completely and assumes an aggressive body posture. But he doesn't threaten.

That's strange, I think.

I walk up to the driver's door of the truck and stop briefly to look inside the truck's passenger compartment. Nothing untoward there. But, the driver is still acting unusual.

I look at the left front tire I saw him working on. It is inflated. Maybe he just installed it, I think, because he was working on the hub cap.

No. No. There is no tire jack installed to the truck, and there is no wheel on the ground, either flat coming off, or inflated going on.

Ding. My low-powered light bulb goes off. This guy isn't the driver, he is attempting to steal the tire. Maybe all of them. I look around for his car. There is a vehicle parked in the median a short distance away on the other side of the oleanders. I see no occupants.

Standing by the driver's door with my suspicions aroused I ask the man, "What's the matter with your pickup? Do you need a tow truck?"

He doesn't answer me. He just stands there looking at me.

I move to the front corner of the left front fender and stop. He stands his ground, but raises the tire iron to waist high.

Without further investigation, and at this distance, I feel I have confirmed my investigative hypothesis—my suspicion.

"Drop the weapon," I say. "Get down on your knees."

He moves into a sort of semicrouch and brandishes the tire iron at me. He still has not said a word.

I elect to draw my side arm. I hold the gun alongside my right leg, pointing the gun barrel down with my finger off the trigger. I don't think I can use the Mace tear gas spray effectively out here because of all the wind from the passing traffic. If I did, I'd probably get a dose of it, too. That's not good for officer safety at times like this.

The guy remains in his threatening position.

I'm now thinking if this guy carries on, it is possible he will be showing up to a gun fight with only a tire iron.

Again, I tell him to drop the weapon and get down on his knees.

He lowers the tire iron to his side, while a contemplative look comes to his face.

"Are you going to shoot me?" he asks.

"Not if you don't try to hit me with that thing. Drop it to the ground, step back three steps, drop down on your knees, and put your hands on top of your head," I say, while holstering my gun.

He drops the tire iron to the side, and goes to position A. I walk around him in a short half-circle, handcuff him, and stand him up. I tell him he is under arrest for tampering with a motor vehicle, for being a pedestrian on the freeway, and for assault on a peace officer.

After checking out the whole situation, I learn he doesn't own the mini-pickup. He wasn't even driving it. He saw it parked there unattended on the freeway, and stopped with the intention to steal all the wheels to sell them.

I booked him for the charges.

Hey. It was only a disabled vehicle.

Tale Number 66 – Surprise! Surprise! Surprise!

Besides the narrow two-lane road through the avocado orchard laden valley of the Puente Hills mentioned in "What Goes Around, Comes Around," another similar roadway near there runs along the crest of a bare ridge, or near it.

This particular roadway seems a bit narrower, because in a lot of places one of the edges has a drop-off of some tens of feet. For the sports car and motorcycle road racing violators, this road isn't as forgiving as the lower road in the valley. If they run off the high road, the car goes over the side at least some feet down an embankment, usually rolling over. If they run off the low road they have a chance as long as they miss the avocado trees.

A car going too fast around a corner on the high road is thrown into the hillside bank, bounces off, crosses the narrow roadway, and then goes over the side. One going the other way too fast for the curve just goes over the side without the benefit of the boost from the embankment. Either way, the occupants are injured or killed.

Consequently, due to the roadway configuration and the abundance of road racing drivers who can't understand this roadway is not a race course (nor do they have the ability or equipment to handle it if it were), a lot of accidents, property damage, and injury, and some fatals, occur on the beat.

The office occasionally put special teams on the high road and environs to try saturation enforcement in an effort to reduce the accident rate and save lives.

One Sunday, I am on such a team.

I think there were three officers, maybe four, on this team. We left for the beat after the 1:45 PM briefing, and drove to one of the very few spots on the roadway where we could park all the patrol cars on the shoulder, and be close to, but not at, a very sharp blind curve, one of many of these types of curves on the road. That's why the road was popular with the road racers. But we picked this particular curve because safe parking was available for us.

The roadway going into, through, and out of the curve is separated by double yellow lines. The curve is posted each way with a yellow warning sign advising of a fifteen mile per hour speed to safely negotiate the curve.

Our enforcement group simply stood by the first parked patrol car and waited, ticket books in hand. Soon the Sunday afternoon road racers arrived.

A car would come sliding around the corner, clear on the wrong side of the roadway, completely left of the double yellow lines. Some of the cars' left wheels would scatter dirt off the cliff's edge. The drivers had no idea if a battleship, tank, or train was around the corner the other way when they raced into the curve.

I'm sure had they known that four Chippies were standing there waiting to flag them in one at a time for their driving indiscretions they would have been a whole bunch legal and safe.

But that was the purpose of our presence: surprise. We wanted the word to get out we might be there waiting at various places on the roadway each day to force them to think about being safer on the road. Random road patrol was not getting the job done. People were being hurt and killed. Property was being damaged. We hoped this team action would help reduce, or even better, stop those damages, injuries, and deaths.

I don't remember how many tickets we wrote for those of you interested in a body count. I know that even rotating outs, we wrote so many tickets between us we got tired of writing them. We had so many drivers we could have used a Take A Number machine for service. But what else coul*ddd* we do? The *cwazy* careless drivers kept coming on the wrong side of the road through a blind curve most of the afternoon.

Oh, some of you will say, "Well, you must have made your quota, then." And, the old snide cop joke answer is, we don't have a quota; we get to write as many tickets as we want.

Bah. Bad joke. But we don't and didn't have a quota. The concern was to encourage driving safety.

When it started getting dark, we left the area, each officer reporting to his regularly assigned beat to begin routine patrol there. Whether we had an effect or not, I don't know. But, I always hoped we did, and saved someone agony and tragedy.

Tale Number 67 – A Night To Remember

It is the weekend night of high school graduation, never a quiet time for law enforcement, especially traffic officers.

I receive a call of an 11-79 about one hour before the start of the commencement ceremony at a high school near my beat.

The crash is at a signalized intersection. Of the two cars involved in the crash, one is driven by a graduating student with another graduating student as the passenger. According to witnesses, the student's car, turning left in the intersection on a green light, violated the right of way of the straight-ahead-bound victim vehicle.

When I arrive, the cars are still in the intersection, front bumpers locked together. The driver of the victim car is standing on the sidewalk. He is a bit banged up, but basically okay. The students are still in the front seat of their car. They are each moderately injured, but look worse off than they are. Several other graduating students have also stopped, and are out of their cars hanging around the crashed cars.

This is not a good place for anyone to be standing, especially noninvolved parties. Even involved parties, if able, should get away to a safer place when cars can't be moved. Other vehicles, driven by drivers who are drunks, looky-looks, or just carelessly going by, can and do hit the crashed cars again with more injuries resulting.

When I exit my car, I try to shoo the bystanders to the sidewalk. But they will have none of it. Their buddies are hurt and they want to be there for their friends' aid and comfort. I want the bystanders out of the intersection. I call another unit for assistance.

In the meantime, some well-intentioned person has gotten in touch with the girlfriend of the wounded passenger to tell her of the accident and injury. (Sound familiar?) Others later say she didn't even hang up the phone. She blasted out of the house, and arrived at the accident location in a cloud of boiling locked-brake rubber. She ran directly to the passenger through the traffic in the intersection, and started her speech of, "Oh, Robbie. Oh, Robbie. Oh, Robbie...." She continues in that manner until my assisting unit arrives.

The assisting officer gets Robbie's girl over to friends in the bystander group, now out of the intersection. She still says her audible mantra through her tears with her friends, just as she did while at Robbie's side.

When the dispatcher assigned the call to me, she told me the ambulance was rolling. It was not there when I arrived. I call dispatch again. I am told the ambulance's ETA is five minutes. I want the victims out of here.

I want them out of here for their well-being and because more graduates-to-be are gathering and oversympathizing with the injured. This overt, dramatic display seems to move the girl who is still "Oh, Robbie-ing" to a higher key. Some hysteria is present and is starting to build quickly.

In the five minutes before the ambulance arrives, a group of now about fifty teenagers is starting to wig out. All the girls are wailing and crying. Their lamentations get a lot of the boys going, too. And now the group won't move much, despite our instructions and encouragement. They fall back a bit, never going to the curb, and then edge forward until they are back where they were before, or closer. All the time, they are crying and wailing.

We certainly weren't going to use crowd control methods on them, so we just keep trying verbally to move them back and out of the intersection. It is a tough fight. They don't want to listen or act. (Oh. I forgot. They *are* teenagers.)

When the ambulance arrives, we make room in the crowd for it and its crew. I tell the crew chief when he exits the rig to make all haste, because the bystanders' temperament balance is swiftly deteriorating to hysteria and I don't think he has enough room in his van for everyone.

They put the two boys on gurneys, put the gurneys into the ambulance, and are gone to the hospital in short order.

At the instant of the departure of the victims, the crowd's hysteria dissipates as fast as one would see a large inner tube deflate when a hole is punched in it.

The kids begin to drift away to their cars, leaving the scene to me, the backup unit and the tow trucks.

As far as I know, the graduation ceremony went off as planned.

Tale Number 68 – Blondies Have More Fun, She Thinks

I am working the Pomona Freeway on afternoon shift.

At the location of this incident, the freeway is four lanes westbound, plus a fifth lane, which is a mandatory exit lane to the surface streets. The fifth lane runs parallel to the freeway lanes. Just before the lane ends to exit the freeway area, it turns ninety degrees to the right to continue to the surface street.

I'm motoring along in moderately heavy traffic in the shoulder lane next to the exit lane. Up ahead, I see a lone passenger car in the mandatory exit lane. It did not exit as required. Instead, the vehicle went out the center of the curve, bumps across a rough area of partial asphalt behind the curve, and through a weedy dirt area kicking up a dust cloud. It then re-enters the freeway.

When that driver re-enters, a car in the shoulder lane is forced to take evasive action, and moves to the lane to the left to avoid a side-to-side collision.

The errant vehicle is now ahead of me in the shoulder lane. I move up and stop the car, which yields to the shoulder.

The driver is a nice-looking girl in her twenties. She has dark brown hair. I tell her why I stopped her, and ask for her driver's license and registration.

While she is looking in her purse for the items, she says, "Are you going to give me a ticket? I don't think you give the blondies tickets. The blondies at work say they don't get tickets. The blondies don't get tickets, do they?"

She continues in that vein the whole time she is looking for and retrieving the documents.

All I say in reply is, 'Ma'am, I give tickets to those who deserve them, brown, black, blond or red, male or female."

I take her documents, tell her to stay in the car, and go to the patrol car's right fender to write a ticket for failure to exit as required by signs or markings. If she hadn't affected the other car, I would have given her a verbal warning because the violation would have been more technical than dangerous.

It takes about ten minutes to write the cite. I return to her driver's window.

Before I can begin my explanation, she starts right in again on The Blondie versus The Brownie situation. She keeps repeating the information faster and faster, and in an increasingly higher tone of voice.

I stand there waiting for her to vent, and to calm down so I can finish.

Pretty quick, she is hyperventilating. All at once, she passes out and falls over in the seat toward the passenger side. Is this for real? is all I can muster to say to myself. I reach through the car window, take her left wrist and take her pulse. She is alive with a good pulse, and seems to be breathing fine. I go back to the car and call dispatch for a code 3 ambulance, and then return to the car's right side window to watch over her to ensure her care.

Quickly, and with my full appreciation, the ambulance arrives. The crew gets out of their rig looking around for an accident. They didn't know what it was they were responding to. I point to the girl on the front seat though the open passenger door. She is still out, and breathing okay. I tell them the story. They shake their heads.

After they check her vital signs, she is loaded, still unconscious, onto a gurney and taken to the hospital.

As a demonstration that I treat everyone equally, and I did, I have the office send the ticket to her by mail.

I never heard of her again.

And I'll bet that dark-haired young lady probably never saw the license plate bracket that reads, "Redheads do what blondes dream of."

Tale Number 69 – A Slacker Gets His Due

In the winter in Fresno County, we get what is called tule fog, as you know. It usually comes in early, stays late, and is very thick. We get some nasty wrecks because of its presence. But this night, the fog didn't start coming in until about 8:00 PM.

I am working the south half of Freeway 99 on the afternoon shift. As the fog moves in at the south end of my beat, I work a little farther north of the fog line so I can patrol in the clear. As the fog creeps farther north, I move farther north, too. Consequently, by about 9:45 PM, I am hanging out right where my beat begins, trying to stay out of the fog unless called.

Ultimately, the time comes to end the shift and head for the office. The fog has moved closer yet, and is ready to engulf my hang-out location on its way farther north.

I congratulate myself on my cleverness and head for the office. I am about three minutes away from the office when dispatch calls.

"65-73, Fresno. Report of a 20002 (twenty thousand two) at 12345 Street Name, in Small Valley Town, north of the county line."

A 20002 is a reference to the California vehicle code section for a misdemeanor hit and run property damage accident. It could be a car into a car, one of which split from the scene. Or more probably, a car hit someone's property and fled. The location given is twenty-five miles from my location. I will have to drive through all that fog I have so cleverly (I think) evaded.

"Uh, Fresno. 65-73. Is it possible to have a graveyard unit handle that? I'm almost to the office," I whine and snivel into the radio mike.

"65-73, Fresno. That's negative. The sergeant assigned the call to you. Graveyard is shorthanded."

Fresno, 65-73. 10-4. Responding." I reply courteously. But once the mike is hung up, I say, "@#$%^&*#!!!" out loud about my luck.

I head south, exiting the freeway to the rural surface highways that run through the vineyards of Fresno County. My top speeds are ten to fifteen miles per hour, and even that is too fast sometimes. At that rate, it is going to take me some two hours, more or less, to get to the accident location. I did hit a few clear spots, but mostly, it is fog, fog, and more fog in varying degrees of visibility, mostly double thick.

The dispatcher calls me several times to check on me. I can't tell her where I am. Despite working the area for several years, I can't distinguish a location or even see the cross street signs. A couple of times I have to get out with my flashlight and walk across the roadway to a street sign to get a fix.

I finally arrive at the location, and go to the house to contact the people who called. They had been inside the house when they *thought* they heard a car hit something. They called it in and then went outside with flashlights to look. They couldn't find anything. I, too, went out, and walked the area in the cold, wet, thick fog looking for a possible-maybe-perhaps accident. I can't find anything either. I call dispatch to report it as UTL. Then, I get back in my patrol car, and drive back to Fresno in that pea soup to the office. My eyes felt like they were put in backwards.

So much for trying to be a slacker.

Tale Number 70 – You Gotta Work With What You Know

I just sit down to eat on my dinner break at home when the phone rings. (We can eat at home if we live on or near the beat we are working.) The ringing of the phone does not portend a long dinner break. My wife then answers the phone.

"It's for you," she says, making a wry face, "It's dispatch."

I take the phone. "Tompkins here. What's up?"

"Tompkins, dispatch. (It's hard to break the radio habit.) You have an 11-79 on The Big Street west of The Other Big Street. It's reported as a truck broken in half, on fire, with the driver trapped inside."

"10-4, I'll be rolling in a couple." The location is about eight to ten miles away in the middle of the beat I am assigned.

I gulp several large mouthfuls of my dinner beef stew while I am putting my gun belt back on, kiss my wife goodbye, and hit the doorway for the car. Pulling away from the driveway, I call dispatch to tell them I am back in service and en route code 3 to the call.

Minutes later, still running with the red light, rear deck amber light, and siren on, and having blown everyone off the road, I am coming down a long gradual hill to the valley plain. I can see smoke from the truck on fire. The truck is parked on the shoulder of the divided highway.

Funny, I think, looking at the scene, the traffic is not backed up there. In fact, there isn't any traffic, or lookylooks, at the incident. Hmm.

I go roaring into the vicinity of the scene, cut the code 3 equipment, and roll up by the truck and stop.

There is no fire engine. There is no ambulance. There is no crowd. There is no truck broken in half, on fire, with the driver trapped.

There is a truck driver, very much alive and uninjured, standing on the sidewalk waiting for a tow truck that he called.

I call dispatch and tell them to cancel any rolling emergency equipment.

It seems the truck broke a radiator hose. In order to inspect same, the driver tilted the cab forward on his *tilt cab* truck and leaned across the inside of the engine compartment under the raised cab. He was inspecting the broken radiator hose that was allowing a lot of steam to escape when, apparently, a passing Good Samaritan saw the tableau, and interpreted the scene as reported.

Right facts, sort of, wrong conclusion. But in spite of right facts and wrong conclusion, I risked my life and limb, and that of others, unnecessarily, to respond to do what I could to assist the reported injured driver.

Like everything else in life, you work with the information you have when you have it. Even if its wrong.

Tale Number 71 – Auxiliary Days Off

All I intended to do was store a disabled truck. I ended up joining the accident statistics.

It is a November evening near the end of an afternoon shift. I am working the south half of State Highway 41, the highway to and from the coastal area. The highway is very busy in the summer, not so much during the winter, especially, during the week.

I am about thirty miles from the office in Fresno when I clear a late enforcement stop and head in. I am glad to go because it is getting foggy.

After driving about a mile, I notice a white garbage truck stopped on the frontage road paralleling the highway on the east side.

The frontage road is a narrow rural way, about a lane and a half wide, and that's being generous with the width. It is separated from the main highway by a shallow ditch and a barbed-wire fence. There is no shoulder on the frontage road, so I know the garbage truck is stopped on the roadway. Its size and position will greatly obstruct passage, if anyone does try to drive through.

Driving on the main highway near the truck's location, I decide not to store the truck. I am late returning to the office, and since I know that road is seldom used, if at all, I think storing the vehicle can probably wait for another unit to handle.

I reach for the mike to call dispatch, intending to ask for a graveyard unit to handle the truck's disposition to allow me to go in now. While I think about it, I keep driving.

But almost immediately, I think if I leave it there, the presently developing tule fog will hide the truck, and someone will hit it. My job is to prevent accidents, not contribute to them. I leave the mike on the hook, make a U-turn, and go back to handle the truck.

Late getting off. Again. Still. Yet. Even.

I pull in behind the white garbage truck and stop just at a car length's away. I put the headlights on bright, put the white spot on the back of the white truck, turn on the red spotlight for parking exemption, put my four-way emergency flashers on, and flip up the switch for the rear parcel deck's amber flashing light. I leave the engine running so the heater will continue to work on this cold night.

I call dispatch. I advise of my 10-20, request the license plate information on the truck, and order a heavy duty tow truck to remove the rig.

The truck, facing north, but more closely positioned to the southbound side of the narrow roadway, has its right rear dual wheels removed. They are not present. One or two jack stands, I don't remember exactly, are under the rear axle.

I exit the unit and begin to walk around the rig with the vehicle storage form, filling in the form's requested information. In a couple of minutes, dispatch calls me with the license information. I return to the car.

I enter the driver's side, leaving the driver's door propped open with my left leg stretched out. I'm sitting on about one cheek, and leaning inside the car the rest of the way to reach the radio mike. As I lift the mike to the tell the dispatcher to go ahead and give me the information, I hesitate. I had glanced in the rear view mirror. Headlights are coming. They are about three blocks behind me in this pocket of clear night air surrounded by the near total darkness and the building fog.

171

I tell dispatch to go ahead with the information. I write the info on the form, and hang the mike up, again looking at the oncoming head lights. The lights are now less than a football field's length away, and the vehicle's speed is at the same fast rate.

The driver has not acknowledged my presence by slackening his speed.

With reaction time and closing distance now short for him, and more particularly, for me, I pull in my left leg, close the driver's door, turn the red spot to the rear, and change the rear deck light from amber to flashing red, which requires a driver to stop. It's just like a flashing red stoplight.

All these newly-added lights do is provide the oncoming driver with a better illuminated target to put between his collision-sight's cross-hairs. I am going to be hit. And hit hard.

Not having the presence of mind to think about the lap seat belt I wore (dumb, dumb, dumb), because of the imminent impact, I brace myself in the seat with steering wheel. I look at the garbage truck closely in front. If I'm rammed into that, I think, I'm history. Even if I just clip it, there is a likelihood it will fall over on me, because it is sitting on jack stands.

Still, going to the left is not an option. No place to go with a ditch and fence. I crank the wheel all the way to the right, grateful I have left the engine running to operate the heater, thus allowing the power steering to work. I look again in the rear view mirror.

Here he comes about fifty to sixty miles per hour.

The impact stops his pickup truck cold. The force shoots my unit around that garbage truck like a jet taking off from an aircraft carrier's catapult. How I missed the right rear corner of that garbage truck, I don't know.

The patrol car is damaged in the rear. A lot. I shot forward about two car lengths to a stop.

When the patrol car stops, I get out. I am hurting. My neck, my total back down to my buttocks, and my arms and shoulders, feel like I have been beaten. I'm not too clear-headed, either. I stumble back to the rear of the car to check out the situation.

The patrol car's rear end, the trunk mostly, is severely bent upward. The trunk lid is still locked, but the lid is buckled up into a ridge allowing one to reach inside the trunk through a large opening.

The pickup front end is smashed down. The male driver, a stocky, balding man of about fifty to sixty years of age, is sitting in the pickup's driver seat moaning and groaning. He is muttering something like "Sphousha, sphousha."

He opens the door and slides out, and then leans in a disoriented manner back against the truck. He is wearing a black suit with a white shirt and black tie. He keeps saying the "Sphousha" word from time to time.

While he looks Hispanic, and I speak a little Spanish, I don't understand what it is he is saying.

It appears to me he is a moderate to severe walking-wounded case, and can function alone for a bit. I return to the patrol car to call dispatch to send up a flare to get some help on the way.

Picking up the radio mike ready to key the talk button, warning words from my academy days come drifting into the vacuum of my head. Words similar to, "Our radios transmit waves that can set off explosives and gasoline fumes." (Even though *they* put the transmitter in the trunk over the gas tank!)

There is no other help out here. None is coming. We are off on a side road in the dark, 150 feet from the new highway, which is devoid of traffic this mid-week, winter, late evening night with fog and darkness all around us.

I am going to have to call in order to get help.

I shuffle back to the trunk and take a deep whiff. I don't smell gas fumes. With great difficulty, I get on my hands and knees and look under the patrol car with my flashlight for gas dripping from the gas tank. There is none. That's a break.

I recontact the driver, and gently escort him to the rear of his pickup truck, leaving him to lean against the tailgate. I give him the "stay" hand command.

Returning to the unit, I take the radio mike cord and stretch it through the driver's window, bending it at the windshield post, and stretching it as far forward to the front of the unit as it will go. I then stretch my arm out as far as it will go while holding the mike. Holding my breath, I hunch my shoulders, squinch up my face, and key the mike button.

Nothing. No explosion of the gas tank. Whew, again. No, double whew.

I call dispatch to advise of the situation. I don't have to request anything. She knows the drill: roll the sergeant, investigating unit, perhaps an assisting unit, ambulance, fire rig—just in case—and two tow trucks.

I shuffle back to the driver of the pickup truck. He has moved back near the open driver's door, and is leaning against the pickup's side. He is still muttering, "Sphousha," or something like it. That bothers me because it just doesn't seem to be injury related. He keeps repeating it.

Thinking that the "sphousha" guy might be an intoxicated driver, and with nothing else to do, because I couldn't handle diddley now, I shine my flashlight inside the pickup truck's cab looking for a booze bottle.

My flashlight beam falls on the floor on the passenger side. There, partially jammed under the dash of the pickup, is a lump of something wrapped in black.

At that time, the driver turns to his right and points inside saying, "Sphousha, sphousha." Jesus! It was his wife. Spouse, dummy, spouse.

Dummy shuffles as best I could around to the passenger side, and tries to open the passenger door. It is jammed. The window is up. I shuffle back around to the driver's side, and ease the driver, who is now leaning/sitting on the driver's seat edge, back to a standing position on the pickup truck's side, putting his arm on the pickup bed rail for support. Then I clamber in across the bench seat to the lump on the floor.

After checking her pulse, which is pulsing okay, I somehow, someway, get her up on the seat. She is unconscious, but breathing okay. I clamber back out, and then the driver and I, each oohing and ow-ing, stretch her out on the seat.

I am beat. I need to sit down myself.

I am shuffling to the patrol car seat to flop down when the requested assistance arrives code 3. Their arrival is a signal that shuts me down. I am all through. I have no more to give.

The lead officer of the investigation unit determines the driver has been drinking, but is not intoxicated. The driver is found at fault for the crash. I don't know how his wife came out.

The couple is of Portuguese heritage. His Portuguese word for wife was not registering with my crash-addled brain. Because he looked Hispanic, I guess I kept wanting to hear some kind of Spanish 101 I knew.

As for me, I "enjoyed" sixty days off the road in recuperation, about half of which I served in a light-duty capacity as the public desk information officer in the area office's lobby. That job is Monday through Friday, with weekends and holidays off, which gave me Christmas at home.

Finally, I got a Christmas off. The hard way.

Tale Number 72 – We Have Lift Off!

My partner and I have a very slow Saturday night on graveyard this summer night in Fresno County. We're looking forward to going home on time because we are going on days off.

We've just finished our end-of-the-shift coffee break and are sitting in the patrol car preparing to head for the office to close out when dispatch calls assigning us to a possible fatal accident.

So much for getting off on time on this bright Sunday morning.

The accident is reported to be at a T-intersection of a north-south road intersecting with an east-west road that runs along a bluff on the south bank of the San Joaquin River. The bank is very high above the river channel, and substantially set back, maybe one-half mile, from the river itself. The area between the roadway along the bluff, and the river proper, first falls by the bluff road as a short-faced cliff, and then goes to receding-river-caused terraces now planted with vineyards, until closer to the river channel itself, when the area becomes wild.

We drive north on the road that will take us to the intersection with the river bank road.

Approaching the stop-sign-controlled approach to the intersection, we see no sign of an accident. We are hopeful it's a bogus call. But as we get closer to the stop sign, we can see across to the river bank road edge. A swath about as wide as a car has been cut in the tall strawlike grass bordering the uncurbed pavement edge. Getting closer, we now see heavy, black, fresh skid marks starting before the stop sign limit line, continuing across that line, through the intersection, and across the river bank road, terminating at the swath cut. Uh, oh.

We get out and walk to the edge of the bluff road to look over to the terraced area beneath us.

Below us, some forty feet in verticality, and some seventy-five to one hundred feet away in horizontal distance, is a two-door sedan. It is facing toward the river, sitting as though purposely parked there. The car is on top of a freshly constructed, large, homemade dirt ramp that was built with a bulldozer. The ramp is used to load and unload farm equipment from a truck bed.

From where we are standing, we think we can see people in the front seat of vehicle.

We scramble down the cliff face, using an adjacent path, and go to the car.

176

People are in the car, all right—a driver and a passenger in the front seat. But, they aren't looking out at the view.

They are both dead, and have been dead for a while. They are cold. The car smells of booze.

If one didn't know better, it would appear the driver drove the car up on top of the dirt ramp, and parked it there so the two could sit in the car and enjoy the river view.

But from all the indicators, the two probably left a bar at closing time. They were zipping up the maybe unfamiliar road, thinking it crossed over the river, which it didn't. The driver saw the stop sign too far past the last minute to get stopped safely. He locked the brakes. The car slid through the stop sign stopping area and across the river bank road, cutting a swath through the dry weeds at the top of the river bank cliff, and then left contact with earth. It then flew like Evel Knivel's motorcycle through the air, landing with no bounce on the soft dirt of the ramp top, rejoining earth.

The occupants were discovered in the very early morning hours by a ranch hand. He had gone out to the vineyard to check on the irrigation water he was running. He couldn't notify anyone then, because he didn't have a phone and none was around. He waited to report the accident until he returned to the main ranch some miles away.

We clear up the scene and go back to the office to do reports. I get home around noon from our scheduled quitting time of 6:15 AM.

Did I miss breakfast, dear?

Tale Number 73 – Bull. Darn It.

When we meet at graveyard briefing, my partner says, "We've got to get off on time. I'm on vacation starting tomorrow."

When we put our equipment in the patrol car after briefing, my partner says, "We've got to get off on time. I'm on vacation starting tomorrow."

When we have our first coffee, and again later at lunch, my partner says, "We've got to get off on time. I'm on vacation starting tomorrow."

In between all those admonitions, he tells me about his vacation plans. And tells me and tells me.

Finally, I tell *him* I am convinced he is going on vacation starting in the morning at 6:15 AM when our shift ends, and I think there is a good likelihood at this hour of 4:30 AM that he is going to make it.

Then dispatch calls.

The call is one of those off-the-wall strange assignments that falls to us once in a career, whether vacation is scheduled or not.

Dispatch: "65-71, report of a loose bull on State Route 180 in the vicinity of the 00000 block. Stand by to direct traffic to keep the cars from hitting the bull. (What about the bull hitting the cars?) The SPCA (humane society) is presently contacting their cowboys (The SPCA has cowboys?), and getting their transportation trailer lined up. (The SPCA has trailers for loose bulls?)"

Us: "Fresno, uh, 65-71. Responding." What else could I say?

It takes us a little more than thirty minutes to respond to the location.

On arrival, we locate the bull in the darkness. He is not on the state highway. He is in the backyard of a double-wide trailer residence on property adjacent to the state highway. The bull has chicken wire with several fence posts attached draped around one horn, and is trailing a substantial length of the wire like a bride's wedding veil. The backyard area is in havoc.

We ask dispatch to call the residents in the mobile home to warn them of the presence of the bull. We kind of figure they know it is there, given the backyard destruction and the chicken wire, but, you know, just in case. When dispatch calls, the residents are in the process of abandoning ship. They tell dispatch they know the bull is there; it has charged the aluminum-sided trailer twice!

We check. Yep.

We assume a position of defense, putting ourselves at a face to face diagonal from the bull, but across the yard. We have our lights off. If the bull charges us he would get the push bumper, front bumper, and the motor before he got to us. We hope. So we sit watching the bull, starting about 5:15 AM.

My partner begins checking his watch every minute like a high school kid waiting for his "best" girlfriend to show up for a date.

He also reminds me, in case he thinks I have forgotten that "We've got to get off on time. I'm going on vacation starting tomorrow," though tomorrow is already here.

Every once in a while, the bull starts to amble away toward the highway. We flash the headlights. He stops and looks and then stands around a bit. Then he starts to walk off again. We click the PA system talk button. He ears perk up and he looks over, stops walking, and then stands around more.

Nice bull. Stand around some more. What the heck are we going to be able to do to keep a bull off a state highway? Go over and say, "Shoo, bull?" Bulls are like the proverbial eight-hundred-pound gorilla; they can go and do whatever they want.

Six fifteen comes and goes. My partner is more fidgety than the bull. He has now resigned himself to the fact he will not be getting off on time.

At 6:45 AM, the bull starts moseying toward the front yard and the highway by going around the west side of the mobile home. He is not stopping for any of our tricks. I drive around the east side and reposition us. We resume surveillance.

Finally, at 7:15 AM, an SPCA truck pulling a covered two-axle trailer pulls up on the shoulder of the front yard. Behind it is a pickup truck with two cowboys, and a double horse trailer. I thought my partner was going to dash over to hug them. He could see the vacation light.

While the cowboys suit up, a CHP day unit arrives to relieve us. I think we tell the guy thank you at forty miles per hour as we drive away immediately for the office.

At the office, I let my partner off at the back door. He gets his stuff and splits. I go ahead, service the unit, then put it in its parking stall. By the time I get inside, he is long gone.

I bet he doesn't know to this day he put the bad mouth on himself by saying those magic words out loud, "I've got to leave on time."

Tale Number 74 – The Highway Hots Club

Male and female human beings' bodies function. They function in ways that spite government laws and cultural mores to the contrary. They function day and night, rain or shine, home or on the highway.

I'm sure like "The Mile High Club"—Denver, at an elevation of 5,280 feet doesn't count here—there is "The Highway Hots Club."

In witness to the above conjecture, the following is offered:

One nice summer afternoon I go past the end of my Freeway 99 beat to the first ramp in the next county, and turn around to head back. After I reenter my beat, I see a Volkswagen camper minivan pulled off onto the southbound shoulder in a wide dirt area. It is parked in the shade of several eucalyptus trees.

I pull in behind the camper and walk forward to check out what appears to be an abandoned, possibly disabled, vehicle.

On making the right side approach, I see the wide cargo door on the right side of the vehicle is open. I am thinking either someone is inside or the door has been inadvertently left open when the occupants left.

I discover the occupants didn't leave.

A completely naked male and female are on a blanket on the floor of the small area inside the door. They are doing—what do the country western people call it?—the mattress boogie in full-time, but without the mattress.

Needless to write, I'm sure, they were oblivious to all. In their oblivion and ecstasy, aided by the passing freeway traffic noise, they had not heard me drive up.

As I start to speak, or cough, or something, the outside speaker of my patrol car radio sounds off with the dispatcher calling another unit. Like the unmistakable sound of a shotgun shell being racked into a pump shotgun, cop radio traffic is unique and attention-getting.

The guy stops his business and cranes his neck up to look out the VW camper's rear window. Then, his peripheral vision must have caught something to his left. He s-l-o-w-l-y turns his head to see the highway constabulary standing there all shiny.

He screams, "Ohhhhhh, s---!"

She screams, "S---!"

They disengage, which I don't think was a problem for him just then, and scramble for cover-up clothes.

After some semblance of decency and composure is obtained, I get their identification. They are husband and wife. They were traveling along from Sacramento going to L. A. when the mattress boogie urge struck. Since they are in a vehicle with almost room enough for that endeavor, they stop to unurge. I'm sure, until my arrival, that was more refreshing than The Uncola, an earlier advertising campaign name for 7-Up.

I give them a verbal warning about a nonemergency stop on the freeway—*I* didn't think it was an emergency—and send them on their way.

Another example occurs one night on graveyard: A passenger car runs out of gas on the freeway in downtown Fresno. The driver pulls the car to the paved shoulder near the bottom of an off-ramp. Of the two males and one female in the car, the driver is the only person who has money for gas. And, what the heck, it was his car, the other two said later. The driver hikes off for gas in an area with not too many open gas stations.

Apparently, he was gone a long time in his search. The couple remaining in the car didn't have anything to do while they waited. They weren't sleepy. The car stereo was broken. It was too dark to read, if they had anything to read. It was just boring to sit there.

So, they decide to break the boredom.

There isn't quite enough room in the right front seat area to maneuver, so the right front door is opened, and the lower corner of the door is jammed into the adjacent ice plant-covered embankment.

Now, they have room to wriggle. Or whatever. (Why the back seat wasn't selected, I don't know.)

Enter graveyard freeway beat unit 65-71.

My partner and I come rolling down the ramp to enter the freeway and see the vehicle parked on the shoulder at the bottom of the ramp. We pull in behind the car, killing our headlights as some officers prefer to do. I see the right side door is open, and make a right side approach to it.

Talk about getting caught flagrante delicto! He is kneeling on the front floorboard, dashboard to his back. She has the seat tilted back, feet on the dashboard. Everyone has his or her eyes closed. Except me and my partner.

I flash my flashlight across their faces, and cough an exaggerated cough.

Zowie! Talk about going to battle stations. Those two move in a blur that would put a roadrunner bird to shame for speed, while disengaging and obtaining clothes to dress to reach a state of acceptable decorum.

They are boyfriend and girlfriend, both over twenty-one, consensually and sensually, passing the time of night. Since the motoring public has not been offended, I suggest they pick a better place, and let the matter go. I offer them a ride off the freeway to find their friend, but they want to wait for his arrival.

I think they mostly want to wait, because neither can walk well.

We tag the car with a yellow disabled vehicle tag, and leave them to wait in their formerly boring way.

Another example: During the same month as the incident immediately above, I am working with the same partner. We encounter a slow-moving car in the shoulder lane of the three lanes of the south half of the 99 Freeway. The speed of the car is about forty-five miles per hour. It is weaving badly and from time to time straddling the line between the slow and fast lanes. It is also straddling the paved shoulder by driving through the shallow concave concrete gutter between the shoulder lane and the paved shoulder.

We stop the car with the usual procedure: Put up the red spotlight, flash the headlights, and put the white spot on the inside rear view mirror.

In doing this, we see only one person, the driver. The driver suddenly starts rustling around, and reaches over to the back seat while trying to pull over to yield.

Because we see the driver rustling around while stopping, we consider that the driver, unknown then if male or female, is trying to stash contraband. Once stopped, we hurriedly go forward; my partner on the left, myself on the right.

We arrive at the front passenger compartment and shine our flashlights inside. We see no contraband, but we do find a young man who is in his twenties, of average height, and of some 260 pounds, seated behind the wheel.

All some 260 pounds is naked. He is not even wearing a watch.

He has a shirt gathered up in a bunch, and has it placed at the reverse "Y" at the top of his legs, trying to obtain a slight degree of modesty. But the shirt is…uh…kind of…uh…standing up.

Because he is unclothed while driving, everything about him is easily accessible. Consequently, he accesses it. The accessing, and the concurrent excessing, causes him to weave because he was almost to the point where he didn't have to access anymore. But our sudden presence created *onanistic interruptus.*

My partner, with the idea in mind of giving the driver the field sobriety tests, tells him to exit the car, not remembering the guy is naked, and also mostly likely not yet in a position to comfortably exit.

"I can't yet," the driver says, ejaculating his reply. "I can't right now."

It dawns on my partner why the driver cannot exit.

We then provide the driver some downtime by standing there chit-chatting across the top of his car.

Partner: "Where do you want to go to coffee?"

Me: "When?"

Partner: "Oh, how about when we clear here?"

Me: "Okay. But let's don't go to the highway chain. Let's go someplace else."

Partner: "Why?"

Me: "I'm burned out going there."

Partner: "Okay."

This chitchat continues for a couple of minutes more. All right. Enough time passed. Back to the business at hand.

With that provided time, and with the driver shifting his corpulence back and forth in the car enough, he gets his shirt on, and most of his pants up. He then gets out and finishes dressing.

When my partner asks him why he is driving in this unclothed state, the driver says he has been at a summer night's swim party at a friend's house. After the swim, he left to go home. Feeling the balminess of the evening after the swim, he decided to drive home au naturel. Somewhere along the way the primal urge struck, and he took matters into his own hand.

Since he isn't drunk or on drugs and has only been inattentive without affecting any traffic, we give him a verbal on straddling, provide him instructions on the need to pay attention to driving and to do his thing someplace else, and then send him along his way. I did tell him that if he kept it up he was going to need glasses.

Last highway hots story.

I am working graveyard with a partner in East Los Angeles. We are assigned a surface street beat. We are driving on a four-lane commercial street that is separated by double yellow lines. It is about 1:30 AM when we encounter a slower car in the fast lane ahead of us.

We had no sooner come upon the car, which has only a driver visible, than it begins to weave over the double yellow center lines, back into the fast lane, over the fast lane-slow lane line, and then back into the fast lane. Because there are numerous cars parked at the westbound curb (we are westbound), we have to let the car proceed some distance to an area where we can affect a safe stop that won't result in a collision with the parked cars.

In a bit, we reach an area where we think the probably intoxicated driver can park the car. We turn up the red and white spotlights.

Exactly at the instant the lights go up, a female head pops up into our view from the area of the driver's side, but from below the seat top. She stops rising halfway up, just clearing the seat top. She looks directly toward us with the white spotlight on her: Her mouth is shaped like a donut hole.

Immediately, my partner, whose out it is for an intoxicated driver, says, "Well, there goes my out for a deuce."

We both realize we probably don't have an alcohol-impaired operator, but rather a driver operating under the influence of fellatio.

With no problem, the car yields quickly into a closed gas station lot. We can see the driver squirming around behind the wheel even while the car is still rolling. The female passenger is rustling around in the front seat, and then she moves around trying to arrange her hair. You know, fluff-fluff here, fluff-fluff there.

On our approach to the front windows, my partner on the left, me on the right, we see nothing unusual. The young couple is sitting quietly and demurely as though in church.

"What's happening, officer," the driver ventures as an opening gambit.

My partner tells him we stopped him for weaving and asks him to exit and to go to the front of the car. The driver complies with no problem. It is obvious even before he gets to the front of the car he is not intoxicated.

"Why were you weaving?" my partner asks.

"Oh, I dropped a cigarette on the floor. My girlfriend was trying to get it while I was driving. I was trying to get out of her way."

My partner tells the guy his story doesn't play, and proceeds to tell him what we think was going on.

His demeanor changes to one of contrition instead of bravado lying.

"I'm sorry. We got carried away," he said.

My partner instructs the guy about the right place for where and when, and decides to take the stop as a verbal warning for lane straddling. He walks around to the girl's window, and tells her she can be cited for interfering with the driver, even if the driver wants to be interfered with.

Since they were back into driving shape, we cut them loose and went back to patrol.

You just never know about humans and their bodily functions.

Tale Number 75 – Close, But No See-gar

I had gone to the east end of my Pomona Freeway beat, had my end-of-the-afternoon-shift coffee break at a highway chain's restaurant, and was heading up the freeway on-ramp westbound to join the traffic throng to head for the barn.

Entering the freeway in the shoulder lane, I am behind a very poor driver. The car is using the shoulder, the shoulder lane, the lane to the left of the shoulder lane, and the lane to the left of that one; three out of the four freeway lanes, plus the shoulder. About as bad as they come, and obviously, an intoxicated driver candidate for inspection.

But I really don't want to stop the car right there. The area is behind a hill, and the hill interferes with radio reception. For those of us who worked the Pomona Freeway here, it was an area notorious for totally dead radio reception and transmission.

I want to continue with the errant car to the other side of the I-605 Freeway, actually my beat area, but more importantly, out of the dead area in case the stop turned sour. But I just can't justify letting the driver continue to drive anymore than necessary. He is very dangerous to himself and the proximate traffic trying to pass him.

So*ooo*, against my better judgment but mandated by necessity, I stop the car.

The driver yields to the nice, wide, level, dark, dirt turnout area frequently and illegally used by drivers to stop on the freeway. The spot is dead center in the bad radio zone. The car is about one hundred feet from the freeway shoulder. The driver is male, and there is a female passenger in the right front seat.

Since it is almost the end of the shift at 10:15 PM, I call dispatch to advise I am making a late stop, and to give my 10-20. My radio will not transmit out, affirming my original judgment of why I didn't want to make a stop here—#$%^&*!! I am out of the radio picture. Alone with three million people and hundreds of cars passing by on the freeway.

I contact the driver, who is seated behind the wheel. He is blitzed. Not intoxicated as earlier discussed, but "drunk as a skunk."

His wife is HBD (Had Been Drinking). She looks like she also is too intoxicated to drive legally, and is possibly drunk within the common meaning.

I direct the driver out, and to the front of his car with his back to his car's headlights. (The better to see, my dear.)

I want to try to administer the field sobriety tests to him, though he is pretty unsteady. While he is objectively drunk enough to book without doing the "monkey drill," I like to have even heavily intoxicated drivers try to perform the tests when possible, in order to have evidence to use in court. Testifying to their performance, better described as poor performance, helps state the case better. It gives jurors something to picture and consider besides just my opinion when deciding on the subject's sobriety.

This driver couldn't hit a bull in the butt with a bass fiddle. He couldn't find his butt in a closet with two people to help him. He is OTL and can't even get started to do anything I demonstrate.

I hook him up. I am escorting him back toward the patrol car's right front seat while walking past the passenger side of his car when his passenger suddenly opens the door, bolts out, and runs and springs on my back.

She starts yelling, "Get his gun! Get his gun!"

He is handcuffed from behind. Drunk as he is, he is trying to back into me to get my 357 caliber Smith and Wesson Highway Patrolman six-shooter revolver from my holster. She too, is trying to grab it periodically when she isn't hitting me in the face with her left fist while holding on with her right hand and a leg lock around my lower waist.

All three of us are doing the whirling dervish dance as I try to keep my gun away from him, remain upright on the irregular surface, and keep the gun from her while I try to get the monkey off my back. (Sorry. Couldn't help it.) I know if I do go down, I am the morning news.

While this is going on, I keep thinking why are they doing this to me? Don't they know who I am? Don't they know I'm the fairest of the fair? Don't they know I'm one of the good guys in a white hat? Don't they know I'm a paragon of reasonableness? No, I don't think they do, nor do they care. You'd better buck up buck-o, or you're going to be a training item at the academy for the cadets.

Luckily, because he is tanked and handcuffed, he can't get it together. And luckily, she is about one hundred and five pounds, including the alcohol that makes her possibly drunk.

Finally in the melee, I get a hard knee hit into his *cajones*, as they say in East L. A. The strike directs his attention away from me to what is important to him. Then, I get enough of her forward to my left side to meet my right fist in her cross-hairs. She decides to get off, lay down, and rethink the matter. Maybe, even take a nap.

While he moans and groans, in a legs-together splayed at the knees semi-crouch, no doubt wishing he had his hands free to assuage and cover his jewels, I hook her up with my other set of cuffs. When I get my breath back, I stand her up, and then put them both into the patrol car. I immediately depart the area, leaving their car there. I only need to drive about five hundred feet to the other side of the I-605 Freeway to get back in contact with the world.

I call dispatch. She advises they took roll call on the air since I wasn't in at the end of the shift, and they had a sergeant out looking for me. I advise I have two in custody out of a resisting arrest, and an officer-needs-assistance battery in the radio dead area. I ask her to have a graveyard unit store the car, and another to meet me at the office to transport and book the couple.

When I get to the office, I deliver Jack and Jill to the transporting and booking unit, throw my paper work into the clerical in-box, and go home to have an adult beverage, one day closer to retirement.

I never got a subpoena for the case. I don't know what happened to them, if anything.

But more importantly, I escaped Jack and Jill putting the brass ring through the hole on this one.

Tale Number 76 – Group View

Each CHP area office has training sessions frequently for the officers assigned to the office. These training days are scheduled and handled differently by each office, depending on the desires of the area commander. The training covers everything from new laws and review of physical arrest procedures to weapons training and first aid. The sessions usually last eight hours, but not always.

One time, after lunch following a four-hour training day in an Los Angeles area office, the attending officers are assigned to go out on beats to supplement the patrol by beat officers. More officers are at the meeting than available patrol cars. Consequently, three of us are in one car and are working the I-605 Freeway between the Santa Ana Freeway and the Pomona Freeway. Not too much is going on.

As usual when cops get together, like other people in their jobs, the talk frequently falls to shop talk. One of our group may have seen something that reminded him of a past enforcement stop, and that tale would remind someone else of an incident to bring up. Not quite round robin, just linked conversation.

During this chitchat our driver turns around south of the Santa Ana Freeway and heads back northbound. As we pass under the crossover of the Santa Ana Freeway, a lone motorcycle rider, wearing "colors," comes on the northbound 605 ahead of us from the Santa Ana Freeway. (Colors is a term used to indicate the rider is wearing some type of clothing bearing an emblem, or other identifying characteristic, reflecting an affiliation with a particular motorcycle group.)

The rider merges into the center lane of three lanes about three hundred feet in front us, and just motors along at sixty-five miles per hour—nothing unusual about his driving.

The conversation in the car at the time is of enforcement stops and encounters those in the car had with members of biker groups.

Soon after the bike rider enters in front of us, one of our group observes, "There's one of them now." We all look at the rider.

Just then the rider, without signaling, heads toward the shoulder lane on a moderate diagonal course. We watch him as he continues through the shoulder lane from the center lane onto the paved shoulder where he impacts the rear center of a set of bottom-dump trailers of a disabled big rig combination parked on the shoulder.

The bike hits the trailer's steel Public Utilities Commission bumper and breaks into several pieces, exploding in flame. The rider, ejected by the sudden stopping, and not being able to go forward due to the presence of the back of the rear trailer he hit, goes up the rear steel wall of the trailer, with blood flying off in different directions. He flies above the top lip of the trailer bin, does a half-turn, and literally heads back down. His face hits the trailer lip as he passes against the wall again. When he hits the ground, he is probably dead. Just like that.

The total elapsed time from the beginning of his lane change to him hitting the ground is probably no more than thirty seconds.

We pull to the shoulder, and lose no time doing what we can do. One officer gets the fire extinguisher to douse the bike, another gets the flares to close off the shoulder lane, and another put a 44 blanket over him.

When the ambulance comes to load him, one of their personnel takes the blanket off. Just then a group of bikers, wearing the same colors as the downed rider, comes up on the freeway from the surface street below. They start to go past the scene, but stop when they recognize some of the scattered bike and then the uncovered rider.

"Hey, that's good old Charlie there," one says to the others.

"Yep, that's good old Charlie," another says to the group.

We hear several more yep-yeps from the biker group. Then, without further ado or ceremony, they fire up their modified motorcycles and roar away northbound on the freeway.

Those loud bike mufflers are probably as close to Taps as Charlie was ever going to get.

Tale Number 77 – I Wasn't Even In Heat

On another day, at the same location as the reported truck that was broken in half, on fire, with the driver trapped, I get a call of a car fire with the fire department responding.

When I arrive, the firemen are already 10-97 and are snaking out their hose to put out the blazing fire in a station wagon. I can't do much other than direct traffic around the scene while the fireman do their thing.

The fire guys, for whom I have the greatest respect because I think their job is more dangerous than mine, have the fire ninety percent knocked down. I grab my clipboard and vehicle storage report form and proceed to fill out the form with the view of having this traffic hazard towed off the highway. I walk around the car filling out the form as I go. I end up at the rear of the station wagon.

I stand there completing the form, not paying too much attention to what is going on. Mistake. Big mistake.

The fire flares up slightly. A fireman rolls the hose back out they had been reeling in, and turns the nozzle to get that just right spray pattern. He hesitates a bit turning the nozzle, and stops on stream mode momentarily on the way to adjusting it to large spray.

In that moment, the high-powered, concentrated water stream ricochets off the car hood. The water propels the burned paint and other debris through the broken out front windshield, though the interior of the car, and though the missing rear window, hitting me full in the clipboard, and knocking me backward.

In one shot, I am filthy dirty and soaked. I hear no laughter.

Thereafter around car fires I am forever careful to stay upstream from the guy with the fire hose and to watch him carefully.

Playing in the hose water in uniform is not as much fun as it is when you're a kid in your bathing suit!

Tale Number 78 – Sad Hands

The ring on the third finger of her left hand is not gold. It is a little band of purplish plastic that is cracked through. The remaining fingers, but not the thumbs, bear rings, too. They are all of a silver-colored metal, most likely not silver. These rings are decorated with a variety of different colored materials; some looks like turquoise, some is a red material, and other rings are decorated in patterns with bits of the colored materials. Around the right wrist is a narrow black elastic band like those used to tie hair into a pony-tail.

The hands wearing the eight rings are very white. They do not appear to have been exposed to much hard work; they are young and not greatly lined. They bear no scars, but a newish-looking tattoo of a five-pointed star is in the web of the right hand. The tattoo is handmade in green ink.

The fingernails of the multi-ring-bearing hands are painted stop sign red. The polish is uncared for and badly chipped. On a couple of nails, the polish is chipped off as far back as the middle of the nail. There is no polish on the nail of the little finger of the right hand, and that fingernail is significantly longer than the rest. The other nails differ in length. Several of them are chewed back to the finger tip. Under most, grime is evident. The first joint area of the first and second fingers of the right hand is stained light brown— surprising to me for such young hands.

The light from the patrol car's white spotlight, reflecting from the inside center mirror of the car, shines brightly in the early morning darkness and illuminates her right hand in the flare of the widened spot. That hand is resting partly on the very white right upper thigh, and partly on the hemline of the red miniskirt she is wearing. The hand is on its right edge with the palm partially facing up and the fingers curled slightly in.

The left hand, in less light than the right, dangles downward with the fingers also partially curled in. The hand dangles in the newly created larger space between the left edge of the front seat of her car and the driver's door post. Blood runs downward over the top of her left hand into a drying large spot on the aluminum trim piece of the driver's door threshold. The blood puddle obliterates the car manufacturer's logo.

The hands, judging from the pungent smell in the general area of the vehicle's cab, were used in the illegal consumption of some kind of alcoholic beverage. Maybe they even helped her to ingest an illegal drug, using the long unpainted nail of the right hand as a scoop.

The person to whom the hands belong is dressed in black calf-high leather boots, the red miniskirt, and a white, long-sleeved, silky blouse. Her driver's license description and photo—and those are usually terrible pictures—are of a pretty auburn-haired, green-eyed girl, nineteen years old. But when I meet her she isn't pretty.

Her neck is slashed across the throat as a result of her head first going into and through the windshield, and then pulling back through the broken windshield glass.

No seat belt.

Her head is tilted far backward, held by the skin of the rear of her neck. Her face is pointed toward the ceiling behind her. She is upright in the seat with a slight lean to the left. Her heart is still pumping in a diminishing effort, squirting blood out of the severed main heart artery in her neck. The blood runs down onto her white blouse and red miniskirt and farther downward.

She had been playing "tag-the-bunny" on the freeway: Weaving in and out while racing a bartender to his home, to see who could get there first. She was driving his car; he was driving hers. She rear-ended a semi-truck and trailer and came to a sudden grinding halt from what witnesses said was a very high speed.

For their wrongful involvement, and it doesn't matter now, the very white, multiring-bearing, chipped-fingernail-polish painted, youthful hands of the formerly pretty girl are lifeless now, and will never again make a wrongful move.

Tale Number 79 – Those Invisible CHP Cars

More times than a civilian would think possible, I have been passed in plain view in broad daylight by speeding cars exceeding one hundred miles per hour in an *adjacent* lane. I kid you not. And by sober drivers.

I'm not talking here about my driving a stealth car. I'm talking about my being in a black and white that has Highway Patrol painted on the rear of the trunk lid, a departmental car with the red and yellow rear window deck lights, radio antenna, and even those with light bar roof racks. Cars full of Christmas tree lights.

When the fast errant cars are chased and stopped, the driver will swear I was hiding behind a billboard somewhere and sneaked up. He might swear it, but he would be wrong about the sneaking up.

I have been as emphatic as possible about the situation, and have been called a liar to my face. I have been called a liar by the defendant in court when I testified I was in such and such lane of the freeway, at sixty-five miles per hour in daylight and good weather, when the defendant blew past me in the adjacent lane.

It is no lie. It is true.

It is true, because the faster a driver drives, including law enforcement, the more narrow the driver's field of vision becomes. Around one hundred miles per hour, the driver gets tunnel vision, and sees only the area and lane directly in front of the driver. It's a nature thing. Driver's have no control over it.

So, heads up! We're out the*rrre*. Hiding in plain view.

Tale Number 80 – Her Name Should Be Lucky

A female driver about twenty-five-years old leaves her house in a rural area of Fresno County to attend a cosmetic party at the house of a friend of a friend. The party house is in another rural area where she has not been before. She is late leaving for the 7:00 PM Saturday night wintertime affair.

Driving out across the wide-open Fresno County farming area, she cannot find the street she needs, despite a hand-drawn map she has been given by her friend. She makes a U-turn to reverse course, and rechecks her route for the street.

In going back the other way, she is no more successful in finding the needed street than she was before reversing course. Nevertheless, she reverses course again to cover the same section of highway. Still no luck.

She says later she reversed course four or five times.

From my contact with her, I surmise that as she reversed course each time, her hysteria level ratcheted up another notch until she was totally psyched out.

She started out frustrated because of leaving late. Then became more frustrated by not finding her street per the map on the first pass, then more frustrated by each succeeding pass as she tried to wing it. Ultimately, she hit the gong by giving up, because of not finding it at all.

By that time, she is totally hyped and in tears. She decides to go back home and call the house where the party is being given. (There were no public phones out where she was, and this was precell phone days.)

In a fit of hysteria, she whips the car around into another U-turn. This turn is at a long straight stretch of two-lane rural road that is bordered on each side by freshly-furrowed acreage. Besides being nearly hysterical and going too fast to make the U-turn, she has a complicating factor she doesn't know about: Her husband had installed bias-ply tires on the front axle of the car, and radial tires on the rear axle. Or vice versa, I don't remember. Each set of tires acts differently to road forces than the other. All installed car tires need to be one type, or the other. Never both.

In any case, when she makes the final U-turn, her passenger vehicle rolls over a couple of times. The first roll flings her from the auto into the field ahead of the car. No seat belt. (Not required.) On the second turn over, the car rolls over the top of her, then returns to a wheels down position in front her.

When I get to the scene from the dispatched call, I find her standing on the shoulder walking and talking. She is a bit tearful. She is covered with dirt and mud and totally disheveled.

Because the rancher who farmed the land plowed nice deep furrows with high-ridged banks, when she was thrown from the car she landed exactly in one of the furrows, but face down. When the car rolled over her, the high dirt ridges of the deep furrows acted like pillows; they cushioned her from the crushing effect of her car's weight. All that happened was she was pushed down into the muddy furrow a bit. She is completely uninjured, just dirty.

Better than winning the lottery.

Tale Number 81 – Help From Heaven

It is 10:00 PM, almost the end of the afternoon shift. I am clearing a late stop, and I am heading back to the office from the far east side of the rural fringe area that surrounds the major metropolitan area of Fresno, where the office is centrally located.

It has been raining hard most of the afternoon and evening.

In a short distance I encounter a passenger vehicle stuck in a half-full feeder irrigation ditch that runs almost immediately adjacent and parallel to the highway. The ditch is only about two feet deep and maybe three feet across.

The driver says his car slid off the roadway during the rain that fell a short time before I arrived.

The rain must have been booze, because he is drunk and his female passenger is drunk. You know: not intoxicated, drunk.

Both are still sitting in the car, and both are belligerent. Apparently, a-look-what-you-did argument between the two that started before my arrival reached its peak just as I arrived. Lucky me.

Almost immediately they turn their belligerence toward me, the Lone Ranger out here in the bush in the dark at shift change with the very likely prospect of no unit available for immediate backup. The units coming on, probably, if they have left the office, aren't this far out yet.

The good thing about the situation is the couple can't get her door open because of the ditch bank. The vehicle is at a slight downward angle with the right side wheels into the ditch.

He keeps wanting to get out. I keep insisting for him to remain in the car until the tow truck comes to extract them.

Remembering my round and round devil dance of several years before with a drunken husband and wife, I decide I'd better make this official, and call for a backup to grace my presence, even if I think one is not available. Things aren't going well already, and I haven't even gotten to the field sobriety tests yet.

I call dispatch. She polls the units on the air checking to see if any are in a position to roll to assist me. There is no response. Uh, oh. She polls, again. Still, no response.

She is just calling me to tell me the bad news, when right after calling my radio sign, I hear, "Fresno, H-14. We'll handle the backup call."

Say what? The "H" in H-14 stands for helicopter. The Birdmen are going to come to my rescue? Well, at least they can fly around in circles up there, shine their bright light down, and yell through their PA system, "Hey, be good down there, you hear." Better than nothing, I think.

"65-21. H-14, bye," the flight officer calls on the car-to-car channel.

"H-14, 65-21, go ahead. This street north of the other street," I say, giving my 10-20.

"65-21. We'll be there in about three."

"10-4," I acknowledge.

In the following three minutes, the driver continues to m----- f--- me and continues to want out of the car. He tries to get out a couple of times, but I keep the door closed with my foot. His wife chips in on the m---- f------ to harmonize.

At the end of three minutes, during which time the driver emphasizes he is going to kick my a-- when he gets out, there is a lot of noise and wind in the air overhead. A spotlight, The Midnight Sun, said to be a million candle-power, maybe more, shines down flooding the ground with its super bright light that takes away all shadows.

To my great surprise, the helicopter pilot, instead of orbiting overhead, slithers the craft sideways checking out the roadway and pole wires and trees, looking for a safe spot to set it down. He finds one five hundred feet away, and puts The Big Whopper Chopper down at the junction of a paved side road. Then he *and* the flight officer run over from the aircraft to my location, fully-equipped to rumble.

I was, and am today, most grateful for their presence, and remain truly amazed the pilot would set that multimillion-dollar craft down for my butt's sake.

Thereafter, including during the field sobriety tests, the physical arrests, transport, and booking at the jail, Mr. and Mrs. Belligerent were Mr. and Mrs. Pussy Cat. Nothing but "yes, sirs," "no, sirs," and "thank you, sirs."

I guess they just wanted to see if I was serious.

Tale Number 82 – Flying Too High

I enter Freeway 99 one Sunday afternoon behind an expensive white American-made sedan. The car is about two hundred feet ahead of me. For a minute I see nothing unusual about the car. At the end of the minute, the vehicle drifts onto the paved shoulder and then drifts back into the shoulder lane of three lanes. Then it drifts over into the lane to the left of the shoulder lane, and again, back to the shoulder lane.

Hmm, something is not right. I put up the red light. The sedan continues tacking northbound. After about a half mile with no response, but continued weaving, I touch the siren a smidgen.

The yield response is way slow, but after another half a mile, the driver pulls the car to the *left* shoulder across two lanes to the center divider, not to the right as required, nor as I desired.

I approach the driver's window on this warm summer's afternoon. The window is up. As I arrive the operator rolls the window down. The odor that comes out that window into my face, blown by the air-conditioner, smells like a bar. Nay, ten bars.

"Wash da matter, offishsir?" the driver inquires with a wobble of his head.

I fill him in on his attempt to drive his vehicle, and subsequently arrest the man for drunken driving. I book him after he takes the required chemical test for which he chooses the breath test.

His breath result is point two six (.26). The threshold level to be considered intoxicated under the law then was point one zero (.10).

This stop is nothing unusual as far as the sighting, identification, arrest, and booking of a drinking driver goes, except the guy is a commercial airline pilot for a major airline on his way to the airport to take over an incoming airliner as the next-in-command relief pilot.

Tale Number 83 – The Devil's In The Dirt

It's a hot summer's day in Fresno, about 6:00 PM in the afternoon. I am working a minor injury two-car accident at a stop-signed intersection located in a residential area.

Three corners of the intersection have houses on them, but the fourth corner, the northeast corner, is a large empty lot.

The lot has the usual conglomeration of loose dirt, weeds, trash, and litter that seems to accumulate on corner lots. It is fenced with a four-foot wire fence on the two inside boundaries (north and east), but the two outside boundaries (west and south) are unfenced and bordered by sidewalks.

A bus stop is located about 150 feet from the corner of the intersection next to a sidewalk, right about where the lot line starts for the adjacent property.

At the time, I'm not too busy. I am waiting for tow trucks to arrive to get the cars unjammed from one another and tow them from the scene. Not much traffic directing is necessary, so I am just hanging out in the intersection, waiting.

While I wait, a city bus pulls up to the bus stop and discharges a nicely dressed older lady in a maroon skirt and a white long-sleeved blouse. She stops to light a cigarette. It strikes me she is coming from work. With the cigarette lit, and the lighter put away, she walks northwesterly on a diagonal across the large dirt lot.

She no sooner steps off the sidewalk, when a tall, moderate-sized dust devil (small tornadolike column of air occurring in desert areas) forms in the northeast corner of the lot to her right. If she noticed it, she didn't react. She walks on. The dust devil, instantly filled with matter from vacuuming the lot area where it formed, lifts the stuff, and spreads it though the column of air some fifty vertical feet, and begins to see-saw around like it is trying to decide which way to go.

After a few seconds it begins to track across the top of the lot on a potential course of convergence with the bus rider where she might rejoin the sidewalk when she finished her diagonal crossing.

After about twenty steps the walking lady notices and reacts to the dust devil. She stops and looks in its direction. Evidently, she is assessing its potential course. Deciding it poses no problem, she continues on her diagonal path.

Apparently, the dust devil made an assessment, too, because it zags a bit to its left toward her direction.

She stops again, but briefly. This time, she too zags a bit to her left to compensate for the dust devil's zag so to keep the distance apart equal.

Now, the dust devil, with more trash, dirt, and litter gathered in its column, zigs a little more to the left, and inches up its speed a click. The lady does not stop this time, but veers more to her left, now making kind of a bent diagonal, and like the dust devil, she too increases her high-heeled pace. The dust devil then veers right and kind of treads water a bit.

The lady looks to her right, and apparently decides she is okay in speed and distance, and proceeds, but now she continues to look to her right at the dust devil to keep her guard. She is now about two-thirds of the way across the lot. She may now think she is out of interception danger. She may now think wrong.

The dust devil suddenly turns sharply left, kicks in the afterburner, and closes the distance between it and its victim. It engulfs her entirely.

She puts her hands up to her face for protection. Her hairdo is pulled upward. Her skirt billows in the manner of Marilyn Monroe, but she keeps her modesty with a crouch, and a quick one-handed pull-down.

In an instant, the dust devil passes her by, zooming out into the street to disappear in the air, letting all the matter fall to the ground and scatter in its dying zephyrs.

The dust devil's victim, now abandoned, stands there filthy dirty, in complete disarray, and covered with the unsightly contents from that column of desert wind.

I could hear her cussing from where I stood. .

Tale Number 84 – Was I On Fire?

I am at the scene of a motorhome fire on the shoulder of the Pomona Freeway. While the location isn't part of my area's command, since it is close to my beat I tell dispatch to advise the responsible area command I will handle it as a courtesy and forward the report.

The motorhome caught fire while it was traveling. The driver pulled it to the shoulder, and then the two women occupants fled the coach and ran far away down the shoulder.

Engulfed as it is on the freeway shoulder—motorhomes and trailers burn quickly—flaming pieces fall off into the dry grass next to the paved shoulder. Then the wind does its thing and the next thing you know, the fire spread quickly down the freeway embankment, and up a low hill of a ridge of hills near the freeway.

The fire blossoms in the wind and begins to spread across the dry grassy hills— just what is needed to warm things up on this hot summer's day.

The fire department arrives. They do what they can from the freeway shoulder with their city-street-equipped fire trucks, but they can't get water to the bulk of the fire on the hillside. They call in a state division of forestry air tanker to drop a rust-colored fire retardant that I call, rightly or wrongly, borate.

On the first run, the air tanker drops a load of borate against the face of the hill. The load billows out and flutters down on the burning hillside. On the second run, either a different air tanker, or the original one now refilled, comes in low to drop another load in the same area. But instead of releasing it between the freeway shoulder, and the lower edge of the fire, the pilot starts the release over the center divider of the four-lane freeway.

Guess where I am? I am standing in the lane to the left of the shoulder lane directing traffic when the plane flies over my head with that loud droning noise common to propeller-driven aircraft.

The stuff comes floating down in clouds and clouds on me, my patrol car, and the now smoldering motorhome. It does not hit the ladies from the motorhome because they are standing out of range, "way down there." Nor does it hit the firemen or their departmental equipment because they have rolled up their operation and hit the road. (I was told some agency with cross-country-equipped fire engines was handling the fire line.)

The stuff just hits lucky ol' Tompkins, who is waiting for the tow truck to arrive to tow the motorhome hulk. I brush off what I can with my fingers, but it doesn't brush well; it's sticky, it also makes you itch, and—sphfffffftt—it tastes horrible.

I continue directing traffic around the scene. I must have looked a sight in my rust-colored uniform.

When the tow truck takes the RV, I return to the office to shower, and resuit in a fresh uniform I just happened to have there because I picked up my cleaning on the way to work.

On the whole, I think I prefer potato chips, or beef-barley soup. Maybe, even clean water from a fire hose.

Tale Number 85 – Told You So, Too

My partner and I arrest an intoxicated male driver with whom we have to really struggle to take into custody and handcuff. It is more than just a tussle, and less than a knock down fight. No blows are struck, but we have our hands full taking the guy off the road.

Even in the patrol car he is a problem. He is trying to kick the dash, and if he could have gotten at it, and he tried, the windshield, too. In the end, we have to secure his legs at the ankles with a tie-down strap.

These types of situations are very, very rare.

California law requires a driver to take a chemical test after being arrested for driving under the influence of an intoxicating beverage, a drug, or both. Even if the driver is belligerent and combative, and requires ten men and strong dog to subdue him, he is still required to take one of the three tests: blood, breath, or urine. And naturally, we are required, despite any arrestee belligerency, to help him accomplish that choice.

Our guy selects the blood test. Of the three, the blood test and the breath test can be taken while handcuffed. Obviously, not so with the urine test, even with females.

His choice of test means we have to go to a hospital where the necessary prearrangements for accommodation, and payment for, a blood withdrawal for a DWI (driving while intoxicated) arrestee have been made by the responsible authorities.

The hospital we commonly use has a good-guy "vampire," as we called him. If we brought in a combative arrestee, the laboratory technician took the blood from the vein in the arrestee's thumb while we left him handcuffed. This saved us, and them, a whole bunch of potential trouble if we had a problem recuffing the arrestee.

Arriving at the hospital's blood lab this night, we find our main man is on vacation. A substitute blood withdrawer is on duty: a doctor.

We walk our guy into the blood lab, one of us on each side of him. We sit him in a chair. My partner sits with him. I go to sign us in.

The doctor comes in with his prep work. He says, "Okay, take off the handcuffs so I can make the withdrawal."

"Uh, doctor," I say, "Can you take the blood with the cuffs on like so and so does?"

The doctor says, "Yes, I can, but I prefer to make the withdrawal with them off. This is a hospital, not a jail."

"Uh, doctor, could I have a word with you in the hallway for just a minute?"

He looks at me like I am going to try to sell him something he doesn't want, but he walks out into the hallway.

"Doctor, we had a hell of a time getting the cuffs on this guy. If we take them off of him in here, he is going to try to get away. We'll have to try to prevent that. This lab will get destroyed because we will have another scramble with the guy. Won't you take the blood from the vein with the cuffs on?"

"Officer, this is not a jail. This is a hospital. I will ask the man to cooperate with you. Because I ask as a doctor of the hospital, I'm sure he will be cooperative with you."

"But, doctor...." He has turned and walked into the lab.

I follow him in. My partner looks at me with the "well?" look.

I look back at him with the "@#$%^&*()#" look.

We stand the prisoner up and walk him over to the chair where the blood is taken from cooperative prisoners.

Before we take the cuffs off and sit him down, the doctor says to him face to face: "Young man, the officers tell me that if they take the handcuffs off of you so I can withdraw your blood, you will try to escape and there will be a fight. Will you promise me you will be cooperative when the handcuffs come off?"

"Yes, sir," the prisoner says demurely.

The doctor looks at me with a "*Ha!*" look.

We take the handcuffs off, seat the arrestee in a chair with a table writing arm like we used to use in high school. I stand to the immediate right of the doctor. My partner stands to the immediate left. The doctor puts the constrictor band on the subject's arm, and then realizes he hasn't brought the disinfectant patch to wipe the guy's skin with. He turns to go get one a short distance away.

The unfettered arrestee comes out of the chair like he is shot from a cannon. He has been sitting on "G," waiting on "O." He tries to make a beeline for the open laboratory door and the hallway beyond. We try to grab him as he starts, but he has the advantage of surprise, knowing when he is going to start. The only thing that assists us a little in detaining him is his shoe soles are slick on the lab's linoleum floor. He has a hard time getting good traction. Nevertheless, he is gunning the engine trying to make up for the slick surface.

My partner and I get him, and we go down in a clump. We all get up. We all go down. We roll here. We roll there. In the end, we get him on his face, and rehandcuffed him behind his back.

The lab is destroyed. All chairs are overturned. The two stainless steel tray tables that usually have all the blood withdrawal paraphernalia on them are overturned with the blood gear scattered everywhere around the floor. Many glass vials are broken. Several coatracklike stands for holding intravenous drip bags are knocked over. All in all, the place is messed up.

Leaving our guy lying on the floor while we stand and get our breath back, we look around for the doctor. He has abandoned ship.

I stick my head out the lab doorway. No one is in sight. I leave my partner in charge of our man, and go to the night emergency entrance desk to tell them we still need the blood withdrawal.

"Where's the doctor?" I ask.

"Oh, he had an emergency. He had to leave," the desk nurse says.

Old "Ha!" *had* to leave. Imagine that.

Another doctor from the hospital comes and makes the blood withdrawal from the subject's thumb vein, after we explain the whole situation and he sees the mess.

He never asks us to take off the cuffs.

Tale Number 86 – And Awaaaay, We Go

My partner and I have been out and about in the darkness of the Long Beach Freeway a couple of hours already on this graveyard shift summer Saturday night when the radio focuses our attention.

A graveyard unit of a CHP area way south of us has a slow speed pursuit, what we call a FTY (failure to yield). They are northbound on the Santa Ana Freeway. The unit is a good distance south of the junction of the Santa Ana Freeway with the Long Beach Freeway.

The pursuing unit keeps putting out their rolling 10-20s while they continue northbound. Their two-car convoy's speed varies from the announced speeds of twenty-five miles per hour to forty miles per hour.

We, like the other units monitoring the radio frequency, are listening to see if we can assist, or if we can put ourselves into position to assist.

Right now my partner and I are substantially out of position in relation to where the chase unit is. Moreover, because they are so far away, we think the pursuit will probably terminate before we are ever in position.

But keeping past experiences in mind, we drive south, turn around for northbound, and just north of where the Santa Ana northbound ramp to the Long Beach Freeway enters, we pull into the center divider, turn off our lights, and wait while listening to the FTY broadcasts.

The unit and the FTY are still northbound on the Santa Ana at twenty-five miles per hour. The unit puts out several more locations, which, over time, bring them closer and closer to our area. Eventually the chase car says, "We're closing on the junction with the Long Beach. Is there an East L. A. unit in position in case he goes that way?"

Well, what do you know.

We announce our position to dispatch, as do several other units that are covering the various ways the FTY can go.

Soon, the chase car announces, "We're taking the transitional to the northbound Long Beach. Our speed is still twenty-five miles per hour."

Really, now. Here we've been sitting la, la-la, la-la, and now we're going to be in a slow speed pursuit. Must be Saturday night.

My partner, who is driving, looks in the rear view mirror, and says, "Here they come."

He turns on our lights, and both rear window deck lights. I put the white spot to the rear. We sit and wait.

The chasee, traveling in the fast lane next to the center divider, approaches and drives past us at twenty five miles per hour. The male driver has his right hand on top of the steering wheel, and his left elbow on the window sill with his hand on the roof line. Just like out for a Sunday drive. As he passes us, he salutes with the International Sign of Peace, removing his hand for just a moment from the roof.

As soon as he is out in front of us, we enter the fast lane behind him from the center divider in front of the original chase car, which will drop off because they don't know the area. At this moment, the FTY driver puts his foot in the carburetor. Zoom.

We are off at twenty-five, forty, sixty-five, ninety, 115 miles per hour. He levels off at about 105. All the while he holds up the roof with his left arm.

What happened to the forty to fifty miles of twenty-five miles per hour? Was that practice?

His passenger carlike pickup truck rolls away northbound on the Long Beach Freeway. We are right behind him with all the emergency equipment going.

Traffic is very light. I call dispatch to request them to notify the Pasadena Police Department of the pursuit because the freeway terminates at Valley Boulevard in that city in about five miles. When the errant driver hits their surface streets, he is in their jurisdiction. We want them to know, but we'll be there.

At Valley Boulevard, we shoot off the freeway, through the red light of the empty intersection at the off-ramp bottom, and onto the surface streets. The FTY driver goes this way and that way, and this way and that way, bumping on the bumps, running lights and stop signs, and sliding around the corners. Finally, he hooks a left at a T-intersection, and accelerates on a side street.

The turn he made is what is called driver error in a pursuit. The side street is only about one long block. It ends in a cul-de-sac at the cliff face of a large hillside cut. The embankment is protected by a large, and hard, yellow-painted sled-type wooden barrier made from what appears to be railroad tie-sized lumber.

The errant driver sees the folly of not knowing his running path, and brings his vehicle to a sliding, screeching halt, almost stopping in time—but not quite. The front end of his vehicle obtains a substantial souvenir from the barrier for playing tag-the-bunny with the cops chasing him.

He is taken into custody with no problem; the arrest is commensurate with a surrender.

The driver is nondrinking. He failed to yield to the original unit for whatever the original violation was because his driver's license was suspended. He didn't want a ticket for that. He was driving slow trying to figure out how to handle the FTY situation.

By the time, he got to me and my partner, he figured he was in trouble, and decided to make a run for it.

I'm sure the driving on the suspended license charge would have been cheaper in fine and time than the total charges for which he was booked.

Besides, he still has to deal with first one, anyway.

Tale Number 87 – Eye Think That's Funny

I have left a coffee shop after meeting an adjacent beat officer for the first coffee break of the afternoon shift, and I'm heading back to my beat. I'm traveling on a busy six-lane street in the city of Fresno.

Stopping for a red light, I casually look around at the traffic and surrounding area, as is my usual way. Looking at the people in the car to my right, I notice they are laughing at something. I don't know what it is.

The signal changes. We move on.

I catch the next signal and stop. The mix of cars has changed around me. Looking around, again, I notice the driver to my left is smiling largely. Hey, everyone must be happy today, I think.

The signal changes. We move on.

I catch the next signal, too. (See, it's not just you who gets red lights!) Now, I am looking around before we get stopped. A couple of young kids in the car to my left are smiling. The boy points in my direction, and says something to the other passengers in the car. Everyone looks toward me and laughs.

What the hell is going on? I ask myself. I'm not getting the joke, if there is one out there.

Because the boy pointed my way, I look in the rear view mirror. I am the joke.

The left lens of my sunglasses fell into my lap when I put them on leaving the coffee shop. One lens is in; one lens is out. The brain compensates for the two differences and the wearer doesn't notice.

Always glad to be of service, and leave 'em laughing.

Tale Number 88 – Lunch, is served

I leave the office following afternoon shift briefing on this nice spring day, and head out for my beat, the state highway that connects the valley to the Pacific coastline. To get to my beat, I take the 99 Freeway.

And that's where I am when I drive by a picnic.

In the grassy center median.

With a family of four.

All are seated on folding chairs at a card table, complete with a white table cloth.

Besides craning my neck almost to the breaking point looking back over my left shoulder when I drive by the picnickers, not believing what I am seeing, I whip my head and neck back the other way looking for a camera truck. Especially, one that is hiding a TV network's secret camera. Surely, this is a trick someone is playing on the beat highway patrolman. Surely.

Nope. Surely, not.

Overshooting the picnickers, I go to the next ramp lickety-split, exit, and then zip back on the northbound side to the meals-near-wheels crew.

I stop in the center median on the other side of the oleanders from the group.

I see a father and mother of forty or so, and a son and daughter of the fifteen-sixteen age group. All are eating lunch as a nice, cozy family group.

Their van is parked in the median with them. Actually, they are somewhat adjacent to the van, trying to get shade from the western sun.

"Hi there," I say, and no more, leaving the talking to the family's leader.

"Hi, officer," the father says, and no more, parrying my opening move.

"Will you folks be much longer? You're not suppose to stop in the median, or on the freeway, unless it's an emergency." I fill in, "This is a very dangerous place for you to have lunch. You are between the two fastest lanes of traffic on the freeway with no safe place to seek refuge if you have to flee because of an out of control vehicle."

"Well, we needed to eat lunch," the father says, "but there is no shoulder. There is only an embankment. This is the only place we found that is almost level where we could set up the table and chairs. And over here, we're away from the trucks."

Hard to argue with the logic.

I ask them if they can close up right then, and move off the freeway to finish lunch in a parking lot, or the like. The father says they are done. In short order, Mom clears the table items into a cardboard box, Dad folds up the table and chairs and puts them in the van, and the whole group embarks into the van to motor on down the southbound freeway to I don't know where.

I guess when you're hungry, you're hungry, and like me, any port in a storm.

Tale Number 89 – Bill's Thrill

Shortly after I get off of three years of working straight graveyard, by choice, in the East L. A. area, I transfer to the Santa Fe Springs Area office a few miles away. This is the office my partner and I were delivering the package to when we ran into the kid brandishing the gun at the gas tanker.

At the Springs, I move to the afternoon shift, and for the most part work that shift. Now, I am out among day people and regular day activities, but it took a while before I felt comfortable getting out of the patrol car on enforcement stops without my flashlight. What do I do with my hands?

Anyway, one day I am the first car stopped at a railroad crossing for the wig-wag signal, waiting for a freight train to come through.

As the engine of the train passes by, *the engineer waves at me!*

Of course, I wave back. I have been waving at engineers my whole life without a return response from any of them, but today, I have "arrived": He waved first.

Tale Number 90 – Care To Dance?

My partner and I are patrolling the Long Beach Freeway on graveyard shift when we stop a vehicle weaving from lane to lane on this summer night.

We make the stop, and my partner makes the contact. He escorts the diminutive female driver to the front of her car, during which journey she walks with some effort to steady herself.

He gives her the field sobriety tests, the ones everyone knows: walk the line toe-to-toe, touch the tip of the nose with the index finger, and stand with one foot elevated about three inches off the ground. He also gives her the ones most people don't know about: finger tip count, hand patting, and saying one's ABCs. He decides she is impaired.

As he tells the driver she is under arrest, he starts to turn her around to handcuff her from behind. (*Everyone* is handcuffed from behind, even those seventy-five years old, or pregnant. It is for officer safety, not punishment for the arrestee.)

At that very moment, the very small women spins left and walks rapidly out into the freeway lanes. She gets as far as the middle of the lane to the left of the shoulder lane before we can grab her.

Luckily, luckily, luckily, we are between traffic groups. But there is a group bearing down on us about a half mile away.

The slight, small women suddenly develops the strength of The Hulk. My partner and I are pulling, tugging, and turning in circles left and right in some kind of mad folk dance, trying without success either to walk her to the shoulder or lift her and carry her there.

She is pulling and tugging and trying equally as hard not to let us accomplish our effort. She is trying all she can to remain in the traffic lane.

The traffic group is getting closer—way to close for comfort.

We silently and collectively decide to stop being gentlemen. We put our maximum panic strength to her and lift her off her feet, and rush to the shoulder. The traffic doesn't slow a whit for us; it goes whizzing by in what seems like a gnat's eyebrow hair away. Zip, zip, zip.

He and I stand there on the shoulder doing a little deep breathing, and looking at each other with the "okay, we dodged another one" look, and then pick up business from where we left off.

Tale Number 91 – Gentleman Jim Ain't Too Happy

I am leaving the office parking lot one midweek day after briefing when dispatch gives me an 11-83 call. The accident is located on a main residential cross street.

I respond code 2: regular speed, obeying the rules of the road, no emergency equipment in use. (To my knowledge there is no code one. Why? Why start at two?)

Arriving at the scene, I find a metallic silver-gray Gentleman Jim pickup truck, with the new car paper tag on the windshield corner, standing in the eastbound lane of the street at an unusual angle to the curb. (A Gentleman Jim pickup is a regular style GMC pickup truck spiffed up with different options of striping and cab décor; it differs from the more famous Chevrolet El Camino passenger car type pickup of the time.)

Glass and other debris are in the street in front of a stop-signed side street. An older maroon passenger car is parked at the curb between the truck and the intersection. The car's front end is mashed in, and coolant is leaking from the radiator.

I look around for the combatants. I don't see anyone. Walking over to the far side of the pickup, I find a man about fifty-five years old sitting on the curb. He is crying his heart out. I walk over to him, squat down, and put my hand on his shoulder.

"Are you hurt?" I ask.

He looks up, still crying. "No-oo," he says with a quiver in his voice, making his answer sound like ho-ho. "I'm just broken-hearted. And angry, real angry." The crying starts to diminish when the anger is mentioned.

"Are you one of the drivers of the vehicles in the accident," I ask.

"Yeah," he says, tears diminishing, anger building.

"This pile of s--- is mine," motioning at the Gentleman Jim pickup, then looking around left and right like he is looking for someone.

"That f-ing kid blew the stop sign and hit me." He starts crying again.

After a bit, I get him calmed down, and back to as normal a condition as possible right then. I get his story:

He ordered the pickup truck through a local dealer. It takes two months to get the truck delivered to the dealer, and then the dealer keeps it for another month installing all the specially-ordered equipment. All the while the man has been building great anticipation about driving the truck, and is champing at the bit to get it. The truck is something he was really, really looking forward to. Early this afternoon, he took delivery, and was driving home from the dealership when the high school student in the maroon car ran the T-intersection stop sign, and hit the brand-spanking new pickup broadside. There is a substantial amount of sheet metal damage, and the frame is probably bent as well.

The truck has been driven one and a half miles.

Big time crying time.

Tale Number 92 – Public Acclamation

My partner and I work all night handling crashes like the rest of the graveyard units. We go from one crash to another, frequently running behind with an accident called in but no unit available to respond. In fact, we were called out of briefing at the beginning of the shift to respond to a crash. We haven't had time for coffee or lunch.

Welcome to Los Angeles in the rain.

When it rains in L. A., and probably in any other big city (I only know about Los Angeles), the freeway frequently takes on a look similar to those roads shown in World War II documentaries. You may know the ones; the fighter plane swoops down and strafes the road with machine gun fire. The cars and the trucks go this-away and that-away, as do the people, thereafter leaving the road littered with vehicles all askew.

This time the weather, and the accidents, taper off about five o'clock in the morning, about an hour before the end of the shift. We beat feet for a local Winchell's Donut House to get coffee and something to eat. (Some of the L. A. public derisively call Winchell's Donut Houses CHP substations.) While we ate, we planned to arrange some semblance of order to all the wet paperwork we had in the car.

I drive into the parking lot, pulling parallel to the building, while snuggling up under the extended roof eave. I stop with the front of the unit even with the front of the building so about half the width of the car is under the eave.

Rain has started again, and we want to leave the driver's window down for fresh air.

While my partner starts sorting his papers, I leave to get our order. Returning with the food, I start to get into the paperwork, also.

We sit there until fifteen minutes before shift-end, working on reports while trying to shake off the tiredness. The hunger we tried to abate with the sweet rations.

At 6:00 AM, I start putting my stuff away. "Ready to roll in and call it a night, partner?" I ask.

"Let's do it. I'm whipped," he says.

I start the engine, drop the transmission in gear, and roll forward to leave.

There is a loud continuous *screeeechhh*, followed by a combined crunching and flexing sound of metal. I have driven the left fender of the patrol car against a four-inch diameter, three-foot tall, concrete-filled, steel pipe, which guards the front corner of the building from being hit. I have smashed the fender metal inward one-inch in depth from the headlight to almost the driver's door opening joint.

"@#$%^&#!"

I didn't see the post when I started up. I knew it was there when I pulled in, and I knew it when I went for the coffee and the donuts. But I forgot about it, hiding it with the body of the patrol car because I parked too close to the pole.

All the folks standing in line for coffee and donuts some twenty feet away hear and see the crash. Each of the fifteen to twenty customers in line whistle and clap, giving me a just reward. I felt small enough to go through the eye of a needle and have plenty of room left over.

But the worst part was backing up to get the unit away from the post. There is more metal grinding and crunching, and so, there is more tribute from my public.

I am very glad to get away from there and back to the office. I would have been glad to leave for the office had I known I was going to be flogged when I got back there, rather than endure another round of tribute.

As it was, my partner, and others, called me "Crash" for a long while. The office gave me a piece of paper to sign that wasn't a commendation. It was placed in my personnel jacket for five years.

All that still didn't hurt like the public tribute.

Tale Number 93 – They're E-v-e-r-y-w-h-e-r-e

I arrest a drinking driver one crisp fall night on the Long Beach Freeway. I call dispatch for a tow truck from the regular rotation list they keep and continue with what I have to do at the scene.

The arrested driver is in the right front seat, handcuffs to his rear, seat belt applied, door closed. (The seat belt is applied in case an errant driver hits the patrol car, which happens more than occasionally, less than frequently.)

I am completing the vehicle storage report for his vehicle when the tow truck arrives. As usual, the tow driver pulls in front of the violator's car, gets out, and begins to hook up the car without contacting the officer. I continue filling out the form he has to sign to take possession of the car.

When the tow driver finishes hooking up the car, he walks back to me at the patrol car's right fender.

A good thing about the right front fender on Dodge patrol cars is when it is crisp or cold, the engine heat billows out from the right front wheel well enveloping one in a dandy blanket of comfortable heat. Arguably, one could be very comfortable in shorts and a T-shirt there in the dead of winter. However, it is not a dandy place in the warm months. But that heat also reveals the boozy smell of drinking people. Billowing upward as the air rises, it pushes a drinking person's breath in our face.

When the tow driver arrives, I think I smell that smell. While he is looking the form over and signing, I definitely smell that telltale smell.

"How much have you been drinking tonight waiting on a tow call?" I ask.

"Nothing," he replies. "Just been sitting home watching TV."

When someone tells a cop that something is not, when the cop knows that something is, two things occur: one, you're telling the cop he's stupid—at your peril—and two, the cop is going to show you he isn't.

"Driver, there are only two of us here. One of us smells of booze, and I (emphasized) haven't been drinking. It has to be you. Step over here and let's do a few tests."

He could not do the tests. I arrest him for drunken driving, hook him up, and put him in the right rear seat behind arrestee number one in the front.

While I am seat-belting the tow driver, the first guy says, "Man, nobody is safe from you guys."

I take that as a compliment. I ask the tow driver who he wants to tow his tow truck, and reach for my vehicle storage report form clipboard.

"Oh, man," he says, "Can't you call and ask them to send the boss out to pick it up? I'm gonna be fired if you tow it, or if he drives it, but he will kill me, too, if his rig gets tied up."

"Sure. I can do that," I say.

I call dispatch. Time for a little occupational fun.

"Los Angeles, 888-73, 11-85 request (tow truck)."

Twenty, twenty-five seconds go by. This is very unusual. Dispatchers usually answer just as the last syllable leaves your mouth. But I know what's going on. I know she knows I have already requested a tow truck. I know she is looking in her radio cards she makes up for each call to make sure what she knows is correct. She's thinking, I know he requested a tow and I know I ordered one. Didn't I? I'm sure she is thinking I have made a mistake, and now, she will have the opportunity to help the poor old boy out, and point out the error of his way.

"Uh, 888-73, Los Angeles. You have already requested an 11-85. It's Big Truck Tow."

"Los Angeles, 888-73. That's 10-4, but I need another Big Truck Tow. Ask the boss to come out with another driver."

By now, I'm sure the dispatcher suspects I've been messing with her.

"888-73, Los Angeles. Is there something the matter with the first tow? Did it get there okay?"

"Los Angeles, 888-73. 10-4. The tow is here, but the driver is inoperable. He's 10-15 (in custody) for deuce."

Now all the former caring inquisitiveness and warmth of concern for the beat officer she takes care of on her frequency disappears in a blink in the dispatcher's tone of voice. She knows I was messing with her. She goes to all business mode.

"888-73, Los Angeles. 10-4," she says stiffly, ending the call.

Sometimes the Devil makes you do it. But at least arrestee number one was impressed.

Tale Number 94 – More Said To Be So's

Here are more tales I've heard other officers tell that are supposed to be true. Keep in mind some of the tale tellers are fishermen.

CHP units working in the wide-open unoccupied desert areas don't have gas stations and the like to pull into to write reports when needed. They don't need them. They can just drive out into the desert off the freeway access roads and park in the peace and quiet of the desert's vastness. But some have to be watchful while they're out there, and it's not rattlesnakes they have to watch for. It's Phantoms.

Officers will be sitting in their cars studiously working on their reports in total concentration. No noise from traffic, people, or cars, just the lovely dead silence of the desert.

Out of the blue, literally, some F-4 Phantom jet pilot on a training flight from air bases out there will spot the noncamouflaged enemy in a standout black and white vehicle in the tan desert. The jet will come in low, low, low just under the speed of sound, and "strafe" the officer and patrol car with the suddenness of the plane's presence, and the substantial accompanying jet noise.

It's my guess that would tend to probably break one's report writing concentration. And bladder control.

Another story.

Two late-middle-aged couples in Southern California decide to go camping and fishing together in Oregon.

One of the couples has a heavy-duty pickup truck with a deluxe camper on the back, the kind of camper with kitchen, bathroom, and shower. They are going to use the rig to travel and camp in.

The group leaves the Los Angeles area and motors north. Somewhere in Northern California, as they have been doing along the way the driver pulls into a gas station to refuel the rig. The ladies, who have been traveling in the camper (not illegal) playing cards and talking, get out to use the gas station's restroom, and to stretch their legs while the men service the truck.

The men finish with the truck, pay the bill, go to the restroom themselves, come back out, get in the truck, and head northbound for Oregon.

When the ladies come out of the restroom, their husbands, and the truck are gone, along with their purses. They are destitute and stranded.

They figure since their husbands left without checking on their presence, no doubt thinking the ladies finished their business and were back in the camper, the boys won't find out their mates are missing until the next fuel stop, possibly some three hundred and fifty miles north, some five or six hours, if they go that far.

The ladies don't know where the campground is the group is heading for. They only know it has a lake. That doesn't narrow it down too much for locating it in Oregon.

The gas station owner calls the CHP, and relates the situation. The CHP office puts out a BOLO for the units north of the area where the ladies are stranded. The CHP also calls the Oregon State Police to pass the info to them.

About a hundred miles north of the gas station, a CHP officer spots the camper on the freeway and stops it.

Contacting the driver, the officer inquires off-handedly if the driver is missing anything.

"No," the driver says curiously, wondering about the officer's approach, he didn't think he was.

The officer asks him to check on his passengers.

Of course, the camper is empty.

The men are shocked. The officer fills them in on their dastardly mistake. They all have a good ha-ha.

Then the driver asks the officer if he will be kind enough to escort them back to collect their wives, because, he says, without police protection he and his friend are going to get killed.

And no doubt, not with kindness.

The last Said To Be So.

A graveyard car receives a late accident call right near the end of their shift. They respond to the scene. Arriving, they find a single vehicle has run off the roadway and is overturned in a vineyard. They look around for victims or witnesses. None is found.

The area involved gets a lot of these types of one-car-off-the-road-into-the-vineyard accidents, and usually the driver and/or passengers flees the scene. We call it "taking leg bail." The officers see nothing special with this one. It's a run-of-the-mill similar type crash matching plenty of the same.

They get their accident investigation info and request dispatch to ask a day sergeant to assign a day unit to store the vehicle so they can try to get back to the office at a reasonable hour to go home.

The day sergeant approves the request, but holds off sending a unit, because morning briefing is still going on. A couple of hours later, he remembers the request, and has dispatch send a unit to recover the overturned vehicle.

The unit arrives at the scene and requests a tow truck, which arrives thirty minutes later.

The tow driver sets about righting the car and getting it back out to the road to tow it. He runs his cable over to the car, hooks it so it will roll the car over, and goes back to pull the lever to wind the cable. The cable winds up. The car turns over onto its wheels. And there is the dead driver from the previous evening.

Uh, oh.

Tale Number 95 – The Bunker

The call the dispatcher assigns me to this nice summer midweek afternoon is of kids throwing avocados at passing cars. As far as the throwing action is concerned, it could be a misdemeanor or felony, depending on whether injury is involved. But, I must also consider the agricultural angle—possible picking and theft of deciduous fruits. After all, California *is* an agricultural state.

I respond to the reported location: A T-intersection in the Puente Hills where a main two-lane north-south rural highway crosses the ridges and passes through the valley where the twisty-curvy road of other stories I've related starts at this intersection. The intersection topography rises on its three sides as low hills of maybe sixty to eighty feet in height.

Arriving at the intersection, I see the fruits of the throwers' labors. (Ouch.) The intersection has easily one hundred hard, green, and expensive avocados strewn about on the asphalt roadway. Some are run over and smashed.

I look left, right, and around for the throwers. I see no one. I call dispatch and advise that the suspects are GOA. (Gone On Arrival). I resume patrol.

A little while later, dispatch calls again with another flying avocado report. I respond to the location again, but this time I come in via the road through the valley, not the main one. I stop about a block's distance short of the intersection. Leaving the car, with advisement to the dispatcher, I approach the intersection on foot to see if I can quietly and unobtrusively spot the assaulters. I approach along the roadway edge under cover of the avocado trees.

At the corner, I stop. I can hear the murmur of voices, but I can't see anyone. Right then, a car passes through the intersection on the main roadway. As it passes under the hillock crest I am standing under, an avocado comes flying in a downward arc from the top to the roadway. Another car passes through the intersection going the other way. In rapid fire order, two avocados come down. None of the fruit hits anything but the asphalt.

Now I know where the snipers are. I walk back about one-half the distance from the intersection corner to the patrol car, and begin hiking up the hillock under cover of the orchard's trees. I take off all my jingle-jangleys, so I can be as quiet as possible.

About halfway up the hill, the voices come in stronger. They become a directional beacon allowing me to come in directly behind the suspects' location.

Getting to near the top of the hill, I stop to survey the area. I see no one, but I keep hearing voices, two, maybe three, seemingly near the crest of the hillock from which one could easily look down on, or throw at, the intersection below.

Where in the heck are these guys? Creeping forward, while straining my ears to hear the voices, I finally find the talkers.

Two young commandos, each about twelve-years-old, have constructed a camouflaged bunker, a pillbox, if you will, right at the crest of the little hill. They used avocado tree limbs for timbers to support fresh leaf foliage to cover their observation/foxhole pit. They have left enough elevation of the roof cover to be able to lob the fruit from the pit without interference with their throwing.

The pit itself, basically a deluxe-sized foxhole for two, is about four feet deep, three feet wide, and six to seven feet long.

I had walked directly up behind them, flanking their surveillance. I stood, looked and listened.

Each has a ready and large supply of avocados stacked in the front left and right corners of the pit, similar to the stacks of cannon balls in forts of yore. They are bemoaning their lack of accuracy, and the concurrent waste of shot. Each is resolving to the other to do better. Both are leaning against the front wall of the bunker, peering down on the intersection. They are totally oblivious to the fact the enemy has breached their security line and he is gearing up to attack their rear.

"What are you boys doing ?" I say, very loudly and strongly without preamble.

They wheel around and fling their butts to the front dirt wall, totally taken aback. (Aback so far I thought I smelled an odor.) They are standing below me in the pit. I am on a little rise on the ground behind and above them. The sun is shining on me in my tan uniform, my hat, my gold hat piece, my gold badge, my sunglasses, and the other metal gear I wear. I must have looked like a military-bearing gargantuan standing there in full regalia as a former Marine at six foot two inches, two hundred pounds, with my arms crossed. And I didn't say ho, ho, ho.

They know they were compromised, and they surrender. There was no white flag. There were no hands in the air. They were withered. Their faces said e-v-e-r-y-t-h-i-n-g.

Because of the extensive fortification preparation, the reserve of ammo on hand, the number of shots fired, and their overheard conversation bemoaning accuracy, I feel the deal warrants a trip to juvenile hall even though they had not hit a vehicle with their tries. Theirs is no kid's game. The potential is there for one or more people to be seriously hurt and/or property damaged.

I handcuff them together, left wrist to right wrist, to prevent a youthful escape attempt in the hills against The Old Man who had huffed his way up the hill. Then I march them to the patrol car and subsequently gave them a ride—

which usually is a thrill for a kid, but not for these two that day.

I gathered from their conversation in the car that being turned over to Mom and Dad wasn't going to be a pleasant affair either.

As the saying goes, "Live by the sword, die by the sword."

Tale Number 96 – The Only Thing Missing Is The White Flag

I am parked at a drive-in having lunch with my beat partner. We are standing outside our units on this summer evening, using the right front fender area for our table instead of our desk.

It is the time of the evening when some cars have their lights on and some don't; some businesses have their outside lights on, some don't.

Suddenly—it always seems it's suddenly in this business—a beat-up older model green two-door sedan goes zipping past us toward the street from the strip mall shopping area behind us. It is going too fast for the crowded area, but not as though the car is fleeing the scene of something. It strikes me it is just a too-fast driver, as some are.

The car goes straight out the driveway and across the two westbound lanes, hitting the raised concrete divider in the middle of the street in a shower of sparks. The car bumps up, over, and down the divider, continues across the two eastbound lanes into, and up and over, the concrete curb on the other side of the street in an equal show of sparks. The car then comes to a stop.

No car on the roadway, though some were approaching, or off the roadway in the parking lot, is affected. Just the stunt driver's car is damaged.

When the car comes to a stop across the street on another shopping area's parking lot, the driver's door opens slowly, and the thirty-something disheveled male driver gets out. He turns and faces us, raising his arms over his head in the surrender position. He stands waiting for us to arrive.

My beat partner, who finished eating before the event started, stuffs his food papers into the bag, hands it to me, and runs across the street to the surrendering, for exactly what, we don't know, driver. I follow in my patrol car using the divider turn pocket.

When I get there, my partner has the guy under arrest for drunken driving and has him handcuffed. Subsequently, the subject is carted off to the calaboose.

The driver was trying to beat the cross traffic to get to the other side, which he did. But he didn't notice the raised concrete divider, because of the beer in his eyes. Also, because of the beer, he hadn't considered the need for a driveway access on the other side of the street until he was flying toward it.

But he knew he had done wrong, and surrendered on the spot.

Tale Number 97 – Showtime

I stop a sporty two-door red sedan one day for speed on the freeway. It has been running at a sustained speed of eighty miles per hour, plus. The speed limit is sixty-five miles per hour.

I make a left side approach to the driver's window and find a pretty brunette behind the wheel. Her gray skirt is hiked up almost to her whatzit, and the zipper of her zip-front, sleeveless, black turtle-necked sweater is pulled down about two-thirds the distance from the top. The evidence indicates that she is sans bra, and has décolleté from here to there.

Before I can speak, she says in a sing-songy, honey-coated voice, "Hello, officer. Was I bad?"

Overlooking the obvious and keeping it strictly professional, I try to be as official as possible without being Barney Fife.

"Ma'am, I stopped you for excessive speed. I paced you in excess of eighty miles per hour. May I have your driver's license and car registration, please?"

She takes her time gathering the documents, particularly looking in the glove box several times, leaning this way and that way. I watch her hands. Not the other. Hands can get a gun in the glove box and kill. But I had no doubt that she could kill with the other, too.

Still smiling and doing what she could do to show off, she gave me the documents. I tell her I am going to write her a citation for the excessive speed and will return.

Back at the driver's window with the citation, I now hear no sing-songy voice. The skirt is pulled down to the top of her knees, and the zipper is now all the way up to the top at the throat. She is in a pout.

She signs the ticket without comment after my explanation, but zips off the signature in a fit of pique to show me she is displeased with me for issuing the ticket.

I think she is more displeased with herself, because her feminine wiles didn't do the trick, so to speak. Never would.

Tale Number 98 – Loose Lips Sink The Speaker

The radio dispatcher is a Chippie's lifeline while the officer is out and about in his or her black and white doing the governor's work. That dispatcher, male or female, is our only link to instant help when things start to go downhill.

To be a dispatcher one has to be able to do ninety-nine things at the same time that eight or ten units on the frequency are requesting, sometimes one officer request after another, as situations develop. Dispatchers have to do them, keep them straight, and also listen for trouble, too.

I don't think I can do their job.

After dispatchers work with the same officers for a while, they can tell by the tone of the officer's voice or his or her breathing whether things are as they should be at the scene.

They are not averse to asking over the air if we are okay, or code 4, and then listening carefully to the answer. If the answer isn't as they think it should be, they tell a supervisor to suggest a drive-by from another unit.

We need them, and count on them, and would be lost without their assistance and concern. But they are human and make misstrakes, too.

In Los Angeles, for example, there is a chain of barbecue restaurants named Chris & Pitts. Officers go there for the same reason as everyone else: good barbecue food, and a change of pace.

One day, a unit apparently was going 10-7 (out of service) for lunch at one of the restaurants. As you know, we can't hear the other units unless we switch to the car-to-car channel. However, dispatchers repeat what we say as a way of assuring clarity of what is said. The dispatcher side of the conversation we can hear.

In this case, the unit said similar to, "Los Angeles, 888-60, 10-7 at Chris & Pitts." And the dispatcher repeated, kind of, for all to hear, "888-60, Los Angeles, 10-7 at Piss & Crits. Oh! Oh. Oh-oh."

There was a certain amount of on-air laughter in tribute.

In Fresno, the sheriff's office sent over a newly-taken stolen car report their office took for a BOLO broadcast to our troops.

Since humans are all influenced by their own environment and culture, there are a lot of things each of us doesn't know that others might. In this case, it is French pronunciation.

The broadcast was for a red Pontiac Gran Prix. Prix is pronounced by the knowledgeable as "pree."

The young dispatcher started out with the usual, "Attention all units" warning, and went on with "add the following vehicle to your stolen car list: a 19-- red two-door Pontiac Grand Prick, California license blah-blah." Over the air, she immediately got back from the troops in the field a few pronunciation reminders, most of which she had to decipher through their laughter.

I think she left work early that night before the shift got in. Since we couldn't pick on her then, we picked on her husband, who was working the shift with us.

It was later reported she was considering changing agencies.

Tale Number 99 – Baby, Baby, Come To Me

My partner and I are returning from booking a DWI driver in the downtown LAPD jail, a place we very seldom had the occasion to go. But we had seen and stopped the driver in the city of Los Angeles proper, and that's where we were required to book him.

Heading back to our beat, we get a call from dispatch to assist a central Los Angeles unit at a crash in their area near the start of our beat. We respond. It is three-thirty in the morning.

Arriving at the scene we observe a passenger car turned over at the bottom of the freeway embankment next to the perimeter fence. The paramedics and the fire department are trying to get the solo female driver out of the car. The doors are jammed shut.

We contact one of the graveyard officers of the requesting unit, and ask what we can do to assist. He tells us that beginning with their arrival, the woman, who is drunk and/or on drugs, keeps saying over and over, "Where's my baby? Where's my baby?" There is evidence in the car there might have been a baby there at the time of the run-off-the-road accident.

The officer tells us he and his partner have made a cursory check of the scene and found nothing, but because of the mature bushy landscaping, he wants a more through search conducted. He and his partner are tied up for the immediate time being. He wants us to do the search now in case the baby is there and injured. We agree but suggest an additional unit be requested, plus the helicopter with the big bright light.

The other officer calls dispatch and makes the arrangements.

When the helicopter arrives and lights up the area like daylight, the five officers, one from the investigating car, my partner and me, and the other two officers line up at arm's length from one another, and from the spot where the car ran off the freeway, move slowly along the embankment in a Texas two-step shuffle toward, and two hundred feet past, the overturned car.

To our great relief we find nothing. Then we turn around and go back over the same ground. Still nothing.

All agree the two assisting units will drive off the freeway and come back alongside the scene on the other side of the freeway perimeter fence where there is a city frontage road. The area between the perimeter fence and frontage road is overgrown with weeds and bushes, and it is thought this area bears checking, also.

We do the two-step up and back over the adjacent area. We find nothing.

While we are making that search, the tow truck arrives to remove the car. The victim has been removed to the hospital. When the car is rolled over, the area underneath it is also clear.

We're batting a thousand.

Having made a best effort, the investigating unit cancels all of us. We thank the CHP flying sun, who leaves to resume routine sky patrol, and then we leave also, but with a lingering sickish feeling maybe we missed the baby and it is still out there.

But later on in the shift, the dispatcher calls to tell us when the investigating unit got to the hospital, a relative of the driver, who had responded there, told the officers the baby was not in the car, but was at home with family while the driver was out and about.

Good news in more than one way.

Tale Number 100 – How Low Can You Go?

My partner and I are just turning the corner to the street the East Los Angeles office is on to go in to end our graveyard shift when dispatch calls to assign us to an 11-83, located on a major thoroughfare by a freeway. We respond. It is my out for a crash.

Arriving at the scene, we find we have a loaded garbage truck jammed about one-third its length inside an underpass that goes under a freeway. The driver forgot to lower his front loader bucket after the last pickup, and left it up over the cab. He was traveling about forty miles per hour when he drove into the underpass. He came to a sudden stop.

A substantial piece of concrete is knocked out at the rim of the underpass by the top edge, and another section is missing on the underpass roof by the rim. The loader bucket and lift arms are twisted forty-five degrees out of kilter. The truck is blocking the shoulder lane of the two westbound lanes, and building commuter traffic is backing up. A bad scene for the heavy commute traffic to come.

Before the accident was reported to the CHP, the driver called his dispatcher to report the incident. Three supervisory personnel responded. The three men and the driver were standing in a group discussing how they were going to get the truck out from the underpass when I arrived and joined the group.

The suggestions being considered were: (1) get a truck with a cutting torch out there and cut the bucket loose from the lift arms, then have another truck with a small crane hook a line to the bucket and drag it off the top of the garbage truck, and (2) have a truck-tractor with a "low-boy" trailer bring a bulldozer out, then use the bulldozer to shove the garbage truck backwards out of the underpass. A third suggestion offered, now escapes me.

The remedies the group is pondering sounds to me like they are just short of the men and matériel needed to land a man on the moon.

Standing with the group, I say, "I have a suggestion. Why don't you just let the air out of the tires and back it out? Then any tow truck with a compressor can refill the tires, and it can be driven back to the yard, or towed if a tire goes."

Time stood still. The traffic noise died. Everything froze in position, except the men's faces, which slowly turned toward me with expressions on them like I had just explained the meaning of life.

When time resumed, the men went to the tires and let all the air out. The driver jumped in the seat, backed the truck out without a problem, made a U-turn while I held up traffic, and drove the truck with the mangled loader bucket into the parking lot of an adjacent closed strip mall. I waved go to the stopped traffic in each direction and it was a done deal.

We headed for the barn one more time.

Tale Number 101 – Funny, You Mention It

I am working the rural area in southern Fresno County one afternoon when I stop a rattletrap of an old two-axle truck with homemade stake-sides on it. The driver gets out and walks back to meet me at the right front fender of the patrol car.

"Good afternoon," I say, "You're missing required lights, mud flaps, and rear license plate, and part of your load is nearly ready to fall off onto the roadway. May I see your driver's license and truck registration, please."

The driver is an older gentleman of maybe sixty years, or so. He takes his very thickly-packed wallet out of his well-used coveralls' back pocket and begins to sort through the contents.

After a bit, he fishes out the truck registration ownership certificate, but no current registration card. The ownership certificate is signed off by the former owner in 1969, the year I joined the highway patrol. It is now 1979. He didn't transfer the title.

He keeps fishing in the thick wad of papers for his driver's license.

After a bit more time, he retrieves a black Photostat driver's license, a type used in California *before* I obtained my first driver's license when I was eighteen. At the time of the stop, I am no longer eighteen. I look at the driver's license. It expired in 1944. I now look from the license to him, from him to the license, wondering if he has shown this to me as a historical piece he thought I haven't seen before to hold my interest while he searches for his current license.

The look on his face says, "No." "Just a minute," he says, apparently reading the look of disbelief on my face. He begins sorting through his lifetime personal archive again. In several minutes, he pulls out a many-times folded sheet of paper and hands it to me, folded.

I open the document on the fender of the patrol car, because I'm afraid the very fragile paper will fall apart.

The document is the original of his United States Army orders dated December, 1946, discharging him at the end of WW II, and authorizing government expense for his transportation to his home of record in California.

I look at this document in equal amazement.

He is looking at me with the "well-now-you-have-it-look."

"Sir," I say, "Do you have anything current with you that allows you to legally drive?"

"Officer, those orders extend my driver's license until I go to DMV to get a license," he says.

Professionally and personally, I am aware of the law he refers to. I used it when I got out of the Marine Corps and came home. I don't remember whether the law extends the license thirty days, six months, or a year from the time the discharge orders are cut, but I am sure the law doesn't provide an extension of thirty-five years.

"Sir, I am going to write you a fix-it ticket for your driver's license, vehicle registration, and equipment deficiencies. You will have to go to DMV to get a new license, and to transfer the ownership of the truck to you."

"Yes, sir," he says, "I understand. That's where I was going when you stopped me."

You Pays Your Dime, You Takes Your Chance

I guess no book written by a traffic cop about traffic enforcement would be complete without something addressed to answer *the* question most often asked of us by family and friends, and people we meet in the daily society of life who learn we are traffic cops. No, not where are the best donut shops.

The most asked question is: How do I get out of a traffic ticket?

The answer is: Don't do the violation. Oh. No laughter.

The real answer is, I don't know. Like all things in life, it depends on the totality of the circumstances, including the temperament and emotional makeup of who you are, and who you end up dancing with at the dance.

You've read where a speeder in excess of one hundred miles per hour was let go with a verbal warning. (More than one, actually.) And, you've read where a simple speed stop got people transported to the pokey. Those variations occur because law enforcement officers have discretionary powers in applying the law, and it is that discretion that allows you to skate sometimes.

I don't think I can provide a how-to. But I can provide some hints and suggestions that *might* ever so slightly assist a noncontrary violator, though always at *your* total risk.

First of all, most courts offer first time traffic violators, and sometimes second time offenders who have gone more than a year without a ticket, the opportunity to go to traffic school. Satisfactory completion of the schooling usually gets the ticket (charge) that brought you to court dropped, maybe with paying some, or all of the fine. This is certainly a worthwhile way to go, and much more sure than the nebulous suggestions below.

And while I'm at it, I'm going to throw in suggestions about where to stop, if possible and safe, and not stop, on a freeway for the cop and for yourself, if the red light does comes on.

First, keep in mind the changing of drivers, the checking of maps, the in-the-field rest room stops, and trying to be a good guy by making your cell phone call while stopped on the freeway, are not emergencies. All those kinds of stops require you to exit the freeway. If you stop on the freeway (anywhere between the perimeter fences and on the ramps) for a nonemergency, you can be, and in most cases will be, ticketed. Once you step out of your vehicle for any reason onto a freeway, you are a pedestrian, and can be physically arrested and booked. Walking to a call box, or off the freeway for help, is considered part of the emergency.

Here, I think I *can* say, don't do the violations above.

Now, keep these few ideas in mind if you are stopped by a police officer's red light:

Always yield to the right as promptly as possible.

Avoid yielding into the freeway center divider, if possible. Especially to change a tire. It is dangerous to stop on a freeway for any reason, but when you are on the shoulder at least you have only one lane of adjacent traffic to deal with. Usually that lane contains the slowest traffic. You have a *slight* edge of safety. And always, always, always, watch the oncoming traffic every second with the idea in mind of fleeing for safety.

If you are having mechanical problems, it is best to drive off the freeway entirely, if you can.

If you are being stopped by a cop on the freeway, avoid stopping in the following areas, if possible: (He or she will not like it if you do so because they are not safe.)

- In the area marked off by the white striping at the beginning of an off-ramp.
- At the bottom of an on-ramp.
- In the area marked off before and after transitional roadways to other freeways.
- On the shoulder of an on-ramp or off-ramp.
- By a guard rail or wall.
- On an overcrossing with a drop below.

If you, and/or an officer, have to get away because something is going down, you want to be in Alaska—wide open spaces. If your car is hit in any of those places listed above, the location makes the accident worse. Stop somewhere away from traffic, where the area is open. In those areas inside the white striping, you are a target for those drivers who suddenly realize they are about to miss their exit, and cut over at the last second. They are always fast, and always seem to have magnetic cars that attract to cars parked in those areas. That would be you if you are parked in those dangerous places.

When the cop's red light comes on, put on your right turn signal. Slow down using your foot brake pedal *so your brake lights come on.* When you try to slow without letting the brake lights come on, figuring you'll give away you were speeding, which the cop already knows because he or she has your speed, it is evident to the cop. You send the message, rightly or wrongly, you are a sneak and a liar.

Remember: You are trying to impress, and truth impresses.

The cop has stopped more people more times than you have been stopped. He or she knows the drill backward, forward, upside down, and right side up.

Truth counts, and it is seldom heard.

If you see a safe place ahead off the roadway for your car and the cop's car, a *little* distance ahead, put on your four-way emergency flashers and go there, slowly. Don't go a mile. A block, or so would be the maximum. Driving out of traffic onto commercial or private property is usually appreciated. More cops are killed by traffic than any other single cause.

If it is nighttime when you are stopped, turn on your interior lights when the red light comes on. This is a courtesy that lets the officer see inside while making the stop. The officer can see who, and how many visible occupants there are and what they are doing. You're telling the officer you have no secrets. He doesn't know if you are the church choir going home, or the New Desperados coming from trouble.

Always stay in your vehicle, unless invited out.

When your car has stopped rolling, and before the officer arrives, roll down your driver's window. Turn off the noise makers, including the kids. If it's raining or foggy, try to time the window roll-down for his arrival at your window. Don't make the officer wait in the rain for you, even if he is in rain gear, while you find the window crank.

Remember: You are trying to display a courtesy of meeting.

Here is the tough one, the one you will not want to do, but it is the best one. Absolutely, the best one to impress. Ask any officer. Once your car is stopped, whether you're one hundred years old or seventeen, socialite or not, unemployed or the president of the bank, put your hands up where they can easily be seen as unthreatening. The driver should put his/her hands on top of the steering wheel, fingers apart. The right front passenger should put his/her hands on the dashboard, fingers similarly apart. The passengers in the back should likewise put their hands on the back of the seats in front of them, fingers separated These positions will go a long way toward impressing the officer you are nonthreatening, cooperating to make the stop safer and easier for him or her, and he or she is welcome.

See, the problem is you know you are good people. But the police officer doesn't know who you are. The officer meets bad people all the time, young or old, male or female, who sometimes try to harm him. They even try to harm him when their kids are in the car with them. As is true in other aspects of life, the bad spoil it for the good. So, the position of your hands, and having the lights on inside your car, will let the cop know you are not a threat to his person. You are saying you care to say so.

Never say, "What's up, officer?" or "Is there a problem here?" Say, "Hello, officer," if you know you are wrong, and if you want to acknowledge the violation, go ahead. "I know, I ran that red light." Or, "I know, I was running 75." Otherwise, just say, "Hello, officer. What did I do wrong?" if you really don't know why you are being stopped. You can imagine your chances of getting a verbal warning if you ask about being wrong, and the officer has you at fifty-five miles per hour in a twenty-five mile per hour zone. BS gets rewarded.

Always sign the ticket if a printed disclaimer on it says it is only a promise to appear in court, and not an admission of guilt.

If you should get careless with drinking, take the chemical test if you are arrested for DWI. Not taking the test is kind of like not signing the ticket. You lose your license automatically for failing to take the test (in California), then you still have to defend the DWI charge, which is separate. And with no test, if you should be below the threshold, you don't have any objective evidence in your favor to argue with, even if it would be beneficial to you. It's then all the experienced officer's viewpoint and testimony. Remember, the field sobriety tests I gave to the blitzed driver?

And lastly, a general courtesy. Always wave at a police officer when you see one. Even though the officer volunteered to be a cop, and it's his or her chosen career, and he or she knows one has to eat dirt sometimes, work holidays, work in the rain, see society's tragedies, handle the mutilated dead, and take abuse, the officer would still like to be home with his wife and/or husband and kids. The officer would just like a little thanks for being out there for you even though it may affect your wallet sometimes. It's nothing personal.

A wave counts a lot.

Epilogue

You have finished the book. I sincerely hope you found it entertaining and informative. I have appreciated your interest and cooperation. Please be careful pulling back into your regular routine when you leave.

Have a nice day.